LESSONS FOR MY SONS

February 2021

Sue & Steve —

Thank you for your friendship
and ongoing committment to
6 Lobal Volunteers. You've made
a big difference in my life and
I am very grateful.
    I wrote this book for our
3 sons, but there may be parts
which you'll find interesting.

Bud

LESSONS FOR MY SONS

or

You Know You're Not Very Good Using Chopsticks

When You Find Rice in Your Tea

BURNHAM PHILBROOK

© 2020 by Burnham Philbrook

LCCN Imprint Name: Burnham J Philbrook, St. Paul, MN

ISBN 978-0-578-79278-1

This book was printed in the United States of America

Interior and Cover design by Matthew Morse

For Jake, Nick, and Drew.
This book is for you, your children, and your children's children.
Hopefully, some of the lessons I've learned during my life journey
will be relevant to your and their journeys.

Contents

PRELUDE

To Jake, Nick, and Drew,

I have enjoyed a blessed life, enriched by the many people who have supported and sustained me. My mother and father offered me unconditional love and acceptance. I grew up in a large family in the same Roseville, Minnesota home where my mother was raised and where my brother and sisters shared who they were and gave what they could. Teachers and professors cared enough to teach me; mentors took me under their wings; friends continue to look out for me; colleagues inspire me. Your mother loves me and cares for me, and each of you makes me so proud.

This is a book of lessons—the things I have learned during my life's journey over seven-plus decades. It is an attempt to share what life has taught me so that you too may learn from it. The lessons are from everyday life—the simple, silly, complex, mundane, and sometimes profound occurrences we all encounter while living on this planet. Every experience noted offered a learning opportunity.

This is not a book of wisdom; although, some lessons learned offered wisdom. This is not an autobiography or even a memoir. It is not a book about Global Volunteers, though that has been a significant part of my journey. (I intend to write that book next.) And this is not a religious book; although, I reference my faith in several chapters.

Additionally, this book is not a confessional. All my great sins have been left unstated; they are contained in another volume, which only God sees.

Much of what I've learned is the result of mistakes made—errors of commission and omission—things I have done that later I wished I hadn't; and things that I didn't do that later I wished I had. Countless lessons are merely from the unpredictable and uncontrollable happenings of the day-to-day. Some lessons I learned early on. Others took years, even decades, before I understood their true significance.

I have met tens of thousands of people in countries all over the world. I've enjoyed conversations with people from every walk of life—presidents and village elders, tribal chiefs and prime ministers, housekeepers and bishops, beggars and thieves, bankers and teachers, cardinals and laborers, farmers and authors, artists and miners, drivers and doctors, lawyers and chefs, pastors and senators, governors and imams, rabbis and priests, movie stars and judges, monks and fishermen, and professional athletes and curators.

I have visited more than one-quarter of all countries on the planet—60 countries and territories—many multiple times, and set foot on a dozen more. These nations represent over two-thirds of the world's population—from the most populous, China, to the smallest, the Holy See. They embody all the major religions, the most widely spoken languages, and the great cultures of all time. I have traveled through five Canadian provinces, visited all fifty US states, and have lived in five states and worked in the District of Columbia. I've flown nearly three million miles and drove from Minnesota through the length of Mexico to Guatemala in a red Ford pickup truck. Travel has been my grand teacher.

I never enjoyed formal education; nevertheless, I completed 21 years of school, plus kindergarten. Perhaps my foremost academic year was kindergarten—that's when I learned about friendship, sharing with others, how to read, being on time, numbers, and the importance of taking a nap. I have toured hundreds of museums, parks, animal sanctuaries, and archeological ruins. I've listened to a thousand speeches and lectures, watched thousands of films and plays, read several thousand books, articles, and posts; perused thousands of newspapers and magazines; viewed and listened to ten thousand newscasts. I've worked multiple jobs—from janitor to CEO—in state and federal government agencies, large multinational companies, small mom-and-pop businesses, and nonprofit organizations.

Far too many of the people named in this book—some who were extremely dear—have passed to eternity. I miss them every day. And others played important roles in my life; each remains forever in my heart.

As you read these stories, vignettes, and essays, and consider my beliefs and values, I hope you will reflect on the depth of meaning contained within them. Not everything may seem relevant to your lives. Some may be irrelevant, boring, or unimportant. But I offer it all with the hope that some parts will resonate with your experience and enlighten your future.

As your life evolves, you will experience your own stories, embrace your own lessons, and develop your own beliefs. I hope you too will share those with your sons and daughters as I am sharing with you.

My father was a wise but quiet man—never one for sharing his thoughts or experiences or giving much advice. He seldom shared with me what he had learned. I loved my father dearly but greatly regret that he did not reveal what he knew because he seemed to know so much. He led a full life, and I believe his life experiences could have been helpful to me. I wish he would have shared his wisdom with me. That is why I am sharing this with you.

All these experiences stimulated my curiosity, enlightened my understanding, increased my knowledge, and helped shape my life. I've written this book for you so you will have no regrets that your father didn't reveal his life lessons to you. And I've written it for your children and grandchildren that they might glean a glimpse of insight into their grandfather and great grandfather.

I suspect some people wonder at what point in their life they might record their learnings. Some write their autobiographies in their 40s, while others wait until their 80s. Because we continue to learn as we live, the best time to record our life lessons is the day before we die. However, we generally don't know that date, so we write when we think it appropriate. I started this book during my 67th year and finished it in my 74th; however, some of the writing was done well before. And I suspect there are lessons I have yet to learn. So, this is not a book about my life lessons. It's a book about my life lessons through today. We will have to wait to see if there is Volume 2.

Caveat: I do not claim ever to have had an original thought. My life has been so filled with lessons and wisdom from others that I don't know when others' thoughts stop and my thinking begins. Consequently, it is possible some ideas contained in this book have originated with others but are not so attributed. For example, this book's subtitle is not original; it's from a Global Volunteers team journal entry written by a teenage volunteer. Nevertheless, it is not my intention to plagiarize or otherwise use someone else's thoughts, ideas, or work and to represent it as my own. These are all my thoughts and writings made today, recognizing that thousands of people have inspired my thinking and words. Hopefully, I have appropriately attributed others' words and ideas.

To all my friends and family, identified or not, I am eternally grateful to each of you for helping me become a better spiritual being. As united citizens of heaven, I am confident we all will be together in the presence of the glorified Creator.

The OPENING

Mother's Day, 1961

The restaurant was packed; it had been all day. Lots of families celebrating Mother's Day. My job was to clean the tables after people had finished. They called me the busboy. It was my first week on the job; I was 14 years old.

I'd been working straight for more than eight hours, so I grabbed some food from the kitchen and sat at a small table in the corner. Before I had taken more than a couple of bites, the owner came by and told me the restaurant was too busy for employees to take breaks. He instructed me to dump the dishwater and help in the kitchen.

The kitchen staff generally washed the dishes in a large kitchen sink, but it was so busy, they had set up an extra metal washing tub as a makeshift sink. So as instructed, I went into the kitchen, grabbed the gray washtub, took it outside, and dumped it in the grass. When I came back in, the owner was standing just inside the doorway.

"What did you do?" he asked incredulously.

"I dumped the dishwater like you told me to."

"That was the soup, you idiot."

And that was the shortest job I ever had.

I wrote this book of stories, vignettes, and essays, and the lessons learned for an audience of three, my living sons. If others find what's on these pages interesting, helpful, or amusing, that's a good thing. I mention a lot of people in these tales. Each story is as I remember it; others may have different recollections.

The Lesson: Double-check before making irrevocable decisions.

The Lesson: If you are fired from a job, you can cry in your soup and blame your "no good" boss; or you can decide to learn from your mistakes and become the best employee in your next job.

If

"Fill the unforgiving minute with
sixty seconds' worth of distance run."

~ Rudyard Kipling, a British poet and novelist

When I graduated from grade school, Jack Bohen, my Godfather and my mother's oldest nephew gave me a congratulatory card that included the poem "If" by Rudyard Kipling. I have read this poem hundreds of times and still have the card. Each time I read it, something new strikes me. I share it in hopes that it will inspire you as it has inspired me.

IF

by Rudyard Kipling

If you can keep your head when all about you
    Are losing theirs and blaming it on you,
If you can trust yourself when all men doubt you,
    But make allowance for their doubting too;
If you can wait and not be tired by waiting,
    Or being lied about, don't deal in lies,
Or being hated, don't give way to hating,
    And yet don't look too good, nor talk too wise:
If you can dream—and not make dreams your master;
    If you can think—and not make thoughts your aim;

If you can meet with Triumph and Disaster
    And treat those two impostors just the same;
If you can bear to hear the truth you've spoken
    Twisted by knaves to make a trap for fools,
Or watch the things you gave your life to, broken,
    And stoop and build 'em up with worn-out tools:
If you can make one heap of all your winnings
    And risk it on one turn of pitch-and-toss,
And lose, and start again at your beginnings
    And never breathe a word about your loss;
If you can force your heart and nerve and sinew
    To serve your turn long after they are gone,
And so hold on when there is nothing in you
    Except the Will which says to them: 'Hold on!'
If you can talk with crowds and keep your virtue,
    Or walk with Kings—nor lose the common touch,
If neither foes nor loving friends can hurt you,
    If all men count with you, but none too much;
If you can fill the unforgiving minute
    With sixty seconds' worth of distance run,
Yours is the earth and everything that's in it,
    And—which is more—you'll be a Man, my son!

The FOUNDATION

*"Would a bird build its nest if it
did not have confidence in the world?"*

~ Gaston Bachelard, a French philosopher

All things worthy of withstanding the test of time require a solid foundation. The foundation is the underpinning, the bedrock upon which all else is sustained and supported. In the absence of a strong footing, all can be lost. That is true for buildings and life. My life has been built on the knowledge that God is our foundation. The lessons in this account reflect my human experience, but they are grounded in the understanding that everything essential is created, sustained, and supported by God. So that is where I begin.

Creation

"In the beginning, God created heaven and earth."

~ Genesis 1:1

Stargazing offers a profound encounter. In the quiet nighttime blackness of Ipalamwa, a small remote village in south-central Tanzania, I've witnessed the constellations of the southern hemisphere and the incredible magnitude of the Milky Way—at least 100 billion stars, as estimated by NASA. How many total planets are warmed by these radiant specs in the sky? We do not know. Although, to date, NASA has discovered more than 4,000 stars with orbiting planets. How many of those planets support life? We can only imagine.

Think about the scale of that for a moment. Our galaxy encompasses 100 billion stars. That's "billion" with a "B." NASA estimates that 17 percent of those stars have an Earth-sized planet. That calculates to 17 billion planets just in the Milky Way.

Scientists believe there are between 100 billion and two trillion galaxies within our observable universe. If the Milky Way is an average galaxy, then multiplying 17 billion planets by the low-end number of 100 billion galaxies results in a total of 1.7 sextillion planets (1,700,000,000,000,000,000,000) in the observable universe. What if 1/1000th of one percent (0.00001) are habitable and support life? That would mean that there could be life on 17,000,000,000,000,000 (17 quadrillion) planets!

And how large is the observable universe? Scientists estimate it's about 46 billion light-years across, or 270.48 sextillion miles (270,480,000,000,000,000,000,000 miles). In comparison, the moon is 238,900 miles from earth, and the sun is 92,960,000 miles away. Moreover, 270 sextillion miles is the distance across the "observable" universe. We do not know how big the actual universe is beyond the observable. Are there limits? Is the universe infinite? Is there a multiverse? We do not know. But some scientists believe that our universe is not alone.

The Lesson: The magnitude of creation is so humongous it is beyond our comprehension.

The Lesson: Our solar system is so small that it is inconsequential compared with the totality of the universe.

The Lesson: As important as you and I might think we are, planet Earth is extremely small potatoes.

The Creator

To say our ancient ancestors' scientific knowledge was limited is an enormous understatement. Nevertheless, as they viewed the night sky, they must have known without a doubt that some Great Being had created the sun, the moon, and the distant stars. Through the morning sunrise, the evening sunset, and the starlit night, the Creator revealed Itself to all those who preceded us.

Contemplating the universe's remarkable display, it becomes readily apparent that this all came from something, for it could not have come from nothing. What in our experience comes from nothing?

This is creation, and creation requires a Creator.

Perhaps the universe started with a "Big Bang." Something had to initiate the bang. Something lit the match. It is not fathomable that nothing self-ignited or that non-ingredients came together from nowhere. It is irrational to conclude that all we see, hear, touch, taste, and feel came from no-thing.

Moreover, I suspect the Creator planned it this way.

Today, with what appears to us as an abundance of scientific knowledge, the Creator continues to reveal Itself as we discover new galaxies in a universe that is expanding at the speed of light. The septillions of stars and planets is the Creator revealing Itself to us. The unimaginable, incomprehensible, humongous magnitude of the universe reveals the Creator. The universe (and possibly multiverse) is the demonstrable sign from the Creator of the Creator's existence. Consequently, there is no need for faith to believe in the Creator. Just look to the stars.

Nor is it necessary to go to Tanzania to see these wonders. The northern hemisphere constellations are equally vivid from the waters of the Lake-of-the-Woods in northern Minnesota. And I have experienced the same in rural deserts, from the tops of mountains, at sea, and anywhere else artificial light does not distract the beauty.

Two hundred years ago, it was not necessary to travel to the wilderness or a remote village to witness the remarkable display of the Milky Way. The nighttime darkness was not interrupted by the lights of the city or even the farmhouse. All humanity could see the Creator's revelation every night. Unfortunately, each of us cannot do the same today.

If you ever question the existence of the Creator study the universe. If you cannot study the universe, then explore the inner ear in all its incredible complexity. Or investigate the Japanese spider crab, Rüppell's vulture, or Dicopomorpha echmepterygis. Try to explain to yourself how they come from nothing.

The revelation of physical creation and its evolution demonstrates the tremendous power of the Creator. But the Creator is much more than power.

Knowing there is a Creator—in our language "God"—is a vital reminder of our role in the universe. The Creator created us—you and me. We know God created us through a big bang and ensuing evolution, or some other theory, because we know we could not have come from nothing. The person you are did not come from nothing.

Knowing God created you is a most affirming revelation. Knowing that God created you as a self-conscious, perceptive, intentional, intelligent, thinking, reflective, and loving being is the ultimate expression of love. These are the reasons we come to the realization "God is love."

Recognizing that there is a God who loves us is foundational to all other lessons of life. In the absence of this knowledge, we wander in the wilderness. But knowing that God created you, out of Its love, offers the energy to sour to the heights, to take knowledge and form it into new possibilities, and to love all of creation in return.

We call God "Father" and use the pronoun "Him" and "He." Perhaps we place on the Creator human characteristics to better understand and grasp the unimaginable ultimate-Power and ultimate-Love. But God is without gender. It just is. Infinite-Power and infinite-Love are how God reveals Itself to us.

Scripture reports that God made us in his image. But knowing our human condition and witnessing the scale of the universe, we can conclude that the Creator probably does not have many human characteristics. Nor do we share many divine attributes. But it is reasonable to conclude that while God may not have made our bodies in Its image, perhaps our souls were made in Its image.

The Lesson: God must exist, or nothing would exist.

The Lesson: We know there is a creator, that is a foregone conclusion—look to the stars. That reality raises the great questions of all time are: Why would It create us? What are we to do with this life? How would It inform us how we should live this life? When does it end, or does it? Where do we go from here? Who am I? Who is God?

On FAMILY

"I sustain myself with the love of family."

~ Maya Angelou, an American poet, singer,
memoirist, and civil rights activist

In this life, there is nothing as important as your family. Family always comes first, and family begins with parents and grandparents. I was extraordinarily blessed with two loving parents who lived into their 80s and 90s, well into my 40s and 50s. They loved me, taught me, supported me, counseled me, consoled me, and loved me some more. They were everything to me—my spiritual role models, coaches, guardians, protectors, champions, cheerleaders, and advisors. My mother and father were married for 60 years, raised 11 children, and offered me the example of the person and parent I have tried to become.

1266

*"We are links between the ages, containing past and pres-
ent expectations, sacred memories and future promise."*

~ Edward Sellner, an American professor and author

I did not know any of my grandparents well. Both of my grandfathers died
many years before I was born. My grandmothers were lovely; however, they
never paid much attention to me, nor do I expect to any of my siblings—there
were just too many of us.

My mother's father—your great-grandfather, John Cardinal Bohen, was born
in 1861 in Camden, New York. Sometime during his grade school years, his
family moved to Wisconsin. After high school, he went to work for Aetna Insurance Company as a salesman.

Maybelle Francis Hanken, your great-grandmother, was born in 1880 and
raised in Trempealeau, Wisconsin. At 17, she was an elementary school teacher
in a one-room schoolhouse in Baraboo, Wisconsin. She earned $25 a month,
about $9,000 annually in 2020.

One day in June 1898, Maybelle and her friend Anna we're walking to the
general store when they saw a good-looking gentleman ride into town on a
beautiful white horse. His name was John Bohen. Shortly after, Maybelle and
John started dating. John was 37 and Maybelle was 18, but age was not a factor;
they were smitten.

John was Catholic and Maybelle Episcopalian. Mabelle's mother, your great-great-grandmother, believed a man and his wife should worship in the same denomination and encouraged her daughter to consider becoming Catholic. Maybelle and John married in December 1898, and Maybelle became a devout Catholic. The following year, they bought a house on Lincoln Avenue in St Paul, Minnesota. They had five sons in nine years and then two daughters. Your grandmother, born on July 14, 1913, was the oldest of the two girls.

John and Maybelle studied osteopathic medicine together. John received his doctorate in 1903. Although Maybelle completed the coursework, she did not graduate because she was pregnant and had two boys under four. John set up practice in St Paul, and occasionally Maybelle assisted him with patients. To make ends meet, John continued selling insurance, work that required extensive travel. Today, osteopathic medicine is one of the fastest-growing health care professions in the US.

After living in the city for 22 years, they decided to move to the countryside. During one of John's longer business trips in 1921, Maybelle bought a two-story, three-bedroom, one-bathroom square house located at 1266 West County Road B in Rosetown (now Roseville), Minnesota. By the time John returned home, she had moved the entire family and all their belongings into the relatively new, three-year-old home. Situated on five acres, they had horses, a cow, ducks, and chickens. A few years later, they added on to the back of the house, building a sunroom, breakfast room, and a fourth bedroom upstairs. This rural environment, Maybelle later recounted, was much better for her children than the city.

Eight years later, Dr. John Bohen died of colon cancer. He was 69. It was 1930, and the beginning of the great depression. Your grandmother was 16 when she lost her Dad.

Your great-grandmother lived at 1266 until 1939 and fortuitously kept one of the five acres when she sold the 1266 property. Maybelle bought 40 acres of woodlands on the Wisconsin side of the St. Croix River, and her sons and sons-in-law built her a log cabin where she lived for four years. But the place was isolated and had few amenities—no electricity, a wood-burning stove, and a hand water pump. In later years as a child, I often visited the rustic cabin in the woods with my parents, siblings, and uncles on weekends, which was great fun. But this place offered too hard a life for a 63-year-old single woman. Maybelle moved to Anoka in 1943.

In 1944, my mom and Dad bought the house and land at 1266 West County Road B. Shortly after, your great-grandmother had her small house physically moved from Anoka to a newly constructed foundation on the land she had not sold, which was adjacent to my parents. So, your great grandmother lived next door for most of my young life, which your grandmother deeply appreciated and enjoyed. But I never got to know Granny Bohen well.

Maybelle sustained herself over her remaining years by crocheting baby clothes, making table centerpieces out of chenille, raising and selling guinea pigs to the University of Minnesota, and babysitting for the neighborhood children. She lived in that small house on County Road B until St. Patrick's Day 1962, when she died at 82 with her seven children by her side. Although her husband was proud of his Irish heritage, Maybelle was an indomitable English woman who wore orange on St. Patrick's Day. So, her children smiled at the coincidence of her dying on the most sacred of Irish holidays. Your grandmother was 49 when her mom died.

My mom lived at 1266 for 71 years, from the time she was eight until age 20, and again from 31 until 90. I lived there for most of my first 20 years. Today, 1266 is one of Roseville's oldest homes listed as #14 on the historical societies Heritage Trail Tour Map.

Your great-grandfather Philbrook was born in Minneapolis in 1884. His mother, your great-great-grandmother, Mary Erpelding Philbrook, died giving him birth. She was just 25. His father, Rufus Burnham Philbrook, named him Archibald (Archie) Thomas Philbrook.

Stories of Rufus, your great-great-grandfather, can be found in the Minnesota Historical Society in a 30-year collection of letters he wrote to his friend, Manly. Rufus Burnham, born in Maine in 1831, was a hunter, trapper, and later a farmer. He walked from his home state to Minnesota in 1863 to find better hunting, settling near Princeton, where he became a trapper. Rufus was not well educated, but he carried with him several books—a dictionary, *The American Poets*, Fowler on *Love and Parentage*, and *Every Man His Own Lawyer*. After many years in the wilderness, he married Mary in 1879; she was 20 and he was 48. They had a baby girl in 1880 whom they named Jewel, and Archie was born four years later. Rufus never remarried after Mary died. He went from hunter to trapper to farmer to single-parent and raised those two children on his own. After working hard all his life, Rufus died in 1898 at 67. Archie never knew his mother and was just 14 when his Dad died.

Your great-grandmother, Mabel Eugenia Linder, was born in New Brighton, Minnesota in 1890, the oldest of four. She quit school after 8th grade to earn money. Always a hard worker, Mabel worked on nearby farms as a nanny, housekeeper, cook, and laundress. In 1906, she went to work for Jewel Philbrook, Archie's sister, as a housekeeper. That's where she met Archie, who was working on the family farm. Soon after, they began dating and got married in 1909; she was 19 and he was 25.

Archie and Mabel rented a farmhouse on North Hamline Avenue in Rosetown, less than a mile from 1266. There, they had three sons and two daughters. Your grandfather, Burnham Leroy Philbrook, was the oldest, born on September 26, 1910. Archie, Mabel, and their children worked the farm, but they wanted a place of their own as the family grew. So, in the spring of 1923, with five children now 13 to 6 years of age, Archie and Mabel purchased a 20-acre truck farm in New Brighton. The family worked side-by-side tilling, planting, weeding, and harvesting vegetables which Archie and his sons took to Minneapolis to sell at the Farmers' Market. They farmed the land until the last child moved out. A few years later, in the spring of 1937, Archie died of peritonitis at 53. Your grandfather was 27 when his Dad died.

Now 47, Mabel rented out their farm and moved into a small apartment in New Brighton over Pinky's Tavern and gas station, which her brother, Leroy, owned. She managed the tavern turning a profit in part by selling beer on Sundays, a violation of state law at the time. The police did not bother her because Mabel tolerated no-nonsense in her tavern and always maintained the peace. The patrons in the tavern down the road continuously had brawls, which kept the police otherwise occupied. A year after the attack on Pearl Harbor, she quit the tavern because there were too few customers given all the young men who had gone off to battle, and it became more difficult to get beer due to most producers focusing on the war effort.

In January 1943, Mabel moved to a small apartment near the University of Minnesota Minneapolis campus. She had several different jobs over the ensuing years, including working in the cafeteria at the US Arms Plant in Arden Hills during the war, where your grandfather also was employed. Mabel paid off the farm mortgage in 1950 and sold the farmhouse and land for $1,000 per acre for a total of $20,000 (over $200,000 in 2020). She retired five years later at 65.

Granny Philbrook was a gorgeous woman in her youth and always kind to me. As an avid baseball and football fan, she got quite excited when the Minneapolis Millers AAA baseball team or the Minnesota Gophers football team played. My Dad often took me to her apartment near the U of M to watch a game on television, and she always had something nice for me to eat. But she didn't talk to me much, and unfortunately, I never really got to know her.

At 75, she moved in with my Uncle Bob and Aunt Bernice Philbrook in New Brighton, where she lived in a basement apartment. Two years later, she became ill with colon and pancreatic cancer and died on Christmas Eve 1967. My Dad was 57 when his mom died.

The Lesson: Love of family is why hard work is necessary.

The Lesson: Your great-grandfathers died at 53 and 69. By today's standards, that is young. But between them and your great-grandmothers, they raised 12 children, had 34 grandchildren of which I am one, and a whole bunch of great-grandchildren including you, and even more great-great-grandchildren. Each of their descendants has their own story of contributing to society and the greater good. And they are not done yet. Their lives live on.

The Lesson: Carrying a forebear's name includes the responsibility to live up to their values and standards. I can only hope that I have warranted being named Burnham after my great paternal grandfather and my Dad, and John after my maternal grandfather.

How Much Did That Cost?

"God could not be everywhere,
and therefore he made mothers."

~ Rudyard Kipling, a British poet and novelist

My mother taught me that the purpose of life is to serve others. And she exemplified that teaching. She volunteered at the Golden Age Home—even after she was older than some of the residents—for the Cancer Society, at her parish church, and as a member of Roseville's Civil Defense. She was present to anyone in need. Even with 11 children, she always made time to help others.

Perhaps the best way to describe my mother is from the eulogy I offered at her funeral. All my siblings were welcome to speak that day, but only my youngest sister, Michelle, and I chose to do so.

Michelle offered an excellent, warm description of mom's faithful and committed relationship with God. How she attended mass daily, her membership in and dedication to the Carmelite Order, her financial support for orphaned children in India, the long list of people she prayed for, and her persistent teaching to all of us about the Gospel, by both word and deed.

In my remarks, I took a different approach. After thanking all for coming—the large church was nearly full—and acknowledging that indeed our mother was a good and prayerful woman, I explained that my assignment was to tell the other side of her story. I then shared nine vignettes about your grandmother. This is her story:

1. Whenever possible, mom attended funeral masses at her home parish, St. Rose of Lima Catholic Church in Roseville, Minnesota. After Mass, she joined her remaining living friends for the funeral lunch in the church basement. However, on Wednesdays, I took her to lunch at her favorite restaurant, provided I was in town. One Wednesday, after we'd been served our food, she told me that she had been to Mrs. McGillicuddy's funeral that morning. She said to me with a sincere face, "They say such wonderful things about you at your funeral. And it occurred to me today that I'm going to miss mine by just a few days."

2. My mother was devoted to all her children. She did things that many moms don't have time to do anymore. For example, she washed, dried, and folded all our clothes, and then put them away in our dressers. She did this even during our teenage years when we were quite capable of doing it ourselves. One afternoon during my sophomore year in high school, my good friend, Ron Rotell, and I were hanging out in my bedroom. Mom came in and started putting clothes in my dresser.

    Ron asked politely, "Mrs. Philbrook, what are you doing?"

    "I'm putting Bud's clothes away, Ronald."

    "Oh! Really? When did Bud start wearing bras and panties?"

3. Our family never had much money, but occasionally mom would splurge—generally on something new she found in the grocery store. No one would accuse her of living on the cutting-edge, but one day she brought home a brand-new product—a can of Ready Whip, the spray-on kind. We didn't have dessert often, but on this day, mom had made pumpkin pie. After dinner, she brought out the pie and the Ready Whip.

    "Oh, Marge," my Dad asked, somewhat exasperated, "how much did that cost us?"

    "It wasn't very expensive, Burnham. Look, I'll show you how it works."

With that, she put her finger on the nozzle, pointed it towards my father's piece of pie, and pressed. But her aim was off, and she sprayed white sticky whip cream all over my father's face. He was not amused.

4. There were a lot of children sitting around our dinner table, but mom always made room for one more. If any of us had friends over around dinnertime, mom would invite them to stay. When there were more people than chairs, she would put a board across two chairs so there was an extra place to sit, and she'd add a cup of water to the soup so there'd be enough for everyone.

5. With so many children, you can imagine her life was hectic, and there was always one more thing to do. When she and Dad would go out, she invariably ran late. So, Dad would sit in the car, waiting for her. One evening, they were going to the funeral of a friend. Mom finally got in the car and told Dad the name of the mortuary. They arrived, and as was her custom, she immediately walked to the casket to kneel and say a prayer. Dad followed. When they got to the casket, they both realized that they did not know the deceased. They were in the wrong funeral home!

6. Mom used to say that she understood the art of the compromise. For example, Dad wanted five children and she wanted six. So, they had 11.

7. But 11 was not enough for her. When I was 16, she asked me if I would like to have a baby brother. It seemed that having a new baby around the house would be like having a new puppy, except I didn't have to clean up after a baby.

So, I said, "Sure."

Then she said to me, "Why don't you tell your father that you'd like a baby brother."

She so enjoyed being pregnant, and she enjoyed raising children. And she was good at both.

8.   Mother loved garage sales. In fact, she liked shopping of any kind, although, due to financial constraints, her store time was mainly window shopping. There's a family legend that describes how she could not pass up a good deal. She and my sister Cynthia stopped by a garage sale one Saturday afternoon. Cynthia put her hat down to try on some headscarves. A couple of minutes later, Mom tried to buy the hat for 25 cents.

9.   Mom could occasionally be a stickler for details. I remember receiving a lengthy voicemail message from her, which she concluded by asking me to call her back. Then, a minute later, she left me another message where she said, "Burnham John, that was your mother." I think she didn't want to take the chance that I might not recognize her voice.

In 1990, your grandmother was selected as Minnesota's American Mother of the Year, an honor of which she was incredibly proud. Your mother nominated her for this prestigious award, and your grandma was forever grateful. I was privileged to join her in New York at the Waldorf Astoria for the closing dinner celebration of the National American Mothers Conference in April, the only one of her children able to attend. Later, Minnesota Governor Rudy Perpich wrote a proclamation declaring May 21, 1990 Margaret Philbrook Day because of her commitment to family and selection as Mother of the Year.

We held several wonderful birthday parties for mom. She loved parties, so we hosted her 80th, 85th, and 90th celebrations at our home. The entire family, including parents of her children's spouses, nieces, and nephews, and all her friends, were invited. Sometimes, we planned these parties for months.

For mom, the essential part of her birthday was attending morning Mass. She considered it the most generous gift when all her children, sons- and daughters-in-law, grandchildren, and great-grandchildren joined her at St. Rose of Lima for Mass. It did not matter if they were Catholic. It did not matter if they choose to receive the Eucharist. It did not matter if they were pissed at another family member. It did not matter if they were angry with God. It only mattered that they came and prayed with her. And for those who attended, she'd buy them breakfast out of our inheritance. It was quite the deal!

Hundreds of people showed up for each of her birthday celebrations, and they were great fun. She held court out on our screen porch, spending as much time with each guest as they desired. There was never a question when you were visiting with my mother that you had her complete attention.

Your grandmother was a wonderful woman—we all miss her dearly. But I am confident that each of you is still on her prayer list.

The Lesson: The purpose of life is to serve others.

The Lesson: Mothers hold the most special place in a son's heart.

The Lesson: Sons are responsible for caring for their mothers; ensuring their safety and security; and being by their side whenever needed.

Aces and Kings

"Blessed indeed is the man who hears many gentle voices call him father."

~ Lydia Maria Child, an American abolitionist and writer

My Dad was much quieter than my mom, more reserved and laid-back. He maintained a wanderlust for the world, always curious and wanting to learn more about other places and other cultures. But, he had so little discretionary money that he was unable to travel. For years he talked about going to Alaska to fish; he loved to fish. But money was an issue. So, for his 80th birthday, I took Dad, mom, and Jake to Alaska for a week of salmon fishing. It was a delightful seven days.

I never understood Dad's enchantment with fishing. He would fish every day if he could. Even on bitter, freezing cold days in the dead of winter, he'd go ice fishing. He never owned an ice fishing house; he would sit outside on a folding chair or a bucket turned upside down, looking into a half-frozen hole he had chopped through the white ice.

One day in my mid-twenties, I asked him why he liked fishing so much. He looked at me and said, "When I'm fishing, I don't have to answer your mother's questions." Then, I understood.

Dad subscribed to National Geographic magazine, and when I was a young boy, each issue included a map of somewhere in the world. Dad gave me those maps. I taped them all over the walls of my brother David's and my bedroom.

As I lay on the top bunk at night, I studied those maps and wondered what it must be like in those places so far away. Perhaps wanderlust is genetic.

Dad also volunteered. He was an early president of the Roseville Historical Society and read for the blind on a special radio network. Every Friday night for over 25 years, he read the news of the day, short stories, and books. Dad had a clear and pleasant voice, delightful to the ear. I was privileged to drive him to the radio studio on the last night he read before his death. He also read Scripture at Sunday mass; parishioners often told me how much they enjoyed hearing him lector.

He enjoyed poetry and could easily be coaxed into reciting, by heart, "*The Cremation of Sam McGee*," which he learned while in school. One of my father's favorite short poems was "*I Held Little Hand Last Night.*" He performed it at my sisters' weddings and sometimes on my mother's birthday. He would lovingly hold your grandmother's hand, look tenderly into her eyes, and say:

> "I held a little hand last night,
> so gentle and so sweet
> I thought my heart would surely break
> So wildly did it beat.
> For no other hand in all the world,
> Greater pleasure brings,
> Than the hand I held last night. . .
> 4 ACES & a KING!"

His recitation always drew laughter and applause.

My mother often told me my father taught me the value of a dollar when I was five and put me on my own when I was seven. There is a lot of truth in that statement. Dad encouraged me to work hard, be prompt, get as much education as possible, share my talents with others, and spend money wisely.

On my 15th birthday, I took the written exam and on-the-road driver's test. I passed both and was issued a license the same day. The next thing I needed was a car. My dream car cost $1,000—a lot of money for a 15-year-old back then, about $8,500 in 2020. I didn't have cash, so I needed to take out a loan that required my father to cosign. Dad persuaded me to buy something less expensive. For $300, I got an eight-year-old brown and beige two-tone 1953 Chevy Belair. Initially, I was not happy with this, but it was good advice. I paid off that loan in 18 months.

Shortly after starting my senior year in high school, I was once again disenchanted with school and decided to quit. My Dad spent several hours with me going over the pros and cons. He did not want me to leave school, but I knew if I did, he would support my decision. He always supported me. We sat together at our dining room table discussing the importance of education and why it did not matter that I did not like school. He believed education offered opportunities that should not be wasted. I decided to stay in school.

I graduated from high school and went on to nine years of higher education. If it hadn't been for my father, I have no doubt I would have quit high school that day and my life indeed would have been different.

My father worked many different jobs, sometimes, more than one at a time. Raising 11 children takes a lot of money, and I still do not understand how he and my mother made ends meet. He was an office worker for General Mills, made bullets during WWII at the Arden Hills Arms Plant, and helped his mom at Pinky's Tavern. He sold *Successful Farming* magazine, sold and installed water softeners, was a bookkeeper for two different small businesses, and managed a convenience store.

He was a good worker and a conscientious employee, seldom took a sick day, and did whatever was necessary to get the job done right. He was a man of his word, and every employer could count on him. My mother also contributed financially working several part-time jobs over the years, but they never had any money.

Dad was diagnosed with pancreatic cancer shortly after his 83rd birthday. The doctors offered him chemotherapy, which they thought might give him another year. But in 1993, chemotherapy took its own severe and painful toll. His other option was to let cancer take its course, which given his condition, probably meant he had four to eight weeks to live. He chose the latter option.

All his children and older grandchildren spent a lot of time with him during those final weeks. As the disease devoured his body, his pain was offset by morphine, which consumed his consciousness. A hospital bed replaced the dining room table in their home so that mom could better care for him. Dad's Godchild and our cousin, Sue Sindelar, was a hospice nurse. She tirelessly cared for him. As he neared the end, Sue called me at my law office on several occasions, telling me death was near and that I should come. I rushed to my parent's home. After the third "false alarm," I told Sue to call me when it was over.

I have never forgotten what Sue said to me.

"Were you at the births of any of your sons?" She asked.

"I was at all their births."

"So, you experienced the miracle of birth."

"Yes," I responded. "Birth is an amazing miracle."

"Well, being in the presence of a loved-one at their death is the same kind of miracle," she explained.

A few days later, Sue called again. I drove to my parent's home and, along with my mother, Sue, and many of my siblings, I was present to my father's final breath. It was a serene spiritual experience. I felt the enormous energy of life amidst the tremendous, overwhelming sadness of my Dad's death. He was 83; I was 46.

The Lesson: A father's principal responsibility is to show by example what it means to be a father.

The Lesson: A card laid is a card played.

The Lesson: Get as much formal education as you possibly can; it will serve you well for the long-term.

The Lesson: Birth and death are extraordinary occasions. They are moments when we are united with, and comforted by, the Creator.

The Lesson: On the death of a loved one, cry until you cannot cry anymore; then cry some more.

Waste Not

Having such a large family with no money to spare, my parents were concerned about wasting things—anything. For my Dad, the most annoying was when one of us wasted food. He worked long hours to support his family, and he did not respond well when one of us wasted something that he had worked so hard to provide.

Our mother would not allow us to chew gum at the dinner table, so to keep it for after dinner, some of my older sisters would put their gum in their glass of milk. One evening, a younger sibling tipped over my Dad's glass of milk. This was not the first time this had happened, and Dad became quite upset. So, my kind and caring older sister, Cynthia, offered my father her glass of milk.

"Here, dad," she said, "Take my milk. I haven't touched it."

When my father drank the last swallow, he saw the gum at the bottom of the glass. "What the Sam hell?" he exclaimed

The Lesson: When you do someone a favor, remember where you put your gum.

The Lesson: Check the facts before you act.

Youngest of the Oldest

"Being a middle child is not something you aspire to; it's some-thing that happens to you."

~ Adam Sternbergh, a Canadian author

Growing up amidst ten siblings—nine sisters and one brother—could be a book in and of itself. Although, at the time, it did not seem special coming from such a large family. It just was what it was.

Numerically, I am the middle child with five older and five younger siblings. There were eight years between my next oldest sister, Sandy, and my younger brother, David—four years on either side. So, I was the youngest of the oldest and the oldest of the youngest. Some might suggest I also have an only child's characteristics because of the many years between my siblings and me—all the makings of a mixed-up kid.

We lived in a two-story house at 1266 West County Road B, which was small for so many people by today's standards. But it was not small when I was grow-ing up. We all fit, doubling or tripling up in the bedrooms. Fortunately, most of my older sisters went away to high school when they were 14—they joined the convent. That offered more room for the rest of us.

There was just one bathroom in our house. When people ask me what that was like, I quip, "it was okay. My sisters put a soup can outside the bathroom door for my brother and me."

All my younger siblings and I were born while our family lived at 1266, and we all grew up there. After I was born, my parents could not agree on my name. Your grandmother wanted to name me "Burnham" after your grandfather, but Dad didn't want any "juniors" in the family. They were at an impasse. So, my birth certificate simply reads, "Baby Boy Philbrook."

When the priest baptized me, he asked my parents, "What name have you given your son?"

My mother immediately replied, "Burnham John." And so it was.

Or at least that's what she thought. On the way out of the church, so the story goes, my Dad turned to mom and said, "His name is Bud." I've been called "Bud" all my life, except when my mother wanted my attention or a teacher at St. Rose called on me.

I don't think any of us knew we were poor until we were much older. That we received government surplus food was never a big deal; I just thought USDA was a peanut butter brand. And we were never hungry. Our parents always ensured that there was food on the table. We wore a lot of hand-me-downs given to us by our wealthier cousins. But the clothes were new to us.

My first bike was an old used big balloon-tired contraption. Rusted when I got it, I decided to paint it. The only extra paint my Dad had was pink. So, I was the sole boy in the area with a pink bike. I couldn't pedal it as fast as my buddies on their new Schwinn bicycles due to the huge tires. But that was okay. I always caught up with them.

Sometimes I felt like an only child. Others were always around, but they were so much older or so much younger that I didn't have much of a relationship with them. By the time I was a freshman in high school, all but one of my older sisters had left home, David was in fifth grade, and Michelle, my youngest sister, was a preschooler.

I just went about my business—going to school, working, hanging with friends, and dating pretty girls—not paying much attention to any of my older or younger siblings. On those occasions when I did eat dinner at home, I often ate alone at the dining room table while my father was at work, and my mother and her brood of five were in the breakfast room. They would eat whatever Mom made that night. I dined on hotdogs drenched in catchup.

Over the years, I have tried to be a supportive brother; although, I certainly could have done more. I've helped my siblings and their children whenever they were in need or asked for assistance. And my siblings have been good to and supported me. For example, Michelle door-knocked for me, along with Dad, during my first campaign for the Minnesota House in 1970. Frannie wished for me. Frannie often reminded me that when she was eight years old and our mother was pregnant with me, she prayed that she would have a baby brother to go along with her four sisters. I'm glad she did. Frannie also graciously let me stay at her home in New Jersey in the summer of 1963 when I was on my way to Europe. Sandy invited me to stay for a couple of weeks at her home in North Carolina after I left VISTA in 1969. Margaret and Anne accompanied mom to my federal court trial for draft resistance in 1971. Cynthia worked on my 1974 campaign for the Minnesota House and loaned me money, so I didn't have to work during the campaign. That was a tremendous gift! Joan held a house party for me in 2005 during my gubernatorial campaign. Kate helped edit *Conclave Conspiracy* in 2011, offering many significant suggestions. Claudette and David have been extremely helpful to Global Volunteers in various ways over many years, and nearly all my other sisters have contributed financially to Global Volunteers. In 2005, along with nieces and nephews, they showed up to serenade my campaign supporters when I announced my candidacy for governor. These are just some of the many ways my siblings have supported me.

We have also always respected each other. Three of my sisters are godparents to one of you, and I am Godfather to four of my siblings' children. My brother

David, Sandy's husband Jay, and Claudette's daughter and my goddaughter Lisa were all in our wedding party. We still honor each other's major birthdays—those that end in zero—and attend graduation parties and family weddings. Fortunately, we are all still living; although, several spouses have passed.

Unfortunately, I have grown apart from some of my siblings over the years, primarily because neither they nor I extended the effort to maintain stronger relationships. On the other hand, I am quite close to other siblings, especially your Uncle David and Aunt Fran. And your Aunt Anne is special and holds each of you close in her heart.

All the same, being one of two boys in a houseful of women was challenging. During an event at the home of one of David's in-laws, a woman approached David and me while we were visiting. After brief introductions, she remarked that she had just learned we had nine sisters. "You must know a lot about women," she said. Without missing a beat, David replied, "I don't know anything about women. Never paid any attention." That sums it up.

The Lesson: Family is a gift, and siblings enrich that gift.

The Lesson: Birth order is not necessarily prescriptive or predictive.

Will You Take Me to the Party?

"You don't marry someone you can live with; you marry some-
one you cannot live without."

~ Aleatha Romig, an American author

Michele Gran and I met at the Minnesota House of Representatives when I
was an elected member, and she was a page. She was 20; I was 28. Your mother
was gorgeous then, as she is now, and wicked smart! One of her job responsibilities was to get things for the members when they needed them. I had her bring
me coffee and hot dogs during floor sessions. When she did, I'd visit with her,
albeit briefly, because the bosses were watching.

Your mom denies that she asked me out on our first date, but it is true. One
evening I was working late in my office, and she stopped by to ask me if I was
going to a legislative party that night. I told her I was considering it, and she
asked if she could go with me. She explained a male page wanted her to go with
him to this event. She said she wanted to go, but not with him. That was February 28, 1975, the day my world changed.

We dated on-again, off-again, on-again, off-again, on-again for five years. Initially, we had to be quite discreet. I was an elected member of the House, and
your mom was an employee; that was not an acceptable relationship. Today it
would be scandalous. We had to be discreet. After the workday, we'd reunite
several blocks from the capital and go to places where no one knew us. We were
so cautious that it was a year before your mom's best friend and roommate,

Terri Hudoba, who was also a House page (and the maid of honor at our wedding), knew we were seeing each other.

During one of those off-again periods, I got engaged to another woman. It seems unimaginable today, but I did do that.

Sometime later, Michele invited me to lunch, and I accepted. When I showed up and on time, it was clear she had been there for a while—her wineglass was nearly empty. Then she told me how disrespectful it was that I had scheduled my wedding date on her birthday.

"I don't care that you're marrying someone else, but on my birthday?!"

With that, she got up and walked out of the restaurant.

I was stunned. I had no idea. I never thought about the date. But I knew I had messed up—big time!

I did not return to work but rather drove to my mother's home. It was evident I was upset, flustered, and flummoxed. As my mother listened to what had happened, she said to me, "If it bothers you that much, you should think carefully about whether you're marrying the right girl."

It wasn't long after that I realized I had made a colossal mistake. Within a few weeks, I broke off the engagement and tried to figure out how I might repair the damage with Michele and hopefully get back together.

Months later, I had not made any progress. She would not answer my phone calls. Threw the roses I sent her into the garbage. Did not respond to letters. Would not open her apartment door when I knocked.

While that was all understandable, I wanted to get back together. But first, I had to at least talk with her.

Your mom and I have a good mutual friend from the legislature days, John Corbid. I asked John for his help. The plan was that he would invite Michele out for a drink, and then I would just happen to show up at that bar, on that particular date, at that specific time. That would allow me to try to break the ice.

When I walked up to their table, your mom looked at me and then said to John, "I thought you were my friend."

She stood up and left the building.

John said to me, "I don't think she likes you."

I continued my efforts to woo her but to no avail. Then one day, out of nowhere, she called to let me know that she would be at an event at the Newman Center on the University of Minnesota campus. Newman was the church where I attended Sunday mass. She said that it would be okay if I went to that event as well. She made it crystal clear that this was not a date; she was not asking me out, and nothing in our relationship had changed. She merely wanted me to know that she would not walk out if I happened to be in the same physical space as she was.

I went to that event, and we talked. She agreed to see me again. We started dating, but there was little trust. As we grew closer over the next several months, we decided to go together on a short trip to Nova Scotia, where she had a friend she hadn't seen in a long time. Because I had a business trip scheduled to Washington DC, we agreed to meet there, attend a performance at the Kennedy Center, and then drive to Maine, where we caught an overnight cruise from Kennebunkport to Halifax.

That night in our room on the boat, I said to her, "I think we should get married." Her response: "Ask me again in the morning." I'd been playing blackjack at the casino and had had a couple of drinks. I think she wanted to make sure I was serious.

We spoke about marriage the next morning, and the following day she accepted my proposal.

But your mom was unwilling to tell anyone, which was understandable given our past. Trust loss is difficult to regain. I wanted to shout from the rooftops that we loved each other, and we were getting married, but I could not say a word. Can you imagine how difficult it is to be engaged to the woman you love but can't tell anyone? I knew if I even whispered it, I'd blow the whole thing.

The Lesson: Do not forget her birthday!

The Lesson: Be gentle, considerate, and respectful to the woman you love—always.

The Lesson: When you love someone, want to spend the rest of your life with her, and raise children together, you must persevere. You cannot let anything deter you; nothing can get in your way or diminish your resolve.

Smokey Joe

"Love is patient; love is kind."

~ 1 Corinthians 13:4-8

Your mom has always loved horses. She'd been riding since she was eight years old when she first went with her mother to St. Mary's Resort in the foothills of Glacier National Park, the summer after her father died. Grandma Gran and your mom returned to St. Mary's every summer for the next ten years. It was during those years that she made good friends from the Blackfeet Nation.

While I was trying to pursue her, and she was still not answering my calls, I decided to take horseback riding lessons to show her that I cared about what she cared about. After we got back together, I continued those lessons, but I did not tell her. I had a bigger plan.

For her 25th birthday, I bought her Smokey Joe, a gentle and lovable light brown appaloosa with white markings. I asked one of her family friends, Mary Bailey, who lived on a hobby farm south of St. Paul, if she would let me give Smoky Joe to Michele at their home on her birthday. Their place was perfect for Smokey Joe. It was out in the sticks and had a long winding dirt driveway protected by pines and oak trees—nothing to spook him.

Mary was reluctant. It was her understanding that Michele did not want to see me. I couldn't tell Mary we were engaged because of your mom's stipulation that we wait before telling anyone. So, I told Mary that we had reestablished our friendship and assured her that it would be okay with Michele. But it had to be a secret. "Michele cannot know I am giving her a horse," I explained to Mary.

Mary relented and agreed to invite Michele and her mother to their home on July 1, 1979. I transported Smoky Joe from the ranch where I bought him to the foot of Mary's long winding driveway. Dayton's department store made a giant green and white bow, which I tied to his head and fastened a big green banner around his neck that read in white letters, "Happy Birthday, Michele." The three of them were outside at the top of the driveway at noon.

I rode Smoky Joe, all decked out in green and white, up the driveway. He immediately caught their attention as we made the final turn. But they did not recognize who was riding due to my cowboy hat and sunglasses. When we got about 10 feet away, your mom finally realized who it was and let out a scream.

She had never had her own horse before; she was excited. It was a wonderful birthday. I think it was because of Smoky Joe that she finally relented to making our engagement public.

As we considered who would be in our wedding party, we concurred that John Corbid should be a groomsman. When we called John, we were both on the call, but he didn't know Michele was on the line. After pleasantries, I asked John if he would be in my wedding.

"Who would ever marry you, Philbrook?" he asked.

"I would," your mom responded.

John recognized her voice and said, "Philbrook, I hope I never have anything you want."

The Lesson: Persistence, persistence, persistence—never give up, never quit. If something is important to you, move whatever mountains you must.

The Lesson: Appreciate the present; have hope for the future, but do not despair because of what you may have done in the past.

The Earth Moved!

"Let there be spaces in your togetherness, And let the winds of the heavens dance between you."

~ Khalil Gibran, a Lebanese-American poet

We made plans to honeymoon on a Windjammer "barefoot cruise" in the Caribbean Sea. That's a cruise where the paying customers work as part of the crew on a small sailing ship. It was your mom's idea; she loves adventure. I agreed; I enjoy being on the water, but I'd never sailed the sea. I mailed in the deposit and began reading about sailing the Caribbean. Your mother made the plane reservations.

Then one evening, several weeks before our wedding, we went out for dinner, and everything changed. Late 1979 was a time when there was a massive exodus of refugees from Southeast Asia. The network news carried stories every day about "the boat people" who risked their lives on small rickety old boats fleeing their countries to sail to freedom. The boats were capsizing, and people were drowning at sea. Their tragic situation brought out the camera crews.

During dinner, she said, "I don't want to go on that cruise. I don't feel right about playing on the water while this terrible thing is going on." She told me that she wanted to do something more significant. Her idea was that we go to a rural village someplace and work with the local people.

I had recently completed the course work for my master's degree in public affairs with a primary concentration in international economic development. I also had practical experience working as a short-term volunteer in a small rural village in India and with American Indians on reservations in the US. But honeymooning in a remote village in a developing country? That sounded a bit strange.

But that is what we did. We spent a week in the rural village of San Miquel Conacaste in Guatemala. We worked with the local people and the staff of a resident North American INGO, the Institute of Cultural Affairs (ICA). It was a fascinating and rewarding experience.

Your mom sometimes tells the story about our first night in the village. Shortly after we arrived, we were shown our room. Our bedding consisted of chaise lounges, the fold-up patio type made of metal and woven plastic. We each got one. After dinner, we went to bed. In the middle of the night, she woke me up and whispered in a terrified voice, "Did you feel that?"

"Feel what?" I responded.

"That trembling. I think it might have been an earthquake"

"Oh, I'm sure it's nothing," I told her. "Go back to sleep."

The next morning during breakfast, your mom asked George West, the ICA staff leader, "What was that trembling last night?"

And he said, "What was it like?"

"It felt like the earth moved," she explained innocently.

George smiled, his eyes twinkling, and said, "Michele, that's supposed to happen on your honeymoon."

Living and working with the local people of that small Guatemalan village enriched us beyond belief. Your mom used her creative writing and public relations skills to develop a brochure the ICA used to acquire local funding for community development projects. I worked with the local people to devise a strategy to encourage the InterAmerican Development Bank to grant the community a loan for a "drip irrigation" system that eventually dramatically improved crop production. It was a week unlike either of us had ever experienced.

But to ensure that you have the proper perspective of our honeymoon, it is important to know we also spent a week at Disney World. That was my idea. We had "a properly balanced" honeymoon.

The Lesson: Do something meaningful to celebrate your marriage. It will inspire you for the rest of your life.

The Lesson: If it's your wife's idea, it's a good idea.

Men are from Mars,
Women are from Venus

"When women are depressed, they either eat or go shopping.
Men invade another country."

~ Elayne Boosler, an American comedian

There was a time when I was young, naïve, and arrogant, and believed I was beyond change. I was well-educated, knew what I wanted to do, and how to do it. Over the years, I've matured and come to realize that I continue to change, continue to learn, and grow almost daily. I embrace the new and look forward to personal growth. I am committed to making my human experience as meaningful and spiritually enriching as possible. And I told your mother that I am also committed to doing this with her.

John Gray wrote an influential book entitled *Men Are from Mars, Women Are from Venus*. Your mother and I read it together. I encourage you to read it.

Among other important things, Gray writes that not talking about our negative and positive feelings in a relationship is like not watering a plant. We all know what that does—it kills the plant. He explains that we cannot expect to repress our negative feelings and expect our positive emotions to remain lively. We cannot expect to grow in love if we do not or cannot talk about all our true feelings.

It's difficult for some men to express their true feelings; it certainly has been for me. Women, on the other hand, do not seem to be plagued by that challenge. However, men can inappropriately express negative feelings, even when we mean no disrespect.

Gray also writes that sometimes men feel exhausted when we hold back so much of what we feel. Perhaps that is why we sometimes feel overwhelmed and so tired.

One of Gray's bright lights is his admission that talking about our true feelings may initially be hard work, but it will become second nature and easy to do overtime. Well, I'm still a work in progress. Perhaps it's gotten easier since we first read Gray's book, but progress is slow. However, that is not an excuse for not being true to who you are.

Your mother and I have struggled with our ability to communicate well with each other. We knew this would be a challenge, even before we were married. We took a couple's communication course before our wedding, and it helped— some. Nevertheless, we continued to struggle. But based on conversations with my male friends, our struggle has not been a whole lot more complicated than other married couples.

Our challenges appear more often as we work together every day. Other couples go about their workday separately and come together on evenings and weekends. From my experience, they too have communication difficulties, but theirs might be easier to deal with. When I ask my friends what they think their marriage would be like working with their spouse every day, they say "no way."

I love your mother to the depths of my bones, and I want nothing more than to grow old with her. We share many things—profound faith, the value of caring for vulnerable children, a common understanding of service, a mutual appreciation of creation, the love of our sons and daughters, the joy of life, political alignment, numerous friends. None of these are superficial or without significant meaning. We often see things differently, but that is good. If I look at a tree and see the wonders of the bark and green leaves while she looks at the same tree and sees the wonders of the squirrels and the birds, those are only different perceptions of the same reality, not observances of different realities.

I hope that each of you and your brides are as blest as we have been.

The Lesson: Love your wife; be kind, gentle, considerate, and caring.

The Lesson: Do your utmost to learn to communicate with your spouse openly and lovingly.

The Lesson: Embrace the concept that a difference of opinion is not necessarily an argument.

Pink and Green

"The smallest good deed is better than
the grandest good intention."

~ Jacques-Joseph Duguet,
a French theologian, author, and philosopher

1984 was a big year for us. We incorporated Global Volunteers; conducted our first service program in Jamaica's Blue Mountains; moved my law office to the 1st National Bank Building downtown St. Paul; celebrated Jake's first birthday, sold our house on Arona; and constructed and moved into our new home on Keller Parkway in Maplewood. The latter was nearly all-consuming.

For several years, your mother and I had visited numerous newly constructed houses across the Twin Cities during the annual Parade of Homes. She liked doing that, and as we toured each house, she would note various features we both liked. One January Sunday afternoon in 1984, your mom and I went out looking for vacant lots to build a new home for our family. We decided the northeast suburbs of St. Paul would be a good location and looked for places that offered ready access to I35E to ease our commutes to work. As we drove around the lakes between Little Canada and northern Maplewood, we got lost due to the winding roads. Then we saw a "Lot for Sale by Owner" sign "with lakeshore." It was a corner lot with numerous mature trees. Your mother noticed a phone number, but I said, "We could never afford that lot. It has lakeshore."

Nevertheless, that evening we called the owner, and to my surprise, his asking price was within our budget. A couple of weeks later, we signed a purchase agreement for the lot at 2634 Keller Parkway. One of my clients was an architect who designed houses; he helped us draw plans that reflected our ideal family home. Then we hired a contractor to build the house and took out a 120-day construction loan.

We put our Arona house up for sale, assuming it would take at least four months to sell. Our plan was to move from Arona to our new home in Maplewood on the first of August, 1984. Not to happen! We received an offer for our full asking price within three days, but the buyer needed to move in no later than April 1, two weeks away. We accepted the deal, packed up all our stuff, put some in storage, and moved the rest into a one-bedroom apartment in Shoreview on a short-term lease.

A few days before the foundation was scheduled to be excavated, we learned the contractor we'd hired could not do the job because he had entered treatment. That was good for him, but a huge problem for us. Spring was prime time for housing construction, and we knew identifying and vetting a new contractor would consume weeks—time we did not have. Interest rates were on the rise in 1984, and the terms of the construction loan required that the house be finished and we close no later than August 10, 1984. If we failed to meet those terms, we would have to renegotiate a new loan, probably at higher interest.

A longtime friend and grade school classmate, Mike Moore, had a road construction business and was an expert at moving earth. Mike agreed to dig the hole and did a magnificent job. Then we had to lay the foundation. I found a local bricklayer who could do the job almost immediately, so we hired him. He constructed the foundation according to the blueprints, and we were off and running.

Lenny Painchaub, another longtime friend and member of our wedding party, was a realtor who sold new homes. Lenny introduced us to several subcontractors he knew—a carpenter with a full crew, a plumber, an electrician, and a concrete guy. I became the general contractor, a role learned OTJ—on the job. I drove from my St. Paul law office to visit the construction site every day over lunch and after work.

Your mother's 30th birthday party was at the new house; although, it was only stud walls and a roof. I bought her a used pontoon boat as her birthday present, and our party guests took turns boating on Lake Gervais. She wanted a kayak, but I tried to convince her that a pontoon boat was better for a family than a kayak. She said, "yeah, better for you!" But she enjoyed evening boating on the pontoon. (Several years later, she bought a kayak—which she still has—from the proceeds of a bet she won when I disagreed with her about at which hospital she gave birth to our first-born. Not too smart on my part.)

We wanted a new home that featured some attributes of old. Architectural Antiques in Minneapolis offered a wide array of light fixtures, stairways, wainscot, doors, windows, buffets, and room dividers salvaged from early 1900 era buildings. When we discovered an old green painted buffet and matching wainscot amid tons of dusty old stuff, we immediately called the carpenter and told him to stop work in the dining room. After modifying the blueprints, they created a space for the buffet.

Your mother spent the summer removing the green paint from the buffet, quickly discovering an undercoat of pink paint. Then she sanded, stained, and varnished the oak wood, turning the 1900 cabinet into a remarkably beautiful piece of furniture. The wainscot was a bit easier—it only had one coat of green paint—but it too required extensive sanding, staining, and varnishing. Phil Ricker, my friend and classmate in grade school, high school, and at the U of M, who was also a groomsman at our wedding and a talented wood craftsman, helped me install the oak wainscot. It was like assembling a complicated puzzle as we modified the multiple pieces to fit a room for which the wood was never intended. After several Saturdays of long hours, the puzzle was complete.

We met the deadline and closed on August 10, 1984, with no time to spare, moving in the following week. That is the story of the home in which each of you grew up and still call 2634.

The Lesson: It never hurts to ask.

The Lesson: When it goes wrong, and it will, find a way to make it go right.

The Lesson: Never underestimate the value of long-time friends. They will help you out and bail you out every time.

Long Marriage

"To be fully seen by somebody, then,
and be loved anyhow - this is a human offering
that can border on miraculous."

~ Elizabeth Gilbert, an American author

We have been married for more than 40 years. However, I confess that I still don't know much about marriage; although, your mother has tried to teach me all those years.

There are tomes written about how to have a happy marriage. Therapists will listen and offer advice, which is sometimes helpful. Well-intentioned family and friends will offer counsel, which may not be useful. Parents will fret and cajole, hoping and praying their children's marriage will not end in divorce.

By today's standards, your mother and I have been married a long time; although we have several friends who have been married longer—my brother David and your Aunt Laura have been happily married two years longer than we have, and my mom and dad were married for 60 years! Especially noteworthy is my sister Kate's marriage to Jack after both of their spouses had died. Kate was 84 and Jack was 92 when they met at an assisted living facility in Chicago. Getting married at that age is a genuine testament to the desirability of marriage.

Younger people sometimes ask, "What's the secret to a long marriage?"

My answer: "I don't know."

However, upon reflection, I've concluded one reason we have stayed married is we never stopped loving each other at the same time. Each of us may have wanted to throw in the towel, but never on the same day.

Marriage is challenging. Do not let anyone fool you into believing otherwise. You must work at marriage.

When we were first married, I didn't understand that. I asked, "Why would I have to work at my marriage? Isn't marriage just a part of life? It's not a job— it's not a course for which you have to take a test."

As I've grown older and more mature in our marriage, there is no longer any question in my mind that you must work at it.

Although marriage is challenging, it is also full of joy—perhaps not bliss, but joy. And, while marriage is full of joy, it is also full of sorrow. Unfortunately and inexplicably, the one we love to the depths of our heart may also be the one to whom we bring the most significant pain. Why? I don't know. Maybe God knows.

One of the biggest mistakes I've made in our marriage is not telling your mother how I feel. I now know the vital importance of letting your spouse know who you are—the whole you. For some men, it is difficult to talk about feelings. But for many women, sharing feelings IS intimacy. If you struggle with talking about your feelings, be sure to show them. When we don't allow the woman we love to understand the totality of who we are, it's the same as saying to her, "I don't want you to know who I am." What kind of relationship does that produce?

If you can talk with her about your feelings, then do that. If you're sentimental, let her know. If you tear up during movies, let her know. Don't wipe away your tears to hide them from her. If you are angry, tell her, but never take your anger out on her. If you are excited, show her your excitement. If you are happy, show her your joy. Don't stuff your emotions. Let her see you as you are. If you do not do that, it's as if you suggest you are someone else, someone you are not.

Having said that, all the above was/is hard for me. Hopefully, it will be easier for you.

The Lesson: True love is not a feeling; it is a covenant.

The Lesson: Never stop loving her, no matter what she says or does. Tell her your sorry when you treat her poorly. Forgive yourself when you mess up.

The Lesson: I hope to grow old with your mother and die in her loving arms. That will be matrimonial bliss.

Mistakes & Second Chances

"No matter how much you love your child,
God loves her more."

~ Author unknown

When I was 19, I fell in love with a wonderful 19-year-old woman. She got pregnant, but even though I pleaded, she did not want to get married. She thought we were too young—just kids—and "kids shouldn't raise kids."

I am honoring her request that she not be identified by name.

Her father raised abortion as an option, but they were illegal in 1966, and she did not want to do that in any event. Instead, she moved to Chicago, where she planned to have our baby and give it up for adoption.

I hired a lawyer, a friend of my parents, to see if I could get custody and raise the child. But that was not possible. In the mid-1960s, there were no laws in Minnesota or Illinois that protected paternal custody rights. I was devastated.

As a student at the University of Minnesota and working part-time as an assistant manager at a movie theater, I did not earn enough money to raise a baby or support a family. So, I got a full-time job at Sperry Univac, a large computer manufacturing company. My hope was that she might change her mind about marriage if she knew I could support her and our child.

On October 16, 1966, my mother called me at work. She had just learned that our baby boy had died in childbirth earlier that morning.

It is not possible to describe the pain I felt that day and all the days since. Even though I had never seen our son, felt him kicking in her womb, or even heard him cry, I felt an overwhelming, excruciating loss.

It was months before the pain became bearable and years before I gave any thought to having other children. But when I did contemplate the possibility of fathering another child, I made an absolute commitment to myself that I would be the best father I could be.

Then God gave your mother and me three sons, all of whom are the joy of my life. I am so proud of each of you. I am blest every day by each of you—just knowing that you are my sons and that I love you. How you raise your children will be the real test of how good a father I have been. But the death of my first son, your brother, has driven me to be the best father I can be to each of you.

The Lesson: We all make mistakes in life, and mistakes present significant learning opportunities. But mistakes offer so much more. Mistakes dangle before our eyes the genuine possibility of renewing our lives by rehearsing the results and then changing.

The Lesson: Be the best possible father to the children you are fortunate to raise.

The Lesson: Help your wife help you become a better father, husband, lover, friend, and companion.

Miracles

"Miracles happen to those who believe in them."

~ Bernard Berenson, an American art historian

We had been married three and a half years when your mother told me she was pregnant. I was thrilled! It was an excitement that only an expecting father can understand.

Your mom and I went to the hospital three times before Jake was born because of false labor pains. When it finally was time for her to give birth, she was in labor at the hospital for 24 hours before the doctor finally decided to do an emergency C-section. I was with her most of the time, as were your two grand-mothers. It was excruciating to watch her in such pain. Even though they gave her meds to confront the pain, she experienced deep agony as women often do when delivering their babies.

Jacob Gran was a big boy, almost 10 pounds. Due to the long labor process, the nurse immediately put him in an incubator. As soon as she closed the glass cover, Jake whizzed all over the inside of the machine. I laughed. I figured it was his way of telling everyone what he thought about the whole delivery process.

Jake had ten fingers and ten toes, and everything else seemed to be in order, so we took him home. And our lives were never the same after that.

Jake was born in March of 1983. I had finished law school the previous December and had taken the February bar exam. We lived at 1514 Arona during his first year. Then we moved to a small apartment while we constructed 2634.

On August 10, 1984, we moved into our brand-new home. Jake was 17 months. Life was good—just the three of us.

Jake was smart, curious, and independent. One day, we went to Rosedale Shopping Mall to get some gifts for Christmas. Your mother set Jake down on the terrazzo floor to look at something, and he started walking away. He walked from one end of the shopping mall to the other and never looked back. We followed at a safe distance, but in total amazement at this little tyke's demonstrable independence.

Four years later, your mom told me that she was pregnant again. I again was thrilled – beyond explanation.

We had decided we wanted two children, hopefully, a boy and a girl, but we would take whatever God gave us. But your mom was done with the labor thing. The doctor told her she should have another C-section, and there was no argument on her part. When we understood that we could pick the birth-date sometime during the last two weeks of May, we selected the 28th. The 28th is special for us—our first date was on February 28, we were married on December 28, and my birthday is August 28. (As an aside, St. Augustine, the great Christian theologian, died on August 28, 430.)

Another big strapping boy, Nicholas Burnham was nearly as large as Jake was at birth. He too had ten fingers and ten toes, so we took him home to 2634. Jake was protective of his little brother but also a bit wary. He didn't seem to understand why Nick found it so much fun to slide headfirst down the carpeted stairs and then hit his head on the tile floor; laugh, and do it all over again.

When your mother told me she was pregnant again, it was a surprise. We never planned to have three children; although, I was thoroughly thrilled.

Nick was less than a year old and too young to understand that he would have a baby brother, but we sat Jake down to tell him. When I explained it to Jake, he looked at me and said emphatically, "no more babies."

Andrew John was also born by C-section in November 1988. Your mother selected November 12 because that was also Grandma Gran's 80th birthday. Your grandmother often told me it was the best birthday present she ever could imagine.

Before Drew was born, we did not know if he was a boy or a girl; although, we were hoping for a girl. On the way to the hospital for his birth, your mother told me, "If it's another red-haired blue-eyed boy, tell them to take me from the maternity ward to the psych ward."

Months after Drew was born, while your mother was holding him, Nick grabbed her mug of boiling tea and it spilled all over his chest. She threw him into cold water in the kitchen sink and then rushed him to our neighbor, Dr. Margaret Hustad's office, the boys' pediatrician. This was serious—third-degree burns. But Nick was a trooper. He put up with all that pain and changing the bandages twice a day for over a month. Your mother nursed Nick back to health, and there are no scars on his chest.

Drew was smaller at birth than his older brothers, but he was also feistier. One day when he was not quite two years old, I heard Nick crying. I asked Nick, "what's the matter, son?"

"Drew hit me."

I asked Drew, "Did you hit your brother?"

"Ya."

"Why would you do that?"

"Because he was going to hit me," Drew said defiantly. Apparently, he thought a preemptive strike was necessary.

I was at each of your births. I loved you from the moment I knew you were conceived. I knew you from the moment you were born. I stood in complete wonder as each of you were born. The miracle of your lives continues to amaze me.

The three of you have brought me more joy than all the rest of life combined. There simply are no words that express the love I have for you and for your mother who gave you birth.

But make no mistake—it was your mother who breast-fed you, who made your breakfast, school lunches, and dinners. She nursed you back to health when you were sick. She comforted you when you were distraught. She held you when you were in pain. She kissed your bruised elbows and scraped knees. She taught you about nature and the love for creation. She raised you to be the fine men you are today.

There is good reason that a man has a special place in his heart for his mother. And your mother is special beyond all mothers.

The Lesson: Children are a breathtaking gift that simply blows the mind.

The Lesson: There is nothing more special to a man than to help raise his sons.

The Lesson: Children can teach their parents as much as parents can teach their children. I have learned so much from each of you, and for that, I am incredibly grateful!

Orange Lake

"We do not remember days, we remember experiences."

~ Cesare Pavese, an Italian poet and novelist

While on a business trip to Florida in 1988, your mother and I decided to take Jake to see the mouse—Disney World. We saw signs along the road advertising free Disney tickets, so we stopped at a Stuckey's to inquire. The offer was free one-day-passes for participating in a two-hour timeshare presentation. That seemed reasonable. What could be the harm? But we both agreed that we were not going to buy anything.

Long story short, we bought a one-week timeshare at Orange Lake Country Club, adjacent to the Disney complex. A few years later, we bought a second week. As it turns out, these were among the smartest decisions we ever made.

At the time when we were first married, I hadn't taken many vacations. But your mom was into vacations—time away from the day-to-day, a chance to experience exciting places, and the opportunity to be together. After a few years traveling to Orange Lake, I too became enamored with vacations, discovering that time away clears the mind and cleanses the soul. Even though I worked some of the time on our family vacations, vacation time allowed me—forced me—to be present to your mother and to enjoy each of you in a unique environment.

Three decades later, we bought two more timeshare weeks in Sint Maarten at a resort situated right on the ocean. I enjoy the water—any water—and thoroughly relish our time in Sint Maarten.

Some advertisers disparage timeshares and the associated costs. But we have found them to be a great value, even though each timeshare week has a substantial annual maintenance fee. Still, the charge is generally less than what it costs for a week of comparable lodging anywhere else, and it forces us to vacation. We hope you enjoy these weeks when you inherit them.

The Lesson: Family vacations are essential, especially when children are young. They are less about what specific things you do and much more about spending time together without all the day-to-day distractions.

The Lesson: "We are not going to buy anything," are famous last words.

Mural, Mural on the Wall

"I'm going down to Florida
to get some sand in my shoes."

~ Johnny Cash, an American singer-songwriter

Your great-great-grandfather came from Maine to Minnesota, built a home, and raised a family in Northeast Minneapolis. Your great-grandfather and grandfather grew up in the same area. I too spent much of my life in this part of the world. That makes me a fourth-generation Minnesotan.

After 65 winters in Minnesota—winters that seemed to get colder, longer, and with more snow as the decades wore on—I decided I could not do it any longer. As a family, we generally tried to escape for a week or two every winter to sunny Florida or some other warm place, but we could do that only when school was not in session. After you all graduated from high school, I started thinking about getting to warmer climates for more extended periods during the dread. Your mother, on the other hand, loves Minnesota winter. She enjoys the change of seasons, the snow, and the cold.

In 2011, Drew, Jake, and I started talking seriously about getting a place in Florida. I knew it would be a hard sell for your mother because that was not something in which she was interested. She didn't particularly like Florida and certainly did not like its conservative politics.

My pitch about the value of buying a second home in Florida was severalfold. First, Jake had finally decided to go to school full-time to get a college education. He had selected the University of South Florida in Tampa, an excellent business school away from the distractions of his many friendships. Our having a family home in the Tampa area would help him achieve that goal.

Second, living and working in the same house as Drew would allow me to mentor him daily. Given his desire to make Global Volunteers his career, this would be good for everyone.

Third, the timing was terrific; the Florida real estate market had bottomed out, and with baby boomers turning 65, the housing market could only improve. Buying a house there would be a good investment. Further, we could use my new monthly Social Security check to pay the mortgage.

Finally, my Raynaud's syndrome was becoming more painful and frustrating. Every winter, it seemed to get worse. Florida's warmth offered a good solution. After a fair amount of discussion, your mother agreed. Everyone was on board.

We started looking for a house in a neighborhood close to the water so Drew could jet-ski, and close to campus so Jake could commute to USF. On the last day of our third Florida trip looking at houses, the realtor showed Drew and me a spacious 4-bedroom single-family residence with a fenced-in backyard, a lovely lanai, and a 3-car garage. It even had a separate private office for me and a substantial recent addition, which could become a fifth bedroom and living area. It met all our needs.

The drawback was the strange murals painted on the walls. Of course, beauty is in the eye of the beholder, so I suspect the owner appreciated all the frescoes. But to us, these were anything but beautiful. They were ugly! However, that did not deter us. They could easily be painted over. A gallon of paint here, a gallon of paint there, and they'd be gone.

The seller's asking price was a different story. Your mother and I had agreed that we would not spend more than a set amount, and the seller wanted a whole lot more than what we could spend. When I told the realtor the amount we were willing to offer, he responded that the seller would never accept such a low number. He told us they had already reduced the price several times, and the current number was their bottom line.

Two days later, the realtor called to tell me that, to his surprise, the seller had accepted our offer. We too were surprised given the realtor's previous declarations.

We hired an inspector to ensure the house was in order, and he returned a thorough report detailing several minor items that required repair. I suggested that we have the repairs completed and take those costs off at closing. The sellers proposed that our offer be reduced by $5,000 to cover the repairs, and I agreed.

Jake and I trailered our 18' Glastron boat behind the Ford Van in time to be in Clearwater for the closing on October 12, 2012. I had all the repairs made for less than $5,000; hired a painter to cover the murals we did not like; although we kept the lovely roses above the fireplace mantel; ordered a minimal amount of furniture; and made plans to move in the first week of January 2013.

Jake, Tiga and Hammy—Jake's two cats, Drew, Drew's girlfriend, Sam—Drew's Siberian Husky, Max—my German Shepherd, and I caravanned from Maplewood to East Lake Woodlands in two cars and a large U-Haul truck. The truck carried our possessions and trailered my 2010 Chrysler 300. It took us three days—an enjoyable and uneventful trip.

All in all, buying and living in this home was a good decision. Jake finished his bachelor's in business with honors and earned an MBA from USF while residing at 335. Working together, Drew learned about Global Volunteers' processes and procedures and was promoted to Director of International Operations when that position opened. Then Drew went to law school at Barry University in Orlando and graduated with a Juris Doctor degree. The value of this property has increased substantially over the past eight years. And my Raynaud's syndrome acts up only when I travel to a cold climate during winter. I continue to spend summers in Minnesota but plan to be in Florida for all remaining winters.

The Lesson: Occasionally, plans work out pretty much as you hoped; but sometimes the results are even better. Our move to Florida resulted in Drew meeting Lauren, the love of his life and the mother of future grandchildren, and Jake and Saron got married while living at 335. Now we have two beautiful daughters! Plans don't work out better than that.

Waking Up Dead

"You're in pretty good shape for the shape you are in."

~ Dr. Seuss, an American children's author, political cartoonist, and poet

When you have a family, it is not enough to merely care for and think about them. You must think about and care for yourself so that you can care for them. A significant part of this is taking care of your health

I have been blest with good health. However, like some others, I stop breathing while I'm sleeping. It's called "sleep apnea." Generally, people with this condition stop breathing for a few seconds. But if it's longer—you've got a problem. Lack of oxygen dangerously strains the heart and can cause strokes and death. Sleep apnea is a serious medical condition that affects 22 million people in the US alone. But those are only the ones who are recorded as being treated. There's reason to believe that millions more Americans suffer from this condition undiagnosed or untreated.

The most common cause of sleep apnea in adults is being overweight or obese. I'm not obese, but I could lose ten pounds. That ten pounds may be the cause; although, there are other potential triggers too—too much caffeine or alcohol.

There is no cure for sleep apnea, but there are effective remedies. CPAP, IPAP, and BiPAP machines force air into the lungs through a tube attached to a facemask worn during sleep. The device prevents the lack of oxygen that is so dangerous. But untreated sleep apnea can lead to death while sleeping. Some people euphemistically call dying in your sleep, "waking up dead."

I have also been diagnosed with atrial fibrillation (Afib), an irregular heartbeat that can lead to blood clots, stroke, heart failure, and other severe heart-related complications. It too can contribute to death during sleep. But this condition can be remedied, and my Afib has been resolved.

It is reasonable to conclude that I may never have been treated for either of these medical conditions if I did not go to the Mayo Clinic for my annual physical. I've had an annual medical physical for over 40 years. However, until 2004, I only saw my primary care physician, and the entire physical process took less than an hour.

Then I learned about the Executive Health Program at the Mayo Clinic in Rochester, Minnesota—90 minutes from home. I started going there for my annual physical. The first year was a three-day affair. They investigated every aspect of my medical health and offered lots of advice about improving my health. Since then, I have adjusted my diet, exercise daily, and take several more meds. All my bad numbers have gone down, and all the good numbers have gone up. And now, I generally spend just two days at Mayo for my yearly physical. It is worth every minute.

The Lesson: Your health is everything. Do not take it for granted.

The Lesson: Get an annual physical at the best healthcare facility you or your insurance can afford. And follow your doctors' instructions—do what they tell you to do. You'll be healthier, feel better, live a longer productive life, and be better able to care for your family.

The Lesson: If you run a business and employ people, get the best employee insurance available—not the best you can afford. This will enable you and them to go to the best healthcare facilities.

Max

"Dogs are the most amazing creatures;
they give unconditional love."

~ Gilda Radner, an American actor and comedian

My mother had a cocker spaniel when I was a young boy. One day, a car hit Blacky as he raced across the street in front of our house. He died from his injuries. My mother was sad for weeks. That little cocker spaniel was our family's dog, but he was really my mother's. They had a special bond that I did not appreciate then but have a better understanding now.

Your mother had two dogs, Rascal and Lucky. They too were family dogs; however, they were really your mother dogs. They both lived long lives, but when they died, your mother grieved for months.

A few months before my 65th birthday, I decided to get a German Shepherd. During my annual physical that year, I told my Doc I wasn't walking as much as I'd like to. My goal was 10,000 steps a day, but I didn't reach that number often enough. He told me to get a dog and to walk it every day. I had never had my own dog, but I wanted a big guy if I was going to get a dog. Rascal and Lucky were terrific dogs, but they were little guys.

I did some research. German Shepherd Dogs (GSD) are big dogs who are extremely loyal, especially to whomever they deem to be their pack leader. GSDs are also beautiful animals and among the smartest of all canines. I found a reputable German Shepherd breeder near Hinckley, Minnesota, and arranged to pick up a pup. I called him Maximus because he had huge feet and huge ears even at 9-weeks-old.

Max was a remarkable creature. He loved people—kids and adults—and he was a good friend, nearly always by my side when I was at home. Even as a pup, he had a "maximus" personality. When Max was in the room, he demanded to be the center of attention. As he grew, his personality grew as well. He would rap his butt against your leg and look back, expecting you to scratch his rear end. If you didn't immediately comply, he would whine until you did. He could learn to do anything and was extraordinarily obedient. Max would sit in front of his food bowl for as long as I would let go by until I said, "Okay." Then he would eat. Max was a huge presence in our lives.

As he got older, I didn't walk him as much as perhaps I should have because he tended to get seriously upset when he saw other dogs. I believe this resulted from when he got bit in the neck by another dog; the owner couldn't handle him. We were in a parking lot, and I had Max on his leash. The other dog came charging at him while I held Max back such that his front feet were off the ground. I tried to pull Max away, but the other dog was too quick and lunged at him, biting him in the neck. It was a serious injury—seven stitches. Max wore a plastic cone-collar for six weeks while his wounds healed. That experience had a lasting impression; he was never the same around other dogs after that.

But he was always friendly with people. When the doorbell rang, he'd bark and run to the door. I'm sure some people waiting out front were scared. He was such a big guy, blackface, dark-colored, and looked as much like a wolf as a Shepherd. All Max wanted to do was sniff them and lick them to death.

It was Saturday morning when I was in Maplewood ready to go to the airport for a flight to Tampa. Jake called. He told me Max was not walking steady; he thought he should take him to the Vet. I told him to go right away.

Jake called again an hour later while I was in the Sky Club at MSP. He said, "He died, dad. Max just died."

I was shocked beyond belief.

I stammered. "What?" "What?" "How could that happen?"

Jake relayed that he and Saron immediately took him to a close-by emergency veterinarian hospital. The Vet came on the line and explained that she believed a mass of malignant blood vessels had ruptured, and Max bled out internally. She said 50 percent of large dogs get cancer, and among those, this scenario is common. She could not be sure without doing some tests or ultrasound, but this was the likely explanation.

After the call, I just sat there—stunned. I didn't know how I felt or what I should do other than get on the airplane. It was an exceedingly long trip.

Jake and Saron met me at TPA around noon, and we drove to the vet. A note on the door said they were in surgery and would not be available until 5 PM. We went home, and I spent the entire afternoon trying to wrap my mind around Max's sudden death. I was devastated.

We returned to the vet at five and saw Max. He looked just as he did alive, but he was dead. It was surreal. I decided to have him cremated, selected a black urn and a paw print, paid $350, and left. His death deeply saddened me. Saron was as distraught as I as she and Max had formed a special bond; she took care of him while I was traveling.

Several months later, I decided to get another German Shepherd. I made arrangements with a Minnesota GSD breeder and, in February 2020, picked up 10-week-old Hawkeye, a nearly all-black puppy. Because it was winter and I was living in Florida, Hawkeye and I flew to TPA; it was almost five months to the day of Max's death.

Like Max, Hawkeye is turning out to be a great friend. He is like Max in that they're both GSDs; however, every dog has its unique personality. Hawkeye also has a huge personality and wanting uninterrupted attention. He is also extremely smart. Hawkeye will never replace Max, but he is a beautiful creature to have in our home and our lives.

The Lesson: I learned how important Max was to me after his death. It reminded me of Anatolia France's insight that, "Until one has loved an animal, a part of one's soul remains unawakened."

The Lesson: I now have a better appreciation of the grief that my mother and your mother experienced when their dogs died. I just did not understand before.

The Lesson: Dogs are members of the family; I've been fortunate to have four as members of our family.

COVID

"A second wave in late summer or early fall that lasts three or four months could make everything we've experienced so far seem mild."

~ Dr. Michael Osterholm, an American infectious disease epidemiologist and regents professor

The spring, summer, and fall of 2020 were among the most challenging times during my life for families in America and around the world. The three of you lived through this, so this essay may be more relevant to your children and their children; although, the lessons learned apply to all.

COVID-19 was a family disease. It struck China first during the winter of 2019 and then attacked the rest of the planet with a vengeance. At the time of this writing, over 50 million people worldwide had contracted the virus, and more than one million had died. Due to the ease with which this contagion spreads, economies shut down, and hundreds of millions of families lost their jobs and livelihoods. Families also lost loved ones, and in some cases, entire families were shattered. For many individuals who contracted the disease, it required months to recover. Some recovered from the virus but never fully regained their health.

Too many leaders initially denied the potential effects of COVID-19. In February 2020, the United States president predicted that "it's going to disappear." Brazil's president refused to track the actual number of cases and deaths caused by the virus, referring to it in April as a "little cold." In May, Tanzania's president was quoted, "We prayed for three days, and the coronavirus is finished."

But it was far from finished. The result was a disaster. Hundreds of thousands died because politicians did not take quick action implementing health experts' advice. Two of the presidents mentioned contracted the disease; the virus was impervious to class, position, or rank.

I did not pay attention to the president of the United States or the governor of Florida. I stayed at home in Florida, walked five miles every day starting at sunrise when few people were out exercising or rode my stationary bike, worked from my home office, and finished writing this book. In the evenings, I watched movies and caught up on my reading. Often, the highlight of my day was driving to the grocery store where a clerk put purchases in the trunk. When I did go out in public, which was seldom, I wore a mask covering my nose and mouth to protect others and myself, and always socially and physically distanced, staying a minimum of six feet from all others as recommended by the Center for Disease Control.

Life literally changed in an instant when COVID struck; it was difficult. Your mom was in Minnesota while I was in Florida, and we did not see each other for months. There was no opportunity to engage with friends or other family personally. Zoom and FaceTime allowed people to visit while seeing each other on their screens, but that does not meet the need for full human connection. Happily, Jake and Saron lived with me in Florida, Drew and Lauren were only 20 minutes away, and I had Hawkeye.

In March 2020, the US government issued a Global Level 4 Health Advisory instructing U.S. citizens to avoid all international travel due to the global impact of COVID-19. This seriously adversely affected Global Volunteers as it shut down all service programs around the world. Fortunately, nonprofits qualified for US government small business loans that helped pay employees' salaries for a couple of months and then kept us afloat until we could generate revenue to resume program activities. Nevertheless, we had to furlough or lay-off too many employees. And many other small businesses and nonprofits just ceased to exist, devastating the families who relied on those enterprises.

The historians will tell the full story of COVID-19. No doubt, they will report that those who failed to respect this virus contributed to the disease's long-term adverse consequences and the economic challenges that followed.

For the most part, our family survived, perhaps even got stronger in our commitment and ability to serve others, especially families and children in need. However, as this book goes to print, the crisis continues. Your Aunt Frannie contracted the virus and I don't know if Global Volunteers will survive.

The Lesson: Life can change quite dramatically and fast. Knowing this can help you survive those remarkable moments.

The Lesson: Listen to and follow the advice of health experts and scientists. They know more than the rest of us about how viruses act and how you can stay healthy.

The Lesson: In a time of crisis, pay less attention to politicians. Too many are self-interested and too often will not provide the best science-based advice.

Tabby and the Mouse

*"They ask us when our friendship ended, and our Love began .
.. We tell them our friendship never ended."*

~ Michele Gran, an American non-profit executive,
philanthropist, and woman extraordinaire.

Extended family includes aunts and uncles, cousins, and nieces and nephews, in addition to siblings, grandparents, parents, and children. But the most significant person in your family is your spouse. You will spend more time with, rely on more, and be closer to your spouse than anyone else.

Your mother and I have been together for the better part of 46 years, although, as noted, it was off and on during the first five. She is my companion, my partner, my wife. No one is more important to me than her. No one has supported me more than she. No one has loved, cared for, looked after, or put up with me more than she. There is no one I love more than she. No one exasperates me more than she, and I her.

When I first met your mother, she was a 20-year-old college student working part-time at the Minnesota legislature. She was gorgeous, vibrant, and wicked smart. But what struck me most was her enormous energy and tremendous capacity to become a genuinely great woman. And that she is!

Your mother is the most caring, kind, and loving person I know. There are so many examples. The care she showed for her mother every day for more than two years during the last months of her life was staggering. She helped bathe, dress, and feed Grandma Gran, did her shopping, drove her to the doctors' offices, ensured her daily medications were correct, negotiated her living arrangements, read to her, and prayed with her. And for all practical purposes, she did this alone. Every day! For more than two years! I was amazed at the love and care your mom showed to your 99-year-old grandmother.

Equally important is the love she has shown each of you. Just giving birth to you is a remarkable expression of love and no small task. After caring you in her body for nine long months, each of you was born by C-section, major surgery with a six-week minimum recovery. I may have changed your diapers and taught you how to throw a baseball, but she nursed you, bathed you, and kissed all your cuts and bruises away. She and I designed 2634 together, and I coordinated the construction, but your mother took the four walls and turned it into a home. And she's painted every room in the house multiple times in multiple colors.

When I was traveling for work, your mother took you camping, hiking, and to the Saint Paul Winter Carnival parades. She taught you the value of life, respect for others, the joy of the outdoors, and how to care for the planet. She taught you to ski, the importance of caring for a pet, and how to wash your clothes—before you were 12. She also lent you her smarts and instilled in you a desire for higher education. With her bachelor's degree from the University of Minnesota's School of Journalism and master's in Liberal Studies from Hamline University, she paved the way so you too would know the value of advanced education.

My mother was overwhelmed when your mom nominated her for Minnesota Mother of the Year. She did this totally on her initiative; I was not involved. That is just what your mother does. When my mom was selected Mother of the Year, she was overjoyed by the honor. I was delighted. Your mom was enormously pleased as well.

When Nick was diagnosed, she read everything about mental illness and became a lay mental health expert. She continues to use her knowledge to support Nick. But she also organized a parents' group, got involved with NAMI, testified at the Minnesota legislature, and has spoken to numerous audiences about mental health and how we can improve adults' health. And she has made many good friendships with and offers support to other moms who deal with illness in their families.

You know well her care of and concern for animals—pets and non-pets alike. My favorite story is about Tabby and the mouse. Tabby was one of our cats when we were living on Arona before you were born. One night, we came home after being out for dinner and a movie, and Tabby was in the backyard playing with a mouse. As you might expect, your mom tried to protect the small rodent. As she attempted to get Tabby away from the mouse, the little guy ran up her pants leg. She started jumping up and down, screaming, "it's in my pants; it's in my pants!" I shouted, loud enough to be heard over her screams, "Take your pants off. Take your pants off." Fortunately, none of our neighbors turned on their outdoor lights, saving us immediate embarrassment. But we never doubted they heard me urging your mother in the middle of the night to take off her pants in our backyard.

Your mother is also among the most organized and creative people on the planet. When we were married, we had a large wedding involving lots of guests and three venues in St. Paul, Minneapolis, and then back to St. Paul. Your mother wrote a 4-page document that detailed the wedding activities, including a church floor diagram identifying who sat where. Then she hand-wrote individual personal instructions on index cards for the 16 people most involved in the ceremony—all the wedding party, our parents, the readers, even the priest. The index cards noted where each person was to be, the time they were to be there, which car they rode in, what to do and when to do it, where to stand in the receiving line, and how they could help clean up after the event. It was amazing! Everything went as she planned; it was a memorable celebration and a beautiful evening for all.

Because of her inspiration, we honeymooned in Guatemala, an experience that helped initiate Global Volunteers. She designed each of your unique birth announcements. Jake's notice was in the form of a mass media news release announcing him as a new PG and Associates member effective March 13, 1983, joining the firm at nine pounds 12 ounces and 22 ½ inches.

Nick's announcement card decreed him a new associate in the firm of P/G Associates, where your mother and I were both senior partners, and Jake was a junior partner. The announcement recorded his date of birth (May 28, 1987), weight (9 lbs. 2 oz.), length (21 ½ inches), and that he was a Catholic Democrat.

Drew was introduced in the Season's Premier of the Updated Remake of the Classic "My Three Sons." He was 6 lbs., 3 oz. and 20 inches in his first performance on November 12, 1988. Also staring was Jake, Nick, Mom, Dad, and Rascal as "the dog." The billing noted that this was a P/G Associates Production.

And your mother has always been a hard and effective worker, receiving outstanding reviews from her managers, and promoted often. Others recognized her enormous talents and commitment. In 1982, the Saint Paul Business and Professional Women's Club selected her as their Young Career Women of the Year. That was a great honor she richly deserved.

As stated previously, I wanted to be a lawyer since I was seven but did not go to law school until after we married when I was 34. It is simply impossible to work and do well in law school, so we lived on your mother's salary with some help from student loans and a partial scholarship. She supported me financially and emotionally throughout those 27 months of law school.

She also held down the fort while I was at USDA. Most weeks, I was in Washington or traveling internationally Monday through Thursday, and she managed Global Volunteers, supported each of you, and kept the home fires burning.

Perhaps most impressive is her integrity. Michele Gran was raised Catholic, attended a German Catholic elementary school and a Catholic high school, and believed deeply in and was profoundly committed to the Catholic Church. She was 110% Catholic. Like most Catholics, when the priest sexual abuse scandals gained public attention, we both became quite concerned. When we learned that most of the victims were young children, our hearts cried out. But when the evidence showed the Catholic hierarchy had covered up the abuse and perpetrated the abuse by transferring the pedophiles from one parish to another, it was too much. Her integrity prevented her from continuing to participate in this organization. It was an excruciating and challenging time for her. While her faith was stable and her love for the Creator was strong, her ties to the Catholic Church were irrevocably severed. Fortunately, she found a home in the Lutheran Church where she worships regularly.

I could write an entire book about your mother; the stories abound. And I know you know how special she is. I write these few vignettes to help you remember that you are the sensitive, loving, and caring men you are today because of her love and attentiveness.

I have learned a lot from your mother over these many decades. The following are but a sampling of those lessons.

The Lesson: True friendship is reaching out and supporting another.

The Lesson: Personal integrity is among the highest of human values.

The Lesson: When someone is in need, you offer your help.

The Lesson: Family always comes first.

The Lesson: When considering the long view, it is far less painful to agree with your mother than not.

On EDUCATION

*"Civilization is in a race between education
and catastrophe."*

~ H.G. Wells, an English writer

I never liked school much. And the older I got and the more time I spent in the classroom, the more I disliked it. But my father convinced me that I had to get as much formal education as possible, or at least get the pieces of paper that offered evidence that I was educated. So, I followed his advice and completed 22 years of schooling—kindergarten through law school. However, the more significant aspects of my education occurred outside the classroom. As important as formal education is, life has been my most influential teacher.

Right Half Over Tackle

"The best way to predict the future is to create it."

~ Abraham Lincoln, an American lawyer
and 16th President of the United States

I attended St. Rose of Lima Catholic Grade School, K–8, in a St. Paul suburb, as did my brother and nine sisters. All my teachers were women, mostly Catholic nuns from the order of Servants of Marry. My 8th-grade graduating class totaled 115 students, two classes of 50 and 15 stuck in with some seventh graders. We never thought there were too many in the classroom—five rows of ten made sense and easy math. Sister Rosalie was our teacher.

The only sports team at St. Rose was boys' baseball, reserved for 7th and 8th graders. I played both years. But several of us wanted to play football too. The school principal, Sister Joan, told us that the school didn't have any money for a football team, and besides, there was no football coach. The assistant pastor, Father Tom Garvey, predicted it would be hard to compete with the city schools, all of which had had excellent teams for decades.

Then someone told us that the parish men's club might be a source of funding. So, during the spring of 7th grade, three of us—Johnny Thompson, Gordy Arneson, and I—attended a monthly meeting of the men's club and made a pitch for why they ought to support our efforts to have a St. Rose of Lima School football team.

I don't remember what we said, but we must've been persuasive. The men's club bought us green and gold football jerseys, and two members volunteered to be our coaches. Father Garvey arranged to get some discarded brown cardboard football helmets from Cretin High School— yes, football helmets made from sturdy cardboard. Each boy came up with the rest of the uniform on his own. I saved money to buy a pair of shoulder pads and wore old jeans and tennis shoes. Some of the guys from wealthier families had real football pants, pads, and cleats.

In the fall of 1959, during our 8th-grade year, St. Rose of Lima inaugurated its football team. If memory serves, everyone who wanted to be on the team made the cut, but some played more than others. I was the starting right halfback in a T formation and scored the first touchdown during our first game—right half over tackle. I broke a tooth on that play but was so excited after scoring, I ran off the field. The coach yelled at me, "Philbrook, get back in there for the point after."

There weren't enough of us to have offensive, defensive and special team squads, so some played all three. I was also the defensive cornerback; caught eight interceptions that year. It wasn't that I was such a great cornerback; the other teams' quarterbacks simply could not throw accurately.

We won most of our games; came in second or third place in the conference. But it would not have mattered if we came in last place. We were just a bunch of young guys who wanted to play football. It was a wonderful experience for me—going to the men's club meeting, making our pitch, helping get the team organized, scoring the first touchdown, even the busted tooth.

I made good friends at St. Rose, some of whom are friends to this day. From our 1960 graduating class, several men and women, along with their spouses, get together every year at one of our homes to catch up. And seven guys from that class gather for lunch and drinks every December in honor of our classmate, Ron Rotell, who died way too young at 63 in 2009. As Gordon Lightfoot writes, we "drink to the living and toast the dead."

St. Rose was a good school. Our class alone produced doctors, masons, nurses, heavy equipment operators, lawyers, sheet metal workers, professional entertainers, businessmen and women, carpenters, architects, educators, pipefitters, and many other professions.

The Lesson: Class-size does not necessarily determine the quality of education.

The Lesson: If you want to do something, go do it. And don't stop until it's done. Perseverance is key. There will be reasons why you shouldn't, can't, won't do something—always! But "you can't score if you don't shoot."

The Lesson: Friendships made early in life can be the most enduring of all.

We Didn't Expect to Get Caught

"And I would have gotten away with it, too, if it weren't for
you meddling kids!"

~ Scooby-Doo, an American animated character

I was a Cub Scout and Boy Scout for several years—St. Rose Troop 622. One year, the troop went on a weekend camping trip. The scoutmaster told us ahead of time that there were four things we absolutely could not do—no leaving camp without permission, no smoking, no drinking, and no fraternizing with girls. I don't remember why we decided to leave camp, but five of us did. We walked into the nearby small town to look around. (Rule #1 broken.)

We decided to buy some cigarettes at a gas station. We made a plan. One of us walked up to the machine and put in the money. Another followed a moment later and pulled the lever for a pack of Marlboros. A third picked up the cigarettes from the tray and ran. The other two were lookouts; although, I have no idea what we were looking out for. We each had a cigarette. (Rule #2 broken.)

We didn't expect to get caught because our plan was to be gone for a short time. That fell apart on the way back to camp when we ran into a group of girls along a sandy beach. I don't know if they were in high school or college-age; they were just a lot older than we were. And they had beer. They offered us a couple of beers to share, and we all drank. (Rules #3 & 4 broken.)

Shortly after, one of the scoutmasters saw us huddling with the older women. (Busted!) That was it. We were sent home and kicked out of the troop. We weren't bad boys. We just didn't follow the rules.

The Lesson: When you don't follow the rules, you'll suffer the consequences.

It's Never Too Late to Say You're Sorry

"Teachers affect eternity; no one can
tell where their influence stops."

~ Henry Brooks Adam, an American author

By the time I was in 8th grade, three of my older sisters had joined the Servants of Mary, the same order of Catholic nuns that taught at St. Rose. My teachers had high expectations of me, given that my sisters were their colleagues. I seldom met those expectations.

A couple of weeks before graduation is a case in point. I was late turning in a science report. I skipped school the morning the assignment was due to finish it at home. Sister Rosalie called my mother, asking where I was. When she learned that I was finishing my homework, she must have been pissed. She refused to accept the report when I got to class after lunch. When she tossed it into the wastebasket next to her desk, my response to her was less than polite. I said something to the effect of, "What the hell did you do that for?"

She immediately sent me to the principal's office. Sister Joan instructed me to apologize to Sister Rosalie and sent me back to her classroom. It made matters much worse when I told Sister Rosalie, "Sister Joan told me I had to apologize to you." The conversation escalated, and I used an expletive to express my feelings.

I was expelled from school for using inappropriate language and being disrespectful—two weeks before graduation.

When the pastor, Monsignor Ryan, learned about my expulsion, he intervened. He ordered that I be reinstated the following week. Later, I learned the Monsignor countermanded Sister Rosalie's and Sister Joan's decision because of my acceptance to attend Cretin High School the next school year. Cretin was a highly respected, all-boys Catholic military school run by Christian Brothers in St. Paul. Apparently, there was competition among the St. Paul area parish priests regarding the number of their boys who got into Cretin. Monsignor Ryan wasn't going to lose one of his over a late science project.

Thirty years later, I invited Sister Rosalie to lunch. We had seen each a couple of times over the years, but never in a one-on-one setting. We enjoyed a delightful conversation during the meal, and as we walked out of the restaurant, I said to her, "I need to apologize to you."

"Why would you need to apologize to me?" she asked.

"I was disrespectful to you years ago, and I want you to know I'm sorry."

"I don't remember that," she said.

"Well, I do, and I am sorry."

"Oh, did you yell at me once?" she asked, apparently remembering.

"Yes, I did."

"Then, I accept your apology."

Over the next 20 plus years, Rosalie Hennessey and I became good friends. We'd have lunch whenever I was in Florida, where she ran a home for unmarried pregnant women. And we'd visit via email. She was quite progressive in her thinking—remarkable given that she was a leader in an order of Catholic nuns—and we enjoyed discussing politics and the state of the Catholic Church. She encouraged me to submit a Global Volunteers funding proposal to a foundation on whose board she served—the proposal was funded. She supported me when I ran for governor of Minnesota, offering helpful advice.

She suggested improvements to my first novel, *Conclave Conspiracy*. And, on the day before she died on a hospital operating table, she emailed me that she was having open-heart surgery the following day and asked for my prayers.

Sister Rosalie taught me in 1st, 7th, and 8th grades at St. Rose and continued to teach me throughout her life. She inspired me to be more than what I was, to do better than what I was doing, and to extend my grasp beyond my reach. She was enormously influential as a teacher, a mentor, and a friend. I think about her often.

The Lesson: There is no percentage in swearing at your teacher, especially a Catholic nun.

The Lesson: It's never too late to say you're sorry.

4th of July

Cretin High School was about a 25-minute drive from our home. During my freshman year, I either hitchhiked to school or walked a couple of miles to the bus stop and took the city bus. In my sophomore year, I bought a car—1953 Chevrolet Bel Air—and drove to school every day. I always worked, so I had money. My dad cosigned a loan for the car, and I paid it off in eighteen months.

Toward the end of my junior year, I decided to quit high school. I hated school and could see no future in it. I wanted to travel the world—I wanted to spread my wings.

My sister, Fran, and her husband Art Dunn, lived in Carteret, New Jersey. I arranged with them to help me get a job on a shipping boat as a laborer, sailing from New York Harbor to Dublin. My plan was to work my way across the Atlantic, save a little bit of money from my wages, and then travel around Europe and perhaps the Near East.

My father tried to discourage me. He told me that if I got an education, I could then travel anywhere I wanted. Fran and Art also attempted to dissuade me, writing a long letter advising that there were no jobs for a 16-year-old in Carteret, telling me I should stay in school, and inviting me to come out east after I turned 18.

All of this was to no avail; I had made my decision. I wasn't looking for a job in New Jersey; I wanted to get on a boat to sail to Europe. When I told them I intended to travel to New York in any event, they decided to let me stay with them.

I packed my bags and took an early June train from St. Paul to Newark. It was an exciting trip; I stayed up all night with some older men and a couple of college students discussing politics, life, and humanity's future.

Art's dad knew some ship captains, and he agreed to introduce me to them. After a few days in Carteret, we drove to the New York City harbor. When Mr. Dunn introduced me to the captain of the first ship we visited, he told him I was from Minnesota. The captain immediately responded, "Ah, a farm boy."

That was amusing. The only farm I had ever been on was my great aunt's hobby farm in New Brighton. I chuckled. I was the furthest thing from a farm boy.

Unfortunately, the Captain did not have any openings for inexperienced laborers, so we went home. A couple of days later, we made the same trip but met a different captain; although, the result was the same. We went out a couple of more times, but it appeared no one wanted to hire a minor as a ship laborer. Still, I was undaunted; there were lots of merchant ships in the harbor.

I needed to make some money while I was looking for an amenable captain. So, I got a job selling magazines door-to-door for Family Publications. I was part of a crew of seven young lads assigned to a territory between Newark and Carteret. We'd go from neighborhood to neighborhood, knocking on doors. The prescribed pitch, which I memorized and still have a copy of, was straightforward:

"Hi! I'm Bud, one of the boys in the neighborhood taking the Publishers' Survey." Then, I'd hand them a card listing 30 different magazines.

"Check 3 that you pick up at the newsstand once in a while, and I'll send you a couple of free copies. NO OBLIGATION. Don't check the ones you're getting now."

After they checked the card, I'd say, "You see, the reason we're giving away free copies is that starting next month, student routes are being formed in the neighborhood for us kids. You know, just like your newspaper. And the terrific part of my route is that if I give you the 3 magazines you checked for free for the next 48 months, would you, like most people I talk to, give me just 45 cents a week for Life and Post? In other words, you'll get Life, Post, plus the 3, all 5 for just 45 cents a week. So, since that's all there is to it, you'll help me build my route. Won't 'cha?"

It was all commission-based, and I did well.

Then, the day immediately before the Fourth of July 1963, our supervisor told us we could take a long break for lunch—there wasn't much doing that day. We were sitting on the grass, eating lunch on a hill overlooking a park, when one of the other boys threw a lit cherry bomb that landed right next to my butt. It exploded. I was pissed. I jumped up and asked, "Who the hell did that?

One of the boys said, "I did. But what are you going to do about it?"

I responded, "I'm going to knock your block off."

Then he pulled out a yellow switchblade and said something to the effect, "Come on, Minnesota boy."

I don't remember much of what happened next, except there was no blood spilled and I ended up with the knife. That night, when I went back to my sister's house, I told them the story, gave my brother-in-law the yellow knife, and reported that I had decided to go home. A month had passed, and it was clear I wasn't getting on a ship to go anywhere. Moreover, I wasn't going to risk my life selling magazines door to door.

Years later, I learned that my mother, father, sister, brother-in-law, and my brother-in-law's father were all in cahoots. They had conspired to allow me to go to New Jersey, but there was no way they were going to let me get on any boat. A couple of years after that, Art gave me the yellow-handled switchblade.

I was 16 years old when I got on that train to New Jersey. Who knows what would've happened had I gotten on a boat to Europe. My guess is I would not have been among the other 273 young men who graduated from Cretin High School in 1964 and may not have received nine years of post-secondary education. My life would have been quite different.

The Lesson: My father was right. I got an education, and I have traveled everywhere I wanted to—60 countries and territories, all 50 US states, nearly all Canadian provinces, and from the north to the south of Mexico—and I'm not done yet.

The Lesson: Get all the formal education you can.

The Lesson: Stand up for yourself when it is necessary.

A Worldly Philosopher

"Knowledge is the only good, and ignorance the only evil."

~ Socrates, a Greek philosopher

As a Catholic Junior ROTC high school, we had military class and religion class every day at Cretin. Some years it seemed like we had religion at 9 AM and military at 10 AM. First, we learned about the importance of loving our neighbors and our enemies. The next hour, we learned how to kill our enemies.

The military field manual detailed how to attach a piano wire to two sticks of wood to decapitate your enemy. (Hopefully, we are not teaching fourteen- and fifteen-year-olds how to do that these days.) The juxtaposition of religion class and military class inspired me to analyze the contradiction of loving your enemy and killing your enemy. A few years later, that analysis caused me to take actions that may well have saved my life and protected my sanity. More about that later.

I was never a good student, but I was curious. And I liked to read, just not the books that my teachers wanted me to read. During my senior year at Cretin, I took trigonometry and analytical geometry as part of my college prep courses. (Calculus was still reserved for college students in the 1960's.) Our teacher, Professor Ireland, would often give us time toward the end of class to do homework. If we finished our work, he allowed us to read whatever we liked, provided it related to mathematics.

I had purchased *The Worldly Philosophers: The Lives, Times and Ideas of the Great Economic Thinkers* by Robert L. Heilbroner. This book, which is now a classic in its 7th edition, examines the history of economic thought from Adam Smith to Karl Marx. One day I took this book to analytical geometry class. After I finished the day's lesson, I opened it to where I last left off. Prof Ireland saw the word "Philosophers" in the title and told me to close the book; philosophy books were not permitted. I tried to explain that this was an economics book, but he would have nothing to do with that—it was clear from the cover: "*Worldly Philosophers.*" A couple of days later, after finishing my homework, I stuck Heilbroner's book inside a magazine about mathematics and started reading. But I got caught again. (Busted.) This time Ireland was pissed. He kicked me out of his class and out of his course. The principal put me in a non-college prep business-economics class.

The Lesson: You cannot both love your enemy and kill your enemy; however, you can kill in self-defense.

The Lesson: When you don't follow the rules, you'll suffer the consequences.

The Lesson: Continue to be curious, regardless of the consequences.

Class Radical

"Education opens the future for those
who otherwise have no hope."

~ Author unknown

Several weeks later, I was called to the principal's office, along with several class-mates—the class president, valedictorian, salutatorian, cadet Colonel, and other high-ranking students. I knew all these guys, and some were friends, but it was unusual for me to be among such an auspicious group in a meeting with Brother Richard.

Brother Richard advised us of a Ford Foundation-funded pre-college program that offered outstanding students the opportunity to take college courses during their last term of high school. Ten of us had been selected by a committee of teachers, military personnel, and administrators to participate in this program. As a result, we no longer needed to attend all our regular classes, provided we enrolled in these special college courses off-campus. Everyone was excited.

I was perplexed.

When dismissed, I asked Brother Richard why they had selected me. We both knew I had a C average and was far from an "outstanding student."

He said to me, "Philbrook, every class needs its radical, and you're this year's class radical." He then reminded me why I was no longer permitted in Professor Ireland's class.

But there was one condition for me to participate in the Ford Foundation program. I was a buck private. In the military chain of command, that was the lowest possible rank. Someone on the selection committee did not want a buck private representing our military high school. So, to take advantage of this opportunity, I had to agree to be promoted to sergeant. Getting out of some classes for the remaining school year sounded good to me, so even though I didn't understand how or why I'd been selected, I accepted the promotion.

I enthusiastically attended the college courses but quickly discovered they held no more interest than my regular high school classes. I was frustrated. Formal education was an absolute requirement to be successful, but how would I be successful if school held so little interest?

Fifty-five years later, I realize what the principal and some other selection committee members might have seen in me, but I certainly did not understand it then.

The Lesson: Sometimes, people see things in us that we do not see in ourselves.

The Lesson: I confirmed that I did not like school, regardless of the level or the packaging.

The Lesson: Some people look out for you even when you're not aware, and you may not know why. You, too, can look out for others.

Not Much of a Student

"What's past is prologue."

~ William Shakespeare, an English poet and playwright

In preparation for college, I took a speed-reading class to help me do better in school. It was two evenings a week, but I didn't apply myself. I did not like sitting in a classroom, listening to a lecture, and then doing homework. In retrospect, I wished I had done better because I enjoy reading, and I wanted to learn. But given my nature and the instructional methodologies of the 1960s, I didn't have what it takes to be a good student.

In the fall of 1964, I started at the University of Minnesota, where I majored in political science and minored in speech and communications in the College of Liberal Arts (CLA). During the second term of my freshman year, I did apply myself and made the Dean's list—3.4 GPA. That was it. Never made the Dean's list again. I didn't need to. I had proven to myself that I could do it, so there was no reason to do it again. Been there, done that.

Silly boy was I.

Most of my time at the U of M was academically uneventful and barely average. I attended class—most of the time; did the readings—some of the time; took the tests—all the time but once; and maintained a 2.5 average on a 4-point scale. I had not improved as a student.

On June 5, 1968, I was cramming for exams in the final term of my senior year. Listening to the news on television while studying for my tests the following day, I heard that US Senator Robert F. Kennedy, a candidate for president of the United States, had been assassinated at a hotel in Los Angeles. As a staunch opponent of the Vietnam War and being from Minnesota, I supported US Senator Eugene McCarthy's candidacy for president. But the fact that they had killed Bobby Kennedy was overwhelming. His assassination was on the heels of Rev. Martin Luther King's assassination a few months earlier and President John F. Kennedy's assassination five years previous.

I stayed up into the morning hours watching the news coverage, then went to bed and did not get up. I was pained to my bones. I lost all interest in everything, skipped the two tests that day and one the following day. I failed all three courses.

Not having enough credits to graduate and falling below a minimum grade point average for courses outside my major or minor, I was suspended from CLA for a year.

The following summer, I retook those three classes and passed them all with a B average—an A, a B, and a C. I graduated on July 18, 1969, with a Bachelor of Arts.

But academically, there was no place for me to go. I wanted to be a lawyer, but no reputable law school would admit someone who'd been kicked out of college and had a 2.5 GPA. And graduate school was also out of the question.

With all that said, 41 years later, the University of Minnesota College of Liberal Arts bestowed upon me one of my treasured honors. The college recognized me as an Alumni of Notable Achievement, one of 20 so honored in 2010. The University reports that "Of the college's 160,000 living graduates, approximately 1% have been selected as recipients." Deeply moved then, I remain so to this day.

The Lesson: When you don't follow the rules, you'll suffer the consequences.

The Lesson: Tragedy, personal and public, affects us all. It is how well you handle the tragedy that makes the difference.

The Lesson: If you fail a course, you can simply accept your failure and move on; or you can retake it and prove that you can master the material.

Preparing Public Leaders of Today

"It is our duty as men and women to proceed as though the
limits of our abilities do not exist."

~ Pierre de Chardin, a French philosopher and Jesuit priest

The year following my college graduation, I ran for a seat in the Minnesota House of Representatives. It was 1970, and at 24 I came in second out of four in the open primary but was defeated by the Republican incumbent in the general election. The legislature was nominally nonpartisan back then, but virtually everyone ran with party backing. I ran as a Democrat on the Democratic-Farmer-Labor (DFL) ticket.

Four years later, I ran again for an open seat and was elected.

While in House committee hearings listening to witnesses testify, it became abundantly clear that I needed to be smarter. I needed a better grip on the subject matter. I needed to know how to weigh the costs and the benefits of proposed legislation to fulfill my public promise to be a responsible legislator.

The School of Public Affairs was a graduate-level institution at the University of Minnesota. I thought the professors there might be able to help me. In conversations with the admissions committee chair, Professor George Warp, I learned the school admitted fifty students each year who were among the brightest and highest ranked students in the country. My undergraduate GPA immediately disqualified me.

I argued that the school's brochure stated that they "Prepare Public Leaders of Tomorrow" and that I was a public leader today. Regretfully he said, I did not qualify.

In mid-September, a week or so before the fall term was to start, I received a call from Professor Warp asking if I would like to join the class of 1975. I did not ask any questions; I immediately said yes and started to prepare for graduate school.

Later, I learned that one of the students, who had been admitted, decided to attend somewhere else. When the admissions committee met to select her replacement, Professor Warp mused that they could ask their fifty-first choice, but the odds were that another school had already accepted the student. They could then ask the applicant who ranked fifty-second, and then fifty-third, and so on. Or, Professor Warp suggested, they could admit a new member of the Minnesota House of Representatives who has a disqualifying GPA, but who argues that if the school prepares public leaders of tomorrow, perhaps they should also prepare public leaders of today. That is how I got into graduate school.

It took me five years to graduate from the Humphrey School of Public Affairs, but my advisor told me that I finished in the top third of my class. Not bad for someone not cut out for the formal educational process.

The Lesson: Always make the best argument you can; you never know when someone will use your argument to advocate your or another person's cause.

A Zero is a Zero & a D is a D

"When you find yourself in a hole, quit digging."

~ Will Rogers, an American cowboy, humorist, and social commentator

My time at the Humphrey School was rather ordinary, except for one incident.

In January 1977, Governor Rudy Perpich asked me to join his administration. He assigned me to the Minnesota Department of Natural Resources (DNR) to represent his position on federal legislation affecting the Boundary Waters Canoe Area (BWCA), a unique wilderness area in northern Minnesota. One spring Tuesday morning in 1977, I got a call from Terry Montgomery, the Governor's chief of staff, advising me I was to travel with the governor to Washington, DC the following morning, where the governor would testify before congress on the federal BWCA bill.

I immediately called a professor at the Humphrey School to tell him that I was unable to take his midterm exam scheduled for the following day because I had to go to Washington with the governor. He suggested I take the exam that evening. That was not possible. My evening would be consumed helping prepare the governor's testimony and answers to potential questions. I proposed that I take the exam immediately upon my return from Washington, but that was out of the question because the professor wanted to "protect the integrity of the exam process." He said something to the effect, "you can take the midterm today, you can take the midterm tomorrow as scheduled, or you can get a zero on the midterm." I had no choice. I accompanied the governor to Washington.

A zero on the mid-term meant that the highest score possible in the course was 67 percent, a D. That is if I aced the final. In that event, I would not need to retake this required course given that a D was a passing grade.

However, these three credits would not count toward the minimum required for graduation. A grade of C or higher was necessary to earn credit. I complained to the dean and my advisor—this was unfair and unnecessary—I could have easily taken the exam when I returned. The professor's concerns about protecting the integrity of his exam from cheaters were needless. I had never cheated on an exam in grade school, high school, or as an undergraduate, and I certainly wasn't going to start in graduate school. I got an A on the final, but a zero is a zero, and a D is a D.

So, my advisor, Professor Arthur Naftalin, offered me an alternative. Art Naftalin was a former four-term mayor of Minneapolis and former Commissioner of the Minnesota Department of Administration. He was both a student and practitioner of government; he understood I had no choice but to accompany the governor to Washington.

Nevertheless, Art advised it would not be in anyone's interest to raise this issue to higher levels. He proposed that he supervise a three-credit independent study on any relevant subject I chose. For a guy who so disliked the formal education process, independent studies were a Godsend. I agreed.

I set about to significantly expand my knowledge of human and economic development in rural communities in developing countries. I earned an A on that independent study, and the 20-page paper I wrote became the basis for my primary Plan B (similar to a thesis or capstone project). That Plan B became the foundation for Global Volunteers' *Philosophy of Service, A Strategy for Development* upon which we continue to rely.

I learned a great deal from Dr. Naftalin during this frustrating time. He was a thoughtful, savvy, brilliant, and worldly academic. It was a gift to be advised by and to know him.

The Lesson: There are people so rigid in their interactions with others that they cannot think beyond the strict confines of their self-imposed walls. Some people don't believe others will commit to a level of integrity where they can be trusted. We must deal with these people throughout life.

The Lesson: Some people recognize injustice and are willing to do something about it to make others whole. These are the saints among us. When you recognize an injustice, do something about it. We can all be saints.

The Lesson: When you don't follow the rules, no matter how arbitrary, you will suffer the consequences.

A Jealous Mistress

"No matter what accomplishments you make,
somebody helped you."

~ Althea Gibson, an American tennis player and professional golfer

In the fall of 1980, I began school, something I had wanted to do for as long as I could remember, but never believed the day would come. My mother often reminded me that when I was seven years old, I told her, "I am going to be a lawyer." I remember betting my boss and mentor at Sperry Univac, Lewie Rydeen, a steak dinner that I would finish law school before turning 30. I lost that bet. Now I was 34 and just starting.

Shortly before classes began, I had lunch with a dear friend, Sam Hanson, who was later appointed to the Minnesota Court of Appeals and then a justice on the Minnesota Supreme Court. I asked Sam what advice he had for me as I was about to enter the profession he loved. "Learn the language," he advised. So that is what I did.

Your mother and I had been married for less than a year when I started law school. We were still newlyweds. But for those two and a half years, I was AWOL—"the law is a jealous mistress"—and I spent virtually every waking hour studying the law. Fortunately, your mother worked while I studied. She enabled me to do that which I had wanted to do since I was a little boy.

Law school was not much better than any other formal education venue. But that no longer mattered. That I did not enjoy school was now merely a nuisance. I worked hard—attended every class, spent long hours in the library, read multiple cases every day, and engaged with my study group—I graduated in twenty-seven months by taking classes year-round.

I enjoyed some courses. Contracts law was intriguing, and criminal procedure explained what the government could and could not do to its citizens. (I earned the AmJur award for Criminal Procedure given to the student with the highest grade in the class.) The faculty and administrators selected me for a partial scholarship, which was much appreciated. I participated on the moot court team and the law review, met some outstanding teachers, made good friends, was admitted to the Silver Gavel Society for academic performance, and was among the top ten students in our class of nearly 200.

Overall, law school was uneventful, but it was all-consuming. There was tremendous relief when I finished; I knew I would never see the inside of a classroom as a student ever again.

But then I had to study for the bar exam.

The Lesson: Every profession, and many organizations, utilize their terms, definitions, acronyms, and jargon. To succeed, learn the language.

The Lesson: Just because you dislike something, or may not be good at it, does not mean you don't have to do it. Suck it up. Do it!

The Lesson: The greatest value of formal education is learning how to learn. It teaches you how to organize information, master specific subject matter, think beyond the pages, communicate ideas, argue a position, create the new, build the future, and teach others how to learn.

50th Reunion

*"I have never let my schooling interfere
with my education."*

~ Mark Twain, an American writer and humorist

In 2014, the Cretin High School class of 1964 celebrated our 50th anniversary. In preparation for the weekend events, the anniversary committee sent out a questionnaire asking all '64 graduates what we'd been up to since graduation. We were asked to write about post-high school education, military service, employment, family and kids, hobbies, and retirement. I wrote the following:

> Michele Gran and I married 35 years ago. I got lucky and married above my rank. She is a wonderful woman and a loving partner. We have three single adult sons—Jake, Nick, and Drew.

> I've never spent a night in jail, although I've toyed with the idea on occasion. Never wore a military uniform after leaving Cretin, although I seriously considered it at one point (ask Phil Ricker). And I've never golfed under 100—not even close.

> I hated school, but Cretin taught me the value of education as a passport to a more meaningful and productive life. So, I earned a BA from the University of Minnesota, an MA from

the Humphrey School of Public Affairs, and a JD from Hamline University School of Law.

I got involved in politics early and served on the presidential campaign staffs of Sen. Eugene McCarthy and Sen. George McGovern, initially in Minnesota, then Illinois and California. I first ran for the Minnesota House of Representatives in 1970 and was elected in 1974. Gov. Rudy Perpich appointed me Assistant Commissioner for DNR in his first administration. Decades later, I spent a year campaigning for Minnesota Governor in the 2006 cycle and conducted 135 house parties across the state. But I was a complete failure raising money and dropped out before the primary. Later, I was appointed Deputy Undersecretary at USDA during President Obama's first administration.

I worked for Sperry Univac (now Unisys) for six years, the Minnesota Public Interest Research Group (MPIRG) for two years, and practiced law for 12 years. In 1984, my wife and I co-founded Global Volunteers, an international human and economic development NGO that we continue to run. We've engaged 30,000 volunteers in 32 countries on six continents. We celebrate our 30th anniversary in December.

I have fond memories of Brother Josephus, Mr. Ireland, and Prof. Clark. I'll never forget the day Josephus nailed Boyer and Sweeney and then backhanded me nearly out of my chair. Apparently, we were sporting more than three. On reflection, I have little doubt we deserved it, but that form of discipline is long gone now.

I published my first novel this year—*Conclave Conspiracy*—and have another book in the making—*Lessons for My Sons.*

I've discovered that writing is something even 'senior citizens' can do. I winter in Clearwater, Florida with two of our adult sons—they are among my best friends—and summer in Maplewood, Minnesota with Michele and our son, Nick. She winters in Minnesota because she loves the snow and cold—go figure. I've traveled to all 50 states and have visited 52 countries, half that number multiple times.

I enjoy good movies and red wine, dancing with my wife, fishing on the Gulf Coast with my sons, shooting pool, taking long walks with my German Shepherd Max, and listening to classical music and audiobooks. I've mostly driven Chevys and Fords. The best cars I've ever owned are Chrysler 300s—a 2005, a 2010, and now a 2013C.

Retyremint: I don't know how to spell it, not sure what it means, and have no desire to experience it.

The honors of which I am most proud and least deserving are being designated a Distinguished Alumnus by Hamline University School of Law and an Alumnus of Notable Achievement by the University of Minnesota CLA. I continue to aspire to be a Christian, attending St. Odilia in Shoreview and Espiritu Santo in Clearwater. I have prayed in pagodas, temples, synagogues, and many Protestant churches all over the world. My mother and father, St. Rose of Lima grade school, and Cretin High School were my foundation; whatever else there is was built on that.

The Lesson: Fifty years goes by in a flash!

The Great Educator

"How shall I talk of the sea to the frog, if he has never left his pond? How shall I talk of the frost to the bird of the summer land, if it has never left the land of its birth? How shall I talk of life with the sage, if he is a prisoner of his doctrine?"

~ a Chinese poet, 4th century B.C.

There is no better form of education than travel. I have learned much more through my journeys than I ever learned in 22 years in the classroom. But it is the people, not the places, who educate. The mountains, oceans, forests, museums, theaters, and cuisine are interesting and often delightful, but the local people and exposure to their culture and way of life are etched in my mind.

In Maliwada, India, observing a village woman rock her dead infant child for more than 12 hours taught me that life everywhere is precious, and when taken young, it is heartbreaking and tragic. Death affects us all; it does not matter when it occurs, where we live, or the culture in which we were raised.

In Pommern, Tanzania, learning from a doctor that malaria was the number one disease in a rural village that 20 years previous had no mosquitoes due to its 5,000-foot elevation taught me that climate change affects even remote places on earth. We are all in this together; we either address our environmental behavior together or perish together.

In Shalpazar, Turkey, visiting with a Muslim imam about his clerical life taught me that his challenges were not much different from how my parish priest described his challenges. We may worship the Creator in unique ways, but the Creator looks upon all of us with the love of a father.

In Jonestown, Mississippi, my friend Mayor Bobbie Walker lost her reelection bid by one vote. That reinforced that every vote counts. We should never underestimate the value of individual action. Go vote!

In Salvador, Brazil, meeting a young girl in a favela, where vast numbers of extremely impoverished families barely eke out a living, literally in the shadow of some of the wealthiest people on earth, reminded me that humanity's indifference to the poor knows no bounds. We are all brothers and sisters united in one Creator. There is no justification for massive poverty.

In the 1990's Russia, I learned that Muscovites opened their apartment windows in the middle of winter to regulate the heat in their flats. They did this because the government centrally controlled the temperature in their buildings. It was their only option for managing the warmth in their personal space. How silly is that scenario?

I have visited ten communist countries, some former and some current, and I can attest that the government would do much better in each if they listened to and better respected their people's wisdom. Most citizens I've met in communist regimes love their countries and respect their leaders. Still, they could do so much better if governments embraced the simple concept that local people know what they need and are willing and able to do what is necessary to achieve what they need for their families. Life is better for all when local people are allowed to be in charge. If some call that democracy, so be it.

Travel also taught me that we are all far more alike than we are different. As I've crisscrossed the planet, I've learned that the differences between us are cause for celebration rather than apprehension, fear, or distrust. The awareness that the Creator designed such a wide variety of races and colors—from the blackest of blacks to the whitest of whites and all the colors in between—should be celebrated.

Regardless of the shade of our skin, the language we speak, our ancestors' race, the culture of our ways, our economic status, the way we dance, our government's political system, or the way we worship the Creator, we are the same people. We laugh, often at the same silly stories. We cry when we experience tragedy and heartbreak. We strive for a better life for our children. We seek freedom, albeit in different ways. We love our families and our friends. We want to help and comfort others, especially those in need. And we all want to realize the fullness of our human potential. And the differences—they are the cause for celebration.

But as I travel, it continually amazes me how much more I need to learn. Although I have visited 60 countries and territories on six continents, including the five most populous nations that comprise more than half the world's people, I still have misconceptions about planet Earth and her people.

My first visit to Romania in 1998 is a case in point. Before preparing for this trip, the little I knew about Romania was mostly wrong. For example, I am embarrassed to admit that I thought Romania was a Slavic nation due to its Eastern European location and its longstanding relationship with Russia and other countries of the former Warsaw pact. Inexplicably, I assumed that it had a high percentage of Muslims because of its proximity to other southeastern European countries with large numbers of Muslims such as Bosnia and Herzegovina, Albania, and Kosovo, even though none of those countries share a border with Romania. In addition, I believed that the Transylvanian Dracula was a vampire.

None of these "facts" are correct. Romania is more like Italy and France than its Slavic neighbors. "Romania" comes from the word "Roman." Romanian is a Romance language, similar to Italian. Its people have long and deep ties to France and Italy.

Much to my surprise, there are few Muslims in Romania. More than eighty percent of the population are Christian Orthodox, and the rest are mostly Roman Catholic and Protestant.

And the historical figure Wallachian Prince Vlad IV, also known as Dracula, is extolled by Romanian historians and Romanian schoolbooks as "a patriot and a champion of order in lawless times." But he is not now and never was known as a vampire.

I don't remember where or how I picked up these misunderstandings, although I suspect the "silver screen" influenced at least one of them. Perhaps I missed the day in school when Romania was discussed, or I didn't read that chapter, the chapter was incorrect, my teacher didn't know what s/he was talking about, or Romania was simply not included in the curriculum. Probably the latter.

But it's not just Romania. My misconceptions about this entire world abound—and I'm a curious and experienced world traveler, with nine years of higher education and nearly three million air miles. I know a lot about the places where I've traveled, but not so much about three-fourths of the world's countries I have not visited.

What's so tragic about this is that I decide what I do in this world based upon what I think I know. And I am not alone in my lack of knowledge.

Americans as a people are notoriously untraveled and misinformed—less than half even have a passport. I suspect other nations and peoples are misinformed as well. It could be that some people are so misinformed about America and Americans that they think we are evil—"The Great Satan"—and they've concluded it is necessary to rid the world of this evil by literally blowing us apart.

The Lesson: St. Augustine may have said it best, "The world is a book, and those who do not travel read only one page."

The Lesson: Travel offers each of us the opportunity to gain a more genuine understanding of other people with whom we share this planet. And they gain a better understanding of us.

The Lesson: Friendships made around the world improve mutual understanding. Then, when serious disputes arise, it becomes less likely to conclude that the best way to resolve the conflict is annihilating the other.

Spaceship Earth

"I've been everywhere, man!"

~ Johnny Cash, an American singer-songwriter

Captain Rusty Schweickart, a former US Air Force fighter pilot, shared the ultimate travel experience, along with a handful of other humans. Schweickart was an aeronautical engineer, a NASA astronaut, and the lunar module pilot on the Apollo 9 mission. He tested the portable life support system used by astronauts who later walked on the moon.

Schweickart wrote about seeing earth from space. He describes orbiting our blue planet and seeing no political boundaries—only a oneness. "...You become startling aware how artificial are thousands of boundaries we've created to separate and define." People "killing each other over some imaginary line that you're not even aware of, that you can't see. And from where you see it, the thing is a whole, the earth is a whole, and it's so beautiful." He later said, "You realize that on that small spot is everything that means anything to you. . . ." "We aren't passengers on Spaceship Earth. We're the crew. We aren't residents on this planet. We're citizens. The difference in both cases is responsibility." Now that's a trip!

The Lesson: I'm never going to see planet Earth from space. However, I have witnessed planet Earth—through her people.

The Lesson: I, too, have seen the oneness of the blue planet; I have learned that we are all far more alike than we are different.

On WORK

"Without ambition one starts nothing.
Without work one finishes nothing."

~ Ralph Waldo Emerson, an American poet, author,
lecturer, and philosopher

There is tremendous dignity in work. Work is something in which to take pride. Doing a job well enriches our self-worth. When we contribute to our society—to the greater good—and, in turn, help support our families, it enhances our self-respect and self-esteem. The type of work is less important than the work itself. Even unsettling and less desirable jobs—picking up trash or cleaning toilets—contribute to the greater good and are therefore honorable.

Work is essential to stay alive, pay for needed things, care for your family, and sustain a functional society. But meaningful work also adds fundamental value to life. Community is best supported when everyone strives to be involved in work that serves others in meaningful ways. Life is so much more fulfilling when you contribute to meaningful work.

All work can be honorable, but some people are required to simply make useless widgets that are neither helpful nor beneficial to society or the common good. Others are relegated to work that is demeaning and even humiliating.

And some are enslaved to do work their masters do not do. Regrettably, societies do not create environments where everyone can perform meaningful work.

I have been blessed in that virtually every job I've had allowed me to be engaged in meaningful work. And Global Volunteers has been the epitome of meaningfulness.

Life's Plans

Some people's lives seem to take them where the winds blow. They may have a general direction, but the uncertain ways of the world cause drift. Life's events direct the road taken. Other people seem able to direct their lives. They set a goal, create a plan, determine a path, execute, and achieve.

I tried to follow the latter track. Early on, I set a goal, created a plan, and did all the other things necessary to achieve. I was determined, committed, focused, and dedicated.

However, the life I've lived is not the life I planned. I have not done what I initially wanted or intended to do.

From my late teens, I desired to be engaged in public policy through elective office or political appointment. My ultimate goal was to be a US senator—perhaps even President of the United States. That's why I ran for the Minnesota House of Representatives and was nominated by the Democratic-Farmer-Labor (DFL) party when I was just 24. Although I lost that year, I was elected four years later—still a young man. I served honorably and with enormous dedication, often working 12-hour days and on weekends. But when I ran for reelection, I was defeated. And I felt the pains of defeat throughout my bones.

Shortly after that, I was appointed Assistant Commissioner of the Minnesota Department of Natural Resources. It was an excellent position that offered the opportunity to affect public policy on significant environmental and wilderness issues. Then, I lost that position too, due to ineffective politics on my part.

Several decades later, I ran for governor of Minnesota and generated tremendous enthusiasm. Hundreds of good and smart people supported me; many volunteered day after day. But I ultimately failed at raising the enormous amounts of money necessary to compete. I simply refused to spend six to eight hours a day—every day—making phone calls to friends, family, special interests, "politicals," and others asking for money.

In 2009, I was appointed Deputy Undersecretary at USDA. That, too, was a prominent position, one with time I could have affected significant policy. But family comes first, and family responsibilities arose that required me to resign my political appointment.

I believe I did everything I possibly could to be meaningfully and effectively engaged in public office, and I desperately wanted to do so, but it was not to be. That wasn't the road I was on.

In my middle 20s, I started praying for wisdom, so I would know what I was to do with my life. I prayed for strength, so I would be able to do what I was supposed to do. And I prayed for grace, so I might do well that which I was to do. I have continued those prayers for fifty years.

Now, in the twilight of my career, I firmly believe my prayers were answered. However, the answer was not what I wanted to hear. I was never successful in doing what I thought I wanted to do.

But the road on which I traveled took me on the most rewarding journey. Every time I veered toward doing that which I wanted to do, I was pushed back onto the track to do what I now believe I was supposed to do.

The opportunity to dedicate my life, in partnership with your mother, to helping children and enhancing the lives of impoverished families around the world while raising our own family has been the best of rides. It may not have been what I thought I wanted to do, but it's been extraordinarily meaningful and rewarding.

All the same, don't let the fact that plans often fall through dissuade you from dreaming and planning. Dream big! Devise big plans based on your dreams. Revise your plans and revise them again. Execute those plans to the best of your ability. Perfect your execution. Fail! Pick yourself up and shake it off. Embrace every disappointment knowing that each failure brings you one step closer to success. Keep dreaming, keep planning, keep executing, keep failing. Now, take joy in your success.

However, if it does not work out as you had hoped or expected, it is OK. If you do your best and focus on serving others to improve their lives, it does not matter if your specific plan succeeds.

Ron Reimann, a longtime dear friend, often reminded me of the words of Daniel Burnham, an American architect, who wrote, "Make no little plans; they have no magic to stir men's blood."

Know also that if you have a big dream, you cannot accomplish it alone. If your goal is big enough, important enough, and you communicate it powerfully, it will stir the hearts and minds of others. They will make your dream a reality. They are the only ones.

The Lesson: The only dream worth dreaming—the only plan worth executing—is one that contributes to humanity through service.

The Lesson: If you pray for something, be prepared to accept the consequences.

Fired!

*"I was once fired as the opening act for Seals and Crofts be-
cause I got loaded and introduced them as
Arts and Crafts."*

~ George Miller, an American comedian

I always wanted to work, earn money, keep busy. My first job was sweeping out the back of Iverson's Rexall drugstore at the Hub Shopping Center (now the Har Mar Mall) in Roseville. I think I was 10 or 11. I got the job because my older sister, Claudette, was a soda fountain clerk there.

Later, when I was 12, I delivered the drugstore sales flyers to mailboxes in the surrounding neighborhoods. I didn't like that job, too many big stray dogs and boring work. That's when I started to steal for the first time. I didn't know it was stealing because I didn't steal things. I didn't steal money. I stole time. I took the fliers and put them in a cul-de-sac underneath the road, and then I'd sit in the shade, relax, and enjoy the breeze. It was stealing because I continued to get paid even though I was not working. I was not fired from that job, although I should have been.

I was fired from the next several jobs. When I was a freshman in high school, I worked at a shoe store but could never figure out the inventory numbering system. Women would ask to see a black pump, and I'd bring out a blue 4-inch heel. Fired!

Next, I worked at the Arden Inn restaurant as a busboy. That's the soup story recounted in "Mother's Day" in the first chapter. Fired!

Then I worked at the Dairy Queen, which was kind of cool because employees could eat all the ice cream you wanted. But the owner discovered I was under-age—you had to be 16 to work back then. I was 15. Fired!

Finally, the summer between my sophomore and junior year in high school and almost old enough to work legally, I got a job at the Midtown Family Theater as a janitor. I decided I would never be fired again. I busted my butt cleaning that movie theater. Then I was promoted to usher. When I returned from New Jersey in the summer of 1963, I was fortunate to be rehired by David Levy, the theater owner, and he promoted me to assistant manager.

The summer between my senior year of high school and college, I worked four jobs—most of them simultaneously. I was a salesclerk at the Coast-to-Coast hardware store; did yard work at the home of a wealthy psychiatrist; continued to work at the Midtown Theater; was a fry cook at the Maid-Rite Hamburger shop during the Minnesota State Fair.

By the time I was a sophomore in college, I had to get a real job. I left the movie theater when Lewie Rydeen, the production control manager at Sperry Univac in Roseville, hired me as a production control dispatcher on the night shift

Sperry Univac was a computer manufacturing company. Lewie had submitted a Cost Improvement Plan (CIP), which had been approved by upper manage-ment. His brilliant idea was simple—save expensive computer parts that were being thrown away and reuse them. When a job of 100 printed circuit boards moved down the assembly line, it was common for the workers to prepare many more than 100 resistors, transistors, diodes, cathodes, etc., required for the assembly to ensure they wouldn't run out if a part were lost or damaged and caused the line to shut down. However, each part cost $5 or more apiece (equivalent to $40 in 2020), and the extras were seldom used because there was no way to retrieve or collect them. So they were discarded.

Lewie's idea was to take all the extra parts and store them in small bins in something like a filing cabinet. When a container became full of a particular part, they would be used for the next printed circuit board job. This CIP also allowed the workers to prepare fewer extra parts for each job. If too many components were lost or damaged while the job moved down the assembly line, a dispatcher could retrieve a substitute part from the cabinet preventing the assembly line from shutting down.

His CIP saved hundreds of thousands of dollars—on paper. Now he had to implement. He hired me to implement it.

I was a full-time student at the University of Minnesota by day and worked the 2nd shift at Sperry Univac—3:30 PM to 12. Every night, I retrieved any extra parts, meticulously put them in their respective bins, and then recovered them when someone on the assembly floor needed one. It was a boring job, but it paid well. I earned $5 a week less than my father was earning at that time. (That equaled approximately $40 a week or $2,000 a year in 2020 dollars. How did that make any sense—a 19-year-old kid earning $2,000 a year less than his dad who had worked hard all his life?)

I generally finished processing extra parts within the first half of my shift. Then there was not much to do other than occasionally retrieve a component that was lost or damaged. I could have done my homework but had learned there was no percentage in stealing time from my employer. Been there, done that. Instead, I read all the company's production control manuals and then reread them again.

Six months later, a promotion opportunity opened up. I told Lewie I wanted to apply. He advised me that there were older, more senior, and more knowledgeable employees in the department, but he appreciated my aggressiveness.

I asked him to test me and to test the others as well. He reluctantly acquiesced and tested all those who applied for the position. When finished, he concluded there was no contest—I was more knowledgeable about Sperry Univac's production control procedures than all those other guys who had been around for several years. I got the promotion. A year later, Lewie promoted me to supervisor when I was just 21, and I became the youngest supervisor in Sperry Univac. Lewie became a most valued mentor.

This I could do, I concluded. I might not be good at school, but I could compete in the workforce.

The Lesson: Don't steal time, or anything else, from your employer.

The Lesson: Work hard at whatever you do!

The Lesson: If you want to get ahead, prepare for the next promotion. Then show your supervisor you have what it takes.

Egg Rolls

"To err is human, but if the eraser wears out before the pencil,
you're overdoing it a bit."

~ Author unknown

One day, a coworker offered to set me up on a blind date with Miss Univac. I generally didn't like the idea of blind dates but figured if she had been selected to represent our company, she must be an attractive and reasonably smart woman. Always willing to go out with beautiful bright women, I told him, "sure."

We double-dated—my friend and his wife, and Miss Univac and me. We went to a fancy Asian restaurant. We sat at the bar, waiting for our table. My friend ordered eggrolls as an appetizer. They were served with an assortment of sauces. I had never had eggrolls, but I guess I'd seen them in a movie. Each of us was served one, and I assumed they were finger food, so I didn't bother using a knife and fork. I picked up mine with my fingers and dipped it into the red sauce. Then I bit into a <u>rolled-up, salmon-colored hand towel</u>!

It's tough to recover from trying to eat a washcloth. There's not much you can say. "Wow, that's a tasty sauce," doesn't quite cut it.

I said nothing, acting as if nothing untoward had happened. Fortunately, I was on the stool at the far end of the bar, next to my date. Had we been sitting at a table, everyone would have seen my stupidity.

I'm not sure Miss Univac even saw me do it. Amazingly, she and I dated sever-al times after that. Neither she nor I ever commented on the salmon-colored hand towel dipped in red sauce ordeal. But that episode is durably implanted in my brain.

The Lesson: A Japanese finger towel is called an oshibori. If you dip your os-hibori into the eggroll sauce, don't try to eat it. If you do, don't tell your date.

The Leson: When you make a fool of yourself in public, don't assume every-one saw you do it. Most people are not paying attention to <u>you</u>!

The Calling

"Be the change you want to see in the world."

~ Mohandas Gandhi, lawyer, anti-colonial nationalist,
political ethicist, and father of the Indian nation

President John F. Kennedy was assassinated in November 1963. His life and death inspired me. I decided I wanted to serve in public office as a way of being helpful to others. My mother had instilled in me that life's purpose was to serve others, and politics seemed a good route to fulfill that responsibility. Kennedy died in the fall of my senior year in high school. The following year, I attended the University of Minnesota and majored in political science and minored in speech and communications.

I first ran for the Minnesota House of Representatives in 1970 at 24; started campaigning eight months after graduating from the U of M. I was a Democrat, having joined the Democratic-Farmer-Labor (DFL) party at 18. I never became involved in the "Young Democrats," which was an option for people under 30 because I always wanted to sit at the adults' table.

I sought the DFL party endorsement at my district convention. First, I had to sit through an endorsing committee made up of party members who then recommended their preferred candidate to the convention. I knew several people on the endorsing committee and was sure they would make a positive recommendation only if they thought I was serious and qualified.

In preparation, I persuaded five friends to grill me for hours as a mock endorsing committee. They asked me questions, I answered. They offered suggestions to tweak my answers; I re-answered. They asked more questions; I answered—until I was exhausted. They were tired too. But it all paid off. Every question asked by the endorsing committee had been reviewed during our mock sessions. I was prepared. I did well. The committee recommended me to the convention.

During the Q & A at the district convention, after each candidate made their speech explaining why they should be endorsed, I was asked about my position on women's rights. I remember responding that in my home, women outnumbered the men 10 to 3; "the women have most of the rights." There was light laughter, but I went on to acknowledge that my parents did not differentiate between gender, and I affirmed that I didn't either. Fortunately for me, I was never burdened with the infliction of thinking women were somehow inferior or superior to men. Another young man opposed me, but the convention delegates, virtually all of whom were old enough to be my parents, endorsed me for the position.

There was an open September primary election with four candidates—the incumbent Republican State Representative, the other twentysomething man who had also sought the DFL endorsement, a a third man whom I don't remember, and me. I came in second with 27 percent of the vote, well ahead of the other two candidates but way behind the Republican incumbent.

Shortly before the November general election, the US government notified me that I was to be inducted into the Army. The Vietnam War was waging during this time—a war which I had long opposed. There was no way I was going to honor the draft notice, even though I knew that refusing induction would subject me to probable prosecution, conviction, and a sentence of two to five years in federal prison. My campaign manager and I decided to advise the state Democratic Party of my decision.

When we met with the DFL state chair, Dick Moe, I told him about the induction notice. However, before I could say anything more, he responded.

"That's great. We never thought we had a shot at winning your district. A couple of pictures of you in uniform at Boot Camp is just what's needed to turn that around."

When my campaign manager, Betty Peterson, explained that I intended to refuse the draft, the chairman's face grew tight and drawn. It appeared he was not a happy man. However, at our urging, he got the induction notice postponed until after the election.

In November, I lost the election. I was disappointed. I was confident my career was to be in public office. Later, I learned that the district was a highly Republican area and that no Democrat had been elected from that district in several decades. Note to self: A good student of politics would have known that basic fact before starting the campaign.

Two days after the 1970 general election, I received a second Notice to Report for Induction to the United States Army. There's more information about refusing to comply with this draft notice in another chapter, so I will leave it at that for now. But I was convinced I was to serve in political office.

As discussed later, I was elected to the Minnesota House four years later, defeated for reelection in 1976, appointed Assistant Commissioner of DNR in 1977, and lost that political appointment in 1978. That was my last foray into politics, other than fundraising and campaigning for other candidates, for the next 26 years.

The Lesson: We can't always do that which we may think we are supposed to do.

The Lesson: When you make a fool of yourself in public, don't assume everyone saw you do it. Most people are not paying attention to you!

The Lesson: Politics can be an unstable profession.

Let's Go to Work

"There are three kinds of people: those who make things happen; those who watch things happen; and those who wonder what happened."

~ Nicholas Murray Butler, an American philosopher, diplomat, and educator

In 1971, Senator Eugene McCarthy, a Democrat from Minnesota, announced his second bid for President. He was someone who made things happen. I joined his campaign as a volunteer and then quit my job at Sperry Univac when John Connolly, McCarthy's Minnesota campaign manager, hired me as a full-time campaign staffer. My initial assignment was organizing the caucus vote in Minnesota's 8th congressional district. I was with the senator on several occasions. Before speaking to a waiting audience, he turned to us and said, "Let's go to work." Then he went out on stage and delivered a most inspiring and entertaining political speech. Unfortunately, Senator McCarthy lost the Minnesota caucuses to Minnesota's other US Senator, Hubert Humphrey.

The next month, I advanced McCarthy's campaign travel for the Illinois primary. I helped raise crowds for events in Chicago; organized a photoshoot with a central Illinois farm family for TV ads; and coordinated a day of multiple events at the University of Illinois, Champaign Urbana, among other things. McCarthy had played baseball as a student at St. John's University and was good at the game. I arranged for him to take batting practice with the Champaign Urbana team, and he did remarkably well for a 56-year-old guy, hitting the ball over the fence a couple of times. After the reporters filmed and shot their images, the campaign manager told me it was an excellent day.

When McCarthy lost the Illinois primary to Senator Edmund Muskie, I was assigned to help open the McCarthy for President Office in Southern California. However, shortly after I drove from Chicago to Los Angeles, Senator McCarthy withdrew from the presidential race and endorsed Senator George McGovern, another candidate for the Democratic presidential nomination in 1972. I was out of a job.

I had met several McGovern campaign staff during my time in Illinois, and they offered me an organizing position with the Northern California McGovern for President Campaign in San Francisco. My job was to organize McGovern supporters in the San Joaquin Valley—the central valley agricultural area between Stockton and Bakersfield. Our goal was to knock on every door in the ten major cities in the valley. I worked long hours, mentored young and older campaign volunteers, busted my butt, learned a lot, and helped squeeze every vote possible out of those cities and small towns. McGovern carried the San Joaquin Valley in the June primary. That allowed him to win California and enough convention votes to gain the Democratic Party nomination for president on the first ballot.

The 1972 Democratic National Convention was in Miami, and I was part of McGovern's convention staff. However, I left the campaign shortly after the convention; I became disenchanted with the way his closest advisors conducted themselves. I remember thinking at the time that McGovern's people made Nixon's crooks look like choirboys. But I never lost my tremendous admiration for Senators McGovern and McCarthy. They were genuine patriots and statesmen—role models for the type of politician I hoped to become someday.

The Lesson: Campaigning for public office is arduous work.

The Lesson: Going door-to-door asking voters about issues which are their primary concern, sending voters candidate position papers which address those issues, following up by phone to determine if they now support the candidate, and then reminding supporters to go vote on election day, as we did for McGovern, is an effective campaign strategy. I used that strategy to win my Minnesota House seat two years later in 1974.

I'd Rather Wear No Pants

"We are a collection of ordinary people collectively capable of
extraordinary things."

~ Jonathan Dyer, an American Author

Following the 1972 presidential election, I was hired by the Minnesota Public
Interest Research Group (MPIRG) as administrative assistant to the Executive
Director, Bob Hudnut, and later promoted to Director of Finance and Communication. MPIRG is a nonprofit, non-partisan organization that works in
the public interest on issues affecting the people of Minnesota. Students from
a variety of Minnesota colleges and universities pay fees to fund the organization. The Board of Directors was comprised of students who hired an executive director who managed a team of scientists, lawyers, and economists.
Reverend Hudnut was a Presbyterian pastor who was on sabbatical from his
ministry. Bob became a dear friend and mentor.

The staff worked as a team on various consumer protection, social justice, and
environmental issues—protecting children from flammable clothing, preventing mining and logging in the BWCA, and raising awareness about question-
able Department of Transportation highway projects. My role was to help get
publicity for these efforts.

The student board of directors and staff decided to support a nationwide boycott against the Farah Pants Company—one of the largest manufacturers of
men's slacks—because the company prevented its mostly immigrant workforce

from forming a union. The worker's average wage was less than $2 an hour (about $11 or $22,000 a year in 2020 dollars). How do you raise a family on $22,000? These employees, 85 percent of whom were Mexican Americans, went on strike.

In support of the workers and the boycott, MPIRG petitioned Dayton's department store in downtown Minneapolis to stop selling Farah pants. Our conversations with management proved unsuccessful. MPIRG's board and staff decided to bring public pressure on Dayton's to help them see the error of their ways.

Bob Hudnut and Father Ed Flavin, a well-known leader in the Catholic Archdiocese of St. Paul, reached out to some celebrities to help bring public attention to this issue. Bobby Bryant was a star cornerback for the Minnesota Vikings, and Rudy Boschwitz was a well-known Republican businessman later elected to the US Senate.

A week before Christmas 1973, we arranged for these four men to hold a news conference on the Nicollette Mall in front of Dayton's largest department store. It was a cold December day. Bernie Bryant, Bobby Bryant's ex-wife who worked for the Catholic Archdiocese, and I painted four cardboard barrels—two green and two red—at Catholic Charities offices. The barrels read, "I'd rather wear no pants at all than wear Farah." With their trousers rolled up to their knees and the painted cardboard barrels hanging from their shoulders over their torsos and bare legs, they met the news media. The dramatic effect was immediate. Boycott efforts were going throughout the country, but ours had a whole lot more color and influence.

The Minneapolis Tribune and local TV evening news ran the story. The Associated Press carried the Tribune's photo of these prominent men not wearing trousers in the middle of a cold Minnesota winter on Minneapolis streets. It was an extraordinary successful tactic. With a caption about immigrants being denied their right to organize, the photo was printed in newspapers and shown on televisions across the country. Not long after, Dayton's stopped selling Farah's clothing. The bitter strike ended two months later when Farah agreed to rehire the 3,000 strikers and negotiate a fair contract with the Amalgamated Clothing Workers of America.

The Lesson: When people of goodwill join on behalf of their brothers and sisters who are being treated unjustly, good things can happen.

It's Time to Go

"Real friends are those who, when you've made a fool of your-self, don't feel that you've done a permanent job."

~ Erwin Randall, an American author

Eighteen months after I quit the McGovern campaign, and while I was working at MPIRG, the incumbent Republican Minnesota State Representative from Roseville, Bob Bell, gave notice of his retirement. I immediately decided to run for that seat. I grew up in Roseville, and due to redistricting, had run in several precincts of this suburb in 1970. I thought I had a good chance, especially since it was an open seat.

Once again, I sought the endorsement of the district DFL party, but this time I failed to gain the necessary 60 percent vote of the convention delegates. I lost by a single vote out of several hundred to Margaret Smith. Margaret was a lovely woman who had supported me four years earlier. But I did not support the legal right to abortion, and she was on the other side of that issue. That was a deal-breaker for her and too many others.

The delegates split along "pro-life" and "pro-choice" groups, with each side dug in hard. Of course, there were those for whom abortion was not a significant issue, and many of them supported me. But the divisions over this issue were so intense that our campaign could not convince even one pro-choice delegate to vote for me. Consequently, there was no DFL endorsement for state representative.

Margaret and I both ran in the primary election. I won by approximately the same percentage of the vote as at the district convention—58 percent to 42 percent. But that was not the end of the problems this divisive issue presented.

After defeating the Republican candidate in the general election, I was privileged to serve in the Minnesota House of Representatives for two years. There are 134 seats in the Minnesota House, and Democrats won 104 of them in 1974. The freshman class was the largest of first-time representatives in decades, and they elected me chair of the DFL Freshman Caucus. As caucus chair, I was responsible for representing these men and women with leadership. Our class held 40 percent of the total Democratic seats, and we concluded we ought to share in the distribution of power.

In a meeting with the Speaker of the House, Martin Sabo, I argued that some members of the freshman class ought to be appointed as committee chairs. Martin said that was a nonstarter. Then, how about subcommittee chairs, or subcommittee co-chairs, or subcommittee assistant chairs—chairs of something—anything. But to each of my proposals, Martin simply said, "No."

The tradition was that new members did not hold positions of power. As I persisted in my argument, and the Speaker continued to deny my requests, John Corbid, one of my freshman colleagues and now a long-time friend, tapped me on the shoulder and said, "Bud, it's time for us to go." So, we left.

The Lesson: Politics is the art of compromise, but only when power is shared. In this case, the Speaker had all the power. There was no need to compromise.

Twins

*"Every sunrise is an invitation for us to arise
and brighten someone's day."*

~ Richelle Goodrich, an American author

Immediately upon President Nixon's resignation in the wake of the Watergate scandal, President Ford assumed office. Ford pardoned Nixon a month later. The pardon hurt the Republicans, and they lost seats in both houses of the US Congress and legislatures across the country. The newly elected Democrats were called "Watergate Babies." Watergate was the primary reason I won in a highly Republican district that year. The district where I won in 1974 was even more Republican than the district where I lost in 1970.

I enjoyed those two years in the House. I worked hard, learned a lot, met some great people, established life-long friends, and fell in love with your mother. I carried several important bills, including the BWCA Protection Act and the Freedom of Information Act, both of which passed the house, but neither became law.

In March 1976, I represented the Minnesota House at a Freedom of Information conference in Washington, DC. Cathleen Douglas, the wife of US Supreme Court Justice William Douglas, was one of the main speakers. Mrs. Douglas and I visited after her presentation and stayed in touch over the next several months. We both attended the 1976 Democratic National Convention in New York City that summer, although neither of us had any official role. We shared dinner one evening, and Cathie invited me to join her in the VIP section of the convention hall at Madison Square Garden. I graciously accepted. It was fascinating to sit among all the highfalutin Hollywood people and former Democratic stars.

Then Jacqueline Kennedy Onassis walked into the VIP area. Everything stopped. The entire convention stood and turned their attention away from the podium to catch a glimpse of the former First Lady. She sat down two rows in front of us.

The VIP section happened to be immediately above where the Minnesota delegation sat, so they got the best view of Mrs. Onassis. I recognized a couple of my colleagues from the House. Then Representative Steve Wenzel started pointing, and it looked like he might be pointing at me. He turned to someone standing next to him, got his attention, and then pointed at me again. I did not acknowledge him; just watched as everyone's attention was fixated on the Kennedy entourage.

US Senator Walter Mondale was nominated Vice President the following night, and there was an after-convention party for the Minnesota delegation. I ran into Steve at the party, and he said to me, "Bud, you won't believe this. There is someone at this convention who looks exactly like you! I saw him last night in the convention hall sitting a couple of rows behind Jackie Kennedy. He is your absolute twin."

I smiled and told Steve, "I'd like to meet that guy."

The Lesson: We all have a twin somewhere.

Defeated

"There's no better exercise for strengthening the heart than
reaching down and lifting people up."

~ John Holmes, an American poet

As a former legislator, I am most proud of my work on the Boundary Waters
Canoe Area (BWCA) legislation, which then-Lt. Governor Rudy Perpich personally asked me to carry on his behalf. Perpich was a good man and a political
friend. We first met during the 1970 election when he ran for Lieutenant Governor and I was running for state representative. After my defeat, he helped
retire my campaign debt. We collaborated in 1972 when I worked for Senator
McCarthy's presidential campaign in Minnesota's 8th CD. Perpich was aware
of my work relating to the BWCA when I was at MPIRG and later supported
my 1974 successful campaign for the House.

Early in 1975, shortly after I took office, Perpich attended a Roseville City
Council meeting where he promoted the United States Bicentennial Celebration, which was to be celebrated across the state and the country the following
year. After his presentation, he and I had coffee in the City Hall cafeteria where
he asked me to carry the BWCA Protection Act. He wrote the major elements
he wanted included in the bill on the back of a white envelope. This legislation,
which was put into legal form by the Reviser of Statutes, was intended to protect this wilderness area from logging, mining, and peat harvesting.

I introduced the bill in the house, and Senator John Milton introduced it in the senate. Rudy, John, and I crisscrossed the state together, promoting the bill. Although this legislation did not become law, Rudy Perpich and I got to know each other quite well as we tried to build support for it.

Early during the week of the 1976 Democratic National Convention, Rudy and I had dinner at a New York restaurant. He had received a message earlier in the day to call Warren Spannaus, then Minnesota's Attorney General and Senator Mondale's close friend, during our dinner. Rudy phoned Spannaus at the appointed time from a street booth outside the restaurant. It was a short call. When Rudy returned to our table, he wore a huge smile. He said, "It's going to be Mondale. Warren just told me." US Senator Walter Mondale was about to be nominated Vice President of the United States.

"What does that mean for you?" I asked.

"If Carter wins, I think I'm going to be governor," he said. "Wendy knows that this is his best chance to become a Senator." (Wendell Anderson was Minnesota's governor at that time.)

We talked some more, and I enjoyed the conversation about my friend possibly becoming governor as early as December.

When I ran for reelection in 1976, I lost by 500 votes. I lost in part because some democrats in my district were upset with my position on abortion. I lost even though I received 2,800 more votes than I had two years previous and received a higher percentage of the vote in my district than Carter and Mondale. Nevertheless, I was fired by the people.

I had not been fired from a job in 15 years—not since I was a sophomore in high school. It was debilitating—excruciatingly painful. The only positive was that I lost to a delightful man, an elementary school teacher and youth hockey coach, John Rose. In all candor, as a Republican, John was much better suited for the district than I, especially given that there were far more Republicans than Democrats in this area at that time.

Georgia Governor Jimmy Carter was elected president in 1976, and Senator Walter Mondale was elected vice president. Shortly after the election, Wendell Anderson, Minnesota's incumbent Democratic governor, decided to become Minnesota's US Senator when that seat was vacated upon Mondale becoming vice president.

The US Constitution provides that when vacancies occur in the Senate, the affected state's governor fills the vacancy. However, it is understood that a governor cannot appoint himself because s/he cannot hold two offices simultaneously. For a sitting governor to be appointed to the US Senate, the governor would have to resign the office first. But then s/he would no longer have the authority to fill the vacancy. The Minnesota Constitution provides that when there is a vacancy in the office of governor, the lieutenant governor immediately becomes governor.

Senator Mondale resigned from the US Senate early to give the new Minnesota Senator a step up in senate seniority. Shortly after, on December 30, 1976, Governor Anderson resigned as governor of Minnesota. Lt. Governor Rudy Perpich immediately became governor. Governor Perpich then appointed Wendell Anderson to the United States Senate. At least that is the order of events the Constitution requires.

Nevertheless, some speculated that Lt. Governor Perpich may have signed the order appointing Wendell Anderson to the Senate before Governor Anderson resigned, thus ensuring Wendy's appointment. In any event, the press concluded and reported that Governor Anderson appointed himself to the US Senate, which eventually cost him big time politically.

On the day of Perpich's formal inauguration, I joined the long line of well-wishers in the governor's reception room at the state capital. When I approached the governor to congratulate him, he indicated he wanted to visit for a moment. We had not spoken since the November election, and he asked me if I had a job. I told him I was fulfilling my state representative responsibilities in the remaining days but didn't have anything beyond that. He asked me to come to his office the following morning at 10. I agreed.

Upon arrival the next day, I was ushered into the governor's ornate office, where we met for 15 minutes. He explained he wanted me to work at the Department of Natural Resources (DNR) and represent him and the state on federal legislation affecting the BWCA. I was thrilled and lifted up. Before that moment, I had no idea what I would do for a job or a career.

I reported to DNR's offices at the Minnesota Centennial Building a few days later, was shown to my office, and took on the role of representing the governor and the state on the boundary waters federal legislation. A couple of months later, Governor Perpich appointed Bill Nye, a wonderful gentleman from Ohio, as DNR Commissioner. Bill appointed me Assistant Commissioner for DNR Administration. Bill was bright, thoughtful, and a strong environmentalist, but not savvy about, and with limited knowledge of, Minnesota politics. In the end, that lack of savvy and knowledge cost him.

Shortly after Bill took office, Governor Perpich, Commissioner Nye, and I flew to Washington DC on the governor's plane to testify on the proposed BWCA federal legislation. Riding in a taxi from the airport to the capital, Bill asked about fishing in the boundary waters.

I jokingly said, "the fishing is so good, you can catch walleye without baiting your hook."

During the hearing, Governor Perpich testified first, then Commissioner Nye. After the formal remarks, there were questions from committee members.

One congressman asked Bill, "So how is the fishing in the BWCA?"

Bill immediately responded, "The fishing is so good, you can catch walleye without baiting your hook."

The governor turned to me with one of his, "I am totally and completely disappointed in you, and I am personally going to physically beat you to a pulp at my first opportunity" looks, which he had perfected.

The Lesson: It is helpful to have friends in high places.

The Lesson: Don't joke around with someone who doesn't know anything about the topic, especially if they're about to testify before Congress.

Joe

"Sometimes God will place a wall on your path to force you to go in another direction."

~ Suzy Kassem, an American poet, writer, and philosopher

Working as Assistant Commissioner in the Minnesota Department of Natural Resources was a tremendous opportunity for me, and I enjoyed the job. My preference was to serve in an elective office; however, being appointed to a significant state agency as a senior executive focusing on environmental issues was a close second. It was also a better use of my skills and experience. I had been managing people, projects, and programs since I was 17.

To my chagrin, Bill Nye made a couple of mistakes that caused him political problems resulting in his resignation. That turned out bad for me.

Governor Perpich appointed Joe Alexander to replace Bill as DNR Commissioner, effective July 1, 1978. Although, nominally a Democrat, Joe was not an advocate for either protecting the boundary waters or continuing me in my job.

Joe and Bill had not gotten along. When Bill was appointed commissioner, Joe was the Assistant Commissioner for Administration, but he had also been a candidate for Commissioner. Shortly after, Bill replaced Joe with me—making me Assistant Commissioner for Administration—and gave Joe a job which Joe aptly described as "vice president in charge of looking out the window."

The day after Governor Perpich announced Joe's appointment, Joe came by my office—literally his former office. After I congratulated him on his new role, he said to me, "Bud, next Monday I'm going to call a news conference. Among other things, I'm going to fire you on live television."

He stood up and left. I was stunned. What had I done to piss him off so?

Later, a mutual friend told me that Joe had concluded that I had conspired to get his job as Assistant Commissioner. He didn't like that I had his job, that I had his office, and that I had his title. And Joe didn't like that he had worked hard to get that job over decades, and I was appointed to the position in under six months in the department. He was going to fire me because he could fire me.

I immediately appealed to Terry Montgomery in the governor's office but was told that the new commissioner was assured that he could have his people in whatever position he wanted. Then I called some former colleagues at the Minnesota House and Senate. They all indicated an understanding of my unfortunate situation and a willingness to help, but they were unsure of what they could do.

Finally, I contacted Senator Nicholas Coleman's office, the Senate majority leader. I knew Nick politically and had campaigned for him when he ran for governor several years earlier. I spoke with one of his aides, who relayed the message to Coleman. The next day, I heard that I could resign rather than be fired and could remain on the job for the next three months, until the end of September. At that time, I had no idea what had happened.

Later, a friend described the telephone call Senator Coleman made on my behalf. He heard only Coleman's side of the conversation; it went something like this.

"Commissioner, I understand that you want your people in your department. However, Bud Philbrook is a friend of mine, and I don't want him fired in the way I understand you intend."

Silence.

"I understand what you're saying, commissioner; however, that's not acceptable to me."

Silence.

"Let me put it this way. I want Bud Philbrook to be able to resign and have his resignation effective three months from today."

Silence.

"Commissioner, let me say this another way. As you know, all appropriation bills for every department come before the Rules Committee, which I chair. I decide which bills are heard and which ones are not. I would consider it a favor if you reconsidered my request for Mr. Philbrook and allow him to resign and stay on the job for the next three months."

Silence.

"Very good commissioner. I appreciate your consideration and understanding in this matter."

This was a difficult time for me. Fired again, twice in less than two years! Even though I had received a three-month reprieve, I had no idea what I would do moving forward.

It is reasonable at times like these to view life as a cup half-filled. However, if we concentrate on the empty part, we focus on the darker side of life—the part that is wanting—the despair, the poverty of the human spirit. I learned that by focusing attention on the portion of life that is filled, then we can be fulfilled—we can see the goodness that life offers. There is no naiveté in focusing on the goodness in life. I guarantee you that the dark side will make its presence known without any effort on your part.

This is particularly important concerning relationships. If we see others as half empty—if we concentrate on their shortcomings, weaknesses, and what they have done or not done—it is more difficult to love, forgive, and fully appreciate the wonder of human creation. Had I focused on the fact that Joe fired me for no damn good reason, I may not have forgiven him.

However, when we focus on the best in others, their human failings and affronts take on less prominence. The goodness in others will overpower their shadowy side if we just recognize and appreciate their goodness. Moreover, if you tell others that you see their positive side, you enhance their decency. By simply letting them know they are good, they will exude even greater goodness. This approach is challenging to do at times, but the benefits can be enormous, especially with people with whom you have an ongoing relationship.

This is also true in how we view ourselves. When we concentrate on our faults, misdeeds, and imperfections, we can become overly self-critical and pessimistic. Some may even despair. However, you can decide to look at your virtuous side. Appreciate the wonder of your creation. Recognize the joy you bring to others, the service you render; the love you give; and the awe you inspire. "Accentuate the positive" is what my mother told me. It is valuable advice.

Joe served admirably as Commissioner of DNR for 12 years, the longest-serving DNR Commissioner in Minnesota history. He was a good man, an excellent public servant, and deeply committed to Minnesota.

The Lesson: A glass may be half-full, but life is neither half-full nor half-empty. Life simply is. How we view life—where we decide to concentrate our focus—makes all the difference.

The Lesson: See the goodness inside you and focus on that aspect of your life.

The Lesson: Every challenge in life strengthens your ability to meet the next challenge.

Minnesota Massacre—1978 version

"Politicians and diapers must be changed often,
and for the same reasons."

~ Mark Twain, an American writer and humorist

I left DNR at the end of September 1978. It was a sad day. I had good friends there, believed that I could make a constructive difference in the department and for the people of Minnesota. Once again, I'd been fired.

As it turned out, I would have lost my job at the end of the year in any event. Governor Perpich lost the election in November, and all his political appointees were terminated. It was called the 1978 "Minnesota Massacre." Minnesota democrats lost both US Senate seats, the governor's office, and 32 seats in the Minnesota house—many of them my friends—primarily due to how Wendell Anderson was appointed to the US Senate and what he did after that.

US senate races cost a lot of money, and statewide campaigns require an enormous amount of time. Under the rules, Anderson had to run for election in 1978; and that gave him less than two years to raise the necessary money and campaign. Senator Anderson spent a lot of time in Minnesota and missed too many votes on the Senate floor. His opponent, Rudy Boschwitz, campaigned on the theme that Anderson "Appointed himself to the office and then didn't show up for work." Anderson lost by a wide margin—56 percent to 40 percent, and Governor Perpich lost 52 percent to 45 percent.

It became clear that if I had won reelection in 1976, I would have lost in 1978, as did many friends who were first elected in 1974. Losing in 1976 was not such a bad deal, especially given that I was able to spend nearly two years in a senior executive position at DNR.

The Lesson: Politics can be an unstable profession.

Blue Jeans and Pinstripes

"In a country well governed, poverty is something to be ashamed of. In a country badly governed, wealth is something to be ashamed of."

~ Confucius, a 5th Century BC Chinese teacher and philosopher

A couple of weeks before leaving DNR, I got a call from a Washington DC Nongovernmental Organization (NGO) which provided services for the State Department. They offered me a one-month gig accompanying foreign political and media officials to meetings with prominent US politicians and citizens around the US. They told me Speaker Martin Sabo had recommended me. I was surprised Martin would do that for me, but greatly appreciative. I left DNR on a Friday and was in Washington, DC the following Monday.

Five men, all my seniors, were assigned to me—a leading political operative from Ireland, a renowned journalist from Egypt, the son of a former president of Columbia, an established journalist from India, and a prominent member of the Israeli Knesset. We enjoyed a great month together. We met with Coretta Scott King, the wife of slain civil rights leader Martin Luther King, Jr., at Ebenezer Baptist Church in Atlanta. George Wallace, the paraplegic governor of Alabama, visited with us about segregation at his office in the capital in Montgomery. Mark White, who was running for Texas Attorney General and later served as governor, described his campaign strategy in his Houston office. Congresswoman Pat Schroeder, the first woman US Representative elected in

Colorado, met with us after a speech she gave in Denver. And Harvey Milk, a member of the San Francisco Board of Supervisors and the first openly gay elected official in California, discussed civil rights issues at his office in City Hall. Milk was assassinated by a former city supervisor one month after we met with him.

Each of these distinguished men and women with whom we met offered incredible insight into the American political process, their personal lives, and our wonderful country. It was a privilege to meet them while also getting to know the five men from around the world.

Shortly after my return from crisscrossing the US, I was offered a contract position at Control Data Corporation in a new subsidiary, Rural Ventures. I got this job because Rural Ventures president was my sister's neighbor, and we had become friends. He knew I had spent considerable time in DC, working on federal legislation and had some knowledge of Indian country. My responsibilities were to sell the concept of Plato agricultural educational software to tribal councils on American Indian reservations and then identify federal government funding sources so the tribes could purchase the software.

Officially, the job started on January 2, 1979; however, I had nothing to do in December, so I worked without pay for the month. That time gave me a running start.

The job required a lot of travel to Indian reservations across the country and multiple trips to Washington DC. On more than one occasion, I had blue jeans and cowboy boots in one suitcase and a blue pinstripe suit, starched white shirt, burgundy tie, and wingtips in the other—one outfit for the reservation, a different costume for DC.

I have always been struck by poverty on reservations. When I first ran for the House in 1970, I visited several Minnesota reservations. During the summer of 1975, I spent nearly a month on the Leach Lake Reservation in northern Minnesota to learn more about issues affecting American Indians. I visited a dozen reservations while at Rural Ventures and lived on the Rocky Boys Reservation in Montana for several weeks during the winter of 1979. Global Volunteers continues to engage volunteers on reservations in Montana and South Dakota. But the poverty in our land of wealth continues to haunt me. On the bright side, I have made good friends in Indian Country, and that's what counted.

The Lesson: The costume you wear or the people you associate with should not make any difference in who you are or what you say.

The Lesson: Respect everyone the same, regardless of their wealth or lack thereof, regardless of their education or lack thereof, regardless of their public stature or lack thereof. Every conversation, every interaction is important. Never lose the common touch.

The Lesson: Some people look out for you even when you're not aware, and you may not know why. You, too, can look out for others.

Pay Back

"You don't learn to walk by following rules. You learn by
doing, and by falling over."

~ Richard Branson, a British business magnate, investor,
author, and philanthropist

One day in mid-August 1979, I ran into Tom Kelm at Control Data offices. Tom was former Senator Wendell Anderson's long time chief of staff and brother-in-law to Control Data's vice chairman. Tom asked what I was doing there, and I briefly explained the outlines of my job at Rural Ventures.

On Friday of that week, my boss, Pat Gorman, called me into his office where I was told by Pat and my other boss, Ralph Thompson, that I'd been fired. They both apologized and expressed their regret. They explained the reason was "big 'D' Democratic party politics." The vice chairman had personally instructed them to fire me.

Pat and Ralph explained it to me this way. Tom Kelm blamed Anderson's 1978 election loss on the controversy over the BWCA federal legislation. Because I was Governor Perpich's representative, I was a key player in that controversy. By inference, I was partially responsible for Anderson's loss. This was payback time.

In any event, I was fired—for the third time in three years. Pat and Ralph arranged for me to be paid according to my contract's terms until it expired at the end of the year.

I was beyond disappointment—something had to change. I was engaged to be married. We were going to have a family. I needed something more stable than a job where I could get fired due to political whim.

That night, your mom and I went out to dinner. I told her I was seriously thinking about going to law school. It was too late in the year for me to do anything right away, but I could study for and take the next LSAT and start law school in the fall of 1980, or possibly even in the coming spring. As always, she was supportive.

In the meantime, I had to inform my friends at the American Indian Development Association (AIDA) that I was leaving my position at Rural Ventures. I did not want them to think poorly of Rural Ventures or Control Data Corporation on my account—the Plato agricultural software could genuinely benefit rural American Indian tribes. So, I did not tell them that I'd been fired.

Dr. Wally Heath, president of AIDA, had become a good friend, and when I told him I was leaving to go to law school, he asked, "When does school start?"

I explained I didn't know for sure, sometime in the spring or next fall at the latest.

"What are you going to do between now and then?" he asked.

"I'm not sure yet," I responded.

Wally expressed unease and suggested he thought something did not seem right.

Because I was still under contract and being paid by Control Data until the end of December and planned to go to law school soon, there wasn't a need to immediately find a job. Although, I knew I would have to find some type of work between then and when law school started. Given the circumstances, I was advised not to be seen around Control Data's offices and could not be out representing Rural Ventures, so I could do whatever I chose for the next couple of months, except take a job somewhere else.

I used those four months to work on my graduate school Plan B—what is sometimes called a thesis—and nearly finished it. Then, shortly before Christmas and a week before we were to be married, I got a call from Pat Gorman; he offered me a full-time position at Rural Ventures. I was stunned. "Why?" I asked. "What changed?"

Pat told me that Bill Norris, Control Data's co-founder and chairman of the board, had received letters from American Indian Chiefs across the country with whom I had worked. The chiefs informed Norris that if they were going to do business with Rural Ventures, it had to be through Bud Philbrook. The American Indian effort was Norris's idea; it was his baby. He was totally committed to it. Norris was not aware I'd been fired. And when he learned, he instructed Pat to rehire me as a full-time employee.

Hamline University School of Law had already accepted me for the 1980 fall term. I had wanted to be a lawyer all my life but had never pulled the trigger. Now, nothing was going to change my decision. I agreed to return to Rural Ventures for the next eight months—January through August—not as an employee, but in the same consulting role I previously had. That was acceptable to Pat.

Although I was fired from Rural Ventures in August 1979, I worked there for almost another full year. Your mom and I were married in December 1979, honeymooned during the first two weeks of January, and enjoyed life as blissful newlyweds until August when I started law school.

The Lesson: Disappointment can cause us to make important life decisions that we might not otherwise make.

The Lesson: Some people look out for you even when you're not aware, and you may not know why. You, too, can look out for others.

An Honorable Profession

"The minute you read something that you can't
understand, you can almost be sure that it was drawn up
by a lawyer."

~ Will Rogers, an American cowboy, humorist, and social commentator

I finished law school in December 1982 after 27 months of classes, and sat for the bar exam the following February. I was confident I had passed the bar, so I started looking for office space immediately after the exam.

In April, I subleased a vacant corner law office on the 18th floor of the American National Bank building in downtown St. Paul. I bought a new prominent walnut lawyers' desk with credenza and a new big brown leather lawyers' chair and never looked back. By May, when I was sworn in, I was open for business as a solo practitioner.

The practice of law was good for our family and me personally. I focused on government relations and business law. Almost from day one, I was never not busy. Some clients were business owners whom I'd known previously. A couple were business guys represented by opposing counsel in transactions on which I represented the other side and liked my work. Other lawyers referred some clients, and several were folks I'd never met but learned about me somehow.

As a business lawyer, I drafted contracts, incorporated businesses, resolved employment issues, negotiated ownership disputes, performed corporate legal audits, represented franchisees, and assisted clients in other transactional matters. I also lobbied at the Minnesota legislature for better education—resources and tuition support for students at private colleges and computer technology for public schools. I did not do criminal defense, divorces, civil litigation, or appeals. Truth be told, I represented one business client in his divorce, but I counseled him that it was in his best financial interest to reconcile. He and his wife decided to stay together, much to my delight. I did not want to learn about divorce law.

I also handled or was involved in three appellate cases. The first was soon after I was admitted to the bar. My dear friend and best man at our wedding, then Minnesota Senator Bill Luther, asked me to take a case before the Minnesota Supreme Court for one of his clients. The court had scheduled oral arguments during the legislative session, and Bill did not have time to do it. Or at least that was the reason he gave me.

I drafted the brief and prepared for the hearing but was a bit concerned about the merits of the case. On the day of the hearing, I was nervous but confident in representing the client. I'm an effective speaker, can be persuasive, and had prepared my opening oral argument and a boatload of succinct and convincing answers for a variety of queries from the justices.

After presenting my argument, I stood and waited for questions. There were none. The silence was deafening.

It quickly became evident that I should sit down. A month later, the court ruled against my client nine to zero. Disappointing, to say the least, but it was a good experience.

I also appealed an employment case to the Minnesota Court of Appeals, which I won. And I participated in a case before the US Court of Appeals for the Third Circuit in Philadelphia, Pennsylvania, which we also won. But transactional law was my bread and butter.

A few years after law school, two other lawyers and I started Philbrook, Anderson & McCormick, Attorneys and Counsellors at Law. We opened offices in downtown St. Paul. Even though the law didn't fulfill my heart, it was the law practice that generated the money that allowed us to commit to Global Volunteers. Three years later, we dissolved the firm when Tom McCormick joined a St. Paul litigation firm, and Tim Anderson hung up his shingle in a small Wisconsin town. I moved to 375 Little Canada Road, a solo practitioner once again, and Global Volunteers found a permanent home.

The Lesson: Follow your heart; it will take you to where you are supposed to go.

Always a Crap Shoot

"Some people are smart in school but dumb on the bus."

~ Author Unknown

I've managed projects and supervised people since I was 17, and I was the youngest manager at Sperry Univac. I have interviewed and hired hundreds of people. I have read books on hiring, contracted with HR consultants, and used candidate qualifying tools. But these have only marginally improved the odds of hiring the best or right person. I have hired the smartest candidate, best-educated candidate, most articulate candidate, prettiest and most handsome candidates, friendliest candidate, the youngest candidate, oldest candidate, and most experienced candidate. I even hired someone whom I thought was all the above.

After more than 50 years of hiring and managing people, I have concluded that what distinguishes the good from the not-so-good, and sometimes the bad is not correlated with education levels, academic grades, scores on qualifying surveys, or relevant experience. What separates the good from the not so good is commitment and character. Commitment to the mission. Commitment to making a difference. Commitment to be the best one can be. Commitment to being a team player. Commitment to getting the job done. Commitment to living life to the fullest. Commitment to helping others live their life to the fullest.

Some people work for money, others for praise, and others for the experience. That level of motivation does not correlate to commitment. What is important is the motivation to contribute to society—a genuine commitment to the common good and the willingness to forsake all for the common good. I believe Scripture calls this "sacrifice."

If you hire those who are willing to sacrifice for the common good, you will seldom go wrong. However, few are willing to sacrifice. The challenge is in identifying the few.

Which brings me to character. Character is defined as the sum of "mental and ethical traits" which identify and describe a person. If you hire employees who are honest, kind to others, respectful, team players, smart, able to learn, curious, and committed, you dramatically increase your odds of hiring well.

Determining if someone has sufficient commitment and good character is complicated. Educated applicants generally know that they should exhibit some of or all these qualities on paper and in an interview. The employer's responsibility is to get beneath the façade of the new suit of clothes and professionally written résumé. However, this cannot be done in one interview session; a minimum of three, perhaps more, is required. By the third or fourth interview, people think they will be hired, and thus their guard may be down a bit, and more of their true self might show through. This process also offers the candidate the opportunity to interview you and to make a personal decision about whether the job is a good fit for them.

There are three tactics and one admonition that can help at this stage. First, be sure that your written materials and oral descriptions of the mission, corporate culture, expectations, etc., have been stated clearly. Do not resort to puffery; do not try to sell applicants by making stuff up.

Second, require the applicant to provide concrete examples of their commitment and character. Ask why they are drawn to this particular position in this organization at this time in their life. What have they achieved academically, professionally, and experientially to prepare themselves to succeed. Try to glean their level of commitment and the foundation for the character traits they have described.

Third, do not talk yourself into hiring someone. Sometimes an applicant will show up who looks so good, and you might conclude that this person owns all the qualities and characteristics you're seeking. However, you must press to know whether they actually possess those qualities or if you just want them to have them. This is dangerous and tricky territory. If you conclude a candidate has a quality or ability because you want them to have it, without evidence that they possess it, everyone will be dissatisfied when you discover they are not what you hoped them to be.

Finally, don't hire family members or friends, or even family members of friends. I hired a guy once because his mother asked me to interview him. His résumé was not sufficient to make the cut for an interview, but his mother was a friend, and I respected her. Out of courtesy, I had her son come in. This guy was one of the smoothest talking people I had ever met; he answered all my questions extremely well and was from good stock—both his mom and dad were high-quality people. I hired him, and a few months later, he was gone. That was my worst hire ever.

Upon reflection, I realized that I did not make that hiring decision based on the candidate's qualifications. Instead, I based it on his parents' qualifications. Both the mother and father were extraordinary people; how could I go wrong! I've also hired my family members, not because they were qualified, but because they were family. Sometimes that works out; however, too often, it does not.

Now use your best judgment and hope that your best candidate has not grown too weary of the extensive hiring process and taken a job somewhere else.

Resist the temptation to believe you have failed if only 50 percent of your hires work out. Be honored by all those who agree to work with you and contribute constructively to the mission. And remember, hiring is a crapshoot.

The Lesson: Some hires are good; some are not. And résumés too often do not offer much information as to which applicants are in which category. Personal interviews help, but when people put on their finest suit of clothes, their best smile, and tell you what they think you want to hear, the crapshoot is in play.

The Lesson: If half the people you hire work out, you have done okay. Treat well those who do work out and keep hiring. Eventually, you will have a cadre of highly committed people of excellent character. Then you can rule the world.

The Hardest Thing

"Quality is not an act; it is a habit."

~ Aristotle, a Greek philosopher

The first time I ever had to fire someone was when I supervised a team of guys on the second shift at Sperry Univac. I didn't actually fire the person; just recommended it. But that had the same effect. He was fired for the offense that I had committed years ago as a young boy; he stole time from his employer. He sat in the shade, relaxed, and enjoyed the breeze—he drank coffee in the lunchroom and visited with co-workers instead of doing his job.

Firing someone is among the most painful work-related things a manager can do. For the person fired, it is generally a terrible experience; however, it can be a meaningful learning opportunity for the employee provided there is sufficient reflection. But it is agonizing for the one doing the firing, as it should be.

Before terminating an employee, be sure you have offered them the full opportunity to improve their performance. In the times I was fired, I was never given that opportunity. I was either legally too young to work, was terminated in a binary political environment—you're either in, or you're out—or the person doing the firing simply did not care.

Performance Improvement Plans (PIPs), when conducted properly, can alleviate the need to fire someone. PIPs describe for the employee where they are failing to perform, detail what they need to change, and offer the employee the opportunity to improve. In most cases, a PIP benefits both the employer and the employee.

Employers invest significant time and resources into every employee, and PIPs create the chance to continue to reap the benefit from those investments. Employees also invest in their employers, and they generally want to continue and do a good job. Otherwise, they would have quit on their own long ago. If employees know what they are supposed to do; are given the tools to do their job; have the skill sets to do the job; are committed to the mission; can enjoy a positive work environment, they will perform well.

I was once asked by a new hire how she could lose points. The employee told me that she assumed every new employee started at zero. When they performed well, they gained points, and when they didn't perform, they lost points. She wanted to know how she might lose points while working for me. I hadn't thought about it that way previously; however, I decided her question deserved consideration. But instead of putting together a list of how an employee can lose points, I created a list of how employees can earn points—what employees can do to perform at their highest:

- **Ask questions—lots of them:** There are no dumb questions. One new manager worked for me for six months and asked me two questions. He made lots of preventable mistakes and did not last a year.

- **Build trust:** Tell the truth. Ensure that the information you provide is reliable. Do not report things because you think your manager wants to hear them. And do not make things up.

- **Demonstrate a strong work ethic:** Come in early; don't take long lunches; don't waste time visiting with anyone about non-work topics; only leave after the workday is complete. Stealing time from an employer is no different than robbing a bank or shoplifting.

- **Stay in your lane:** Do your job; do not get involved in someone else's job unless assigned to do so. If you believe you have more to offer, suggest that to your manager, but don't go off on your own.

- **Be collaborative:** Even though you need to stay in your lane, it is crucial to collaborate with your team and other teams to achieve the company's goals.

- **Do the job:** Assuming the job description is clear and you have the necessary tools, you are expected to do your job. It is a simple contract—you do the work, and your employer fairly pays you according to the terms of the employment agreement.

- **Walk your talk:** Talking a good game is okay; however, you must perform. Productivity always trumps activity. Results are what matters.

- **Be creative:** Suggest ideas. Think through problems. Out of what may seem like silly ideas can come elegant solutions.

- **Be proactive:** Anticipate what needs to be done before being told what to do. Proactivity is a vital quality; although, too often too rare.

- **Respect everyone:** It is essential that employees respect their colleagues, respect their managers, respect the organization, and respect themselves.

The Lesson: Hire the best people you can and treat them fairly and with respect. Do this, and you will limit the number of times you must fire someone.

The Lesson: Treat everyone the same—with dignity and respect. And as Rudyard Kipling wrote, "keep your virtue and don't lose the common touch."

Leadership

"Leaders are made, not born. Leadership is forged in times of crisis. It's easy to sit there with your feet up on the desk and talk theory. Or send someone else's kids off to war when you've never seen a battlefield yourself. It's another thing to lead when your world comes tumbling down."

~ Lee Iacocca, an American automobile executive and author

Leading is challenging but also extraordinarily rewarding. In my experience, nearly everyone can become a leader. Like Iacocca, I do not believe leaders are born. I think all leaders are made; although, some may have more natural talents than others.

I started learning about leadership early on. In high school, I was one of the instigators and the general manager of two St. Rose of Lima Youth Group plays—*Cheaper by the Dozen* and *You Can't Take It With You*. I also was privileged to have a leading role in both plays. While still in college, I was promoted to supervisor, the youngest at Sperry Univac, at age 21. I led the San Joaquin Valley McGovern county leaders to victory in the 1972 California Democratic presidential primary. I was elected Chair of the Freshman Caucus of democrats in the Minnesota House of Representatives in 1975. And I have led Global Volunteers for nearly four decades.

During those many years, I have learned ten primary leadership lessons; although, I have not always applied them because I first had to learn them. Some who have worked with me might rightfully say, "He never led that way when I worked for him." That may be true; I had not yet learned all these lessons.

Hopefully, this list will help you become a better leader at an earlier age than I. Each of the following can be learned, practiced, and developed.

The Lessons:

1. **Think big:** Leave the small ideas to someone else. They are often just tactics necessary to achieve a much larger goal. But keep your eyes on the details because, as Willie Sutton, the bank robber, said, "Success in any endeavor requires single-minded attention to detail and total concentration."

2. **Plan before acting:** Think every project through. Write down your goals and your strategy to achieve your goals. Test various approaches. Timeline each action item. Employ Gantt charts. However, know that plans become obsolete the moment first implemented. Listen carefully to President Eisenhower, who instructed, "planning is everything; the plan is nothing." The process is essential; it defines the goals and the desired outcomes. The planning process requires you to think through how, what, where, when, who, and perhaps even why you will do something. Employing Objectives and Key Results (OKRs) is an excellent and effective planning tool.

3. **Collaborate:** Seek guidance and listen carefully. Know that everyone around the table possesses wisdom, especially subordinates who may report to someone who reports to someone who reports to you. Employees do not demand you adopt what they propose, but they do expect you to listen. In that positive environment, they will offer extraordinary ideas. And always get a second (or third) set of eyes on anything you publish.

4. **Communicate clearly:** If your team does not understand your directions, they cannot implement them. Organize your thoughts carefully. Write down what you intend to communicate. Use short, concise sentences.

Practice what you intend to say. After saying it, follow-up in writing. Do your absolute best <u>not</u> to communicate decisions on the fly in the hallways.

5. **Delegate:** Delegate to subordinates the authority and responsibility to do their job, remembering that you are accountable. When you delegate, you contribute to people's self-confidence and desire to do better, and you no longer must do everything. However, you must have qualified people who can do the job. So, you must first hire, train, and mentor good people, and then delegate.

6. **Nurture your team:** Be kind to, encourage, and support your team. Mentor those who show promise. Clearly explain things that you know how to do that your people may not know. Respect confidences. Be fair and just. Praise and award quality work. Hold people accountable—they expect it. And "praise in public and correct in private." Subordinates may follow out of fear, but colleagues will do what needs to be done out of love and respect.

7. **Be optimistic:** Remember, "the glass <u>is</u> always half full!" It is hard to prevail if you think you're going to fail.

8. **Believe in yourself and show you care:** Confidence is a prerequisite to leadership. If you do not believe in what you are doing, no one will believe in you. But you must show you care. People need to believe that you care before they will care about what you believe.

9. **Persevere:** Perseverance is the fuel of leadership. "You cannot score if you do not shoot." Do not give up.

10. **Pray for wisdom, strength, and grace:** If you're truly doing God's work, God will help.

In addition, there are some no brainers:
- Tell the truth.
- Treat others as you would like to be treated.
- Don't ask someone to do that which you would not do yourself.

135 Parties

"Action removes the doubt that theory cannot solve."

~ Sun Tzu, a Chinese general and philosopher

Before deciding to run for Governor of Minnesota in 2006, I was ambivalent about campaigning for office again. For years I felt an urge, a need, a desire to serve in high public office. However, at the same time, I did not want to run for office. I did not enjoy campaigning and had no desire to subject myself or our family to the tremendous scrutiny and challenges of competing for statewide office.

I was intensely satisfied with my work at Global Volunteers; although, there were times when it grew tiresome. Nevertheless, the political bug was there. I judged that no recent governor or president had the educational or experiential training that I've had. The world is complex, and few politicians experience the breadth of international knowledge combined with the deep understanding of local issues—education, economic development, environmental protection—and a grounded philosophy of local initiative, local leadership, and local action, that I have. Consequently, I felt compelled to at least offer my candidacy.

But I was still ambivalent. On the one hand, I did not want to subject myself and our family to the grueling task of campaigning and serving in such a problematic and intrusive climate. On the other hand, I was reasonably confident that if I ran, I could win. The possibility of a statewide grassroots political campaign focused on important public policy issues energized me. I believed I could outwit, out-organize, outwork and out-finesse any other candidate. The competitive side of me would drive me to win, and my sense of responsibility would require me to put all my strength and commitment into the effort. You will note that I did not include that I could out-fundraise any of the other candidates.

In 2004, I finally decided to run for governor of Minnesota. I was concerned about where Minnesota was being taken; the incumbent Republican governor had discarded many Minnesota core values. I knew Minnesotans could and wanted to do better. I focused the campaign theme on three main pillars—the 3Es—protecting the Environment, improving Education, and enhancing the Economy. These were the things I was most concerned about. And, I wanted voters to have ready answer to the questions, "What does Philbrook stand for?" 3E's made that easy.

However, there were divisive issues some people cared about. I learned in my campaigns for the Minnesota House that the legal right to abortion was an important concern to many, and I needed a thoughtful position on that issue. My personal view on abortion is consistent with the Catholic teaching that sacred life begins at conception. That had not changed from my days in the Minnesota House. Nevertheless, I had concluded that the government should not impose any religious belief on others. The Catholic Church teaches sacred life begins at conception; other faiths teach otherwise. The law should not be used to force anyone to comply with another's religious views.

This position complies with my Christian faith. Jesus never taught his followers to impose their religious beliefs on others, especially through government edict. I have found nothing in Jesus' words that instruct the government to make abortion illegal, just as there is nothing in Jesus' words that require the government to feed the hungry or visit the imprisoned. I believe He instructs his followers not to participate in abortion, and to feed the hungry and visit the imprisoned, but does not require Caesar to do the same. With that said, it is my judgment that, with the exception to protect the life of the mother, late term abortions should be illegal because it is adverse to a just society and the common good to kill viable human life. That is the same reason I oppose capital punishment—not out of my religious belief that all life is sacred but because it is destructive to a just society. This position is similar to Joe Biden's position when he ran for president of the United States in 2020.

I chose to run as a democrat; however, I have never been supportive of the party process whereby a relatively small number of people, selected through the caucus system, decide who can run with party support. That process I find undemocratic. So, I decided to bypass the DFL endorsement process at the state convention and run in the primary.

I started by visiting with people I knew, seeking their advice and counsel, developing a campaign strategy, and organizing a campaign team. We decided to do hundreds of house parties all over the state and use those parties to learn about the needs of the people, elicit support, and raise money.

Each house party involved me offering a brief explanation of why I was running for governor, a description of the 3Es, and the qualities I would bring to the office. But most of the event focused on what the participants saw as pressing needs in Minnesota. I asked specific open-ended questions, and people responded. I took notes and filled volumes. After conducting about 50 parties in various areas of the state, I concluded I had heard about most of the essential needs people cared about and had been offered lots of good ideas on how to meet those needs. Furthermore, the 3Es fit nicely with the concerns and ideas expressed during these conversations. From that point on, I seldom heard anything unique and did not get a new answer or a new question.

The support generated from these parties was phenomenal, but the money was severely lacking. After one year and 135 house parties, I had raised only $250,000—that was peanuts. The plan to rapidly advance support across the state was a success, but most of my supporters were not party activists. They were Democrats and Independents, perhaps even a few Republicans, but they did not understand the necessity of writing substantial checks supporting my campaign. Virtually everyone gave me $50 or $100. But I needed checks of $1,000 and $2,000. Your mother and I loaned the campaign $40,000 but there was no strategy to be repaid.

About a year into the campaign, a professional political operative offered to do opposition research on me to determine if he wanted to become involved in our effort. I agreed—it would be good to know what negative stuff was out there. A couple of weeks later, he reported that a group of five former Global Volunteers employees intended to tell the media that I was a terrible employer. They were primarily disgruntled former employees led by someone I had fired during her probationary period; although, one person on the list was particularly surprising and disappointing.

This was not good given that one of my campaign arguments was that I had successfully co-founded and managed a nonprofit business and had employed and mentored numerous young men and women. Many current and former employees would have offered positive testimonials; nevertheless, I was concerned about the reflection any negative criticism might have on Global Volunteers and our ability to fulfill its mission.

At this point in the campaign we had generated genuine enthusiasm and support from thousands of people who had attended house parties. But my complete failure at raising the necessary money to conduct a competitive campaign and the potential of an unfounded negative attack stared me in the face. Your mother was concerned from the beginning that, due to the state of politics at the time, someone would come up with something personal, even if it were false or a half-truth.

A few days after receiving the oppo-research report, I decided to end the campaign. I was simply unwilling to risk damaging Global Volunteers' reputation. Too many people had worked too hard to help children in need to take the chance. Equally important, I was broke, and the campaign was broke. Our family did not have any more money to loan the campaign, and there was no reason to believe we would ever recover the funds already loaned.

Furthermore, while I am neither shy nor introverted, I am not motivated by public acclaim. That said, I did not want to suffer the embarrassment of public criticism for things I never did. After a year of campaigning across the state and nine months before the primary election, I withdrew from the race. I could not raise the necessary money; I could not self-finance; I refused to put Global Volunteers and our family's reputation at risk.

The Lesson: Elective political office is not for the faint-hearted. Candidates of all parties are subjected to public ridicule and embarrassment. Candidates are often charged with things they never did or miscues exaggerated to shine the most negative light. The higher the office, the more sensational the allegations. If you or your spouse are unable to take this type of heat, you should not run.

The Lesson: Political positions evolve with knowledge, reflection, and time.

The Lesson: Running for statewide office costs a lot of money. If you are unable or unwilling to do what is necessary to raise the money, you shouldn't even start.

The Lesson: It is tremendously helpful to have a firm understanding of what you value. Sometimes, you may want something; however, when that which you want impedes something you value more, the decision to forgo the want is made easy.

The Lesson: Requiring candidates to spend their time raising money rather than explaining to voters why they should be elected to office is counterproductive. The current process too often results in elected officials who do not, perhaps, cannot make the common good their primary goal because they must focus on raising money. Many barriers dissuade good people from running for office. Public funding of campaigns would eliminate one big obstacle.

Conclave Conspiracy

*"Imagination is more important than knowledge. Knowledge
is limited. Imagination encircles the world."*

~ Albert Einstein, a German-born theoretical physicist

Writing *Conclave Conspiracy* was the most long-term fun I have ever had. I started this novel in 2008 and published it in 2014. It was work; it even generated some income. But the process of writing was extraordinarily enjoyable.

The backdrop of this piece of fiction is written on the back cover of *Conclave Conspiracy*:

> Three Catholic popes have died in less than a year. Foul play had not been eliminated and is suspected by many. But before the Vatican can deal with these suspicions, there's something else to take care of—a new pope must be elected.
>
> After seventy-seven excruciating days of deliberation, the conclave of cardinals finally reaches its decision—and it's a shocker. For the first time in 1,000 years, a layman—from the US—will lead the church. Before the white smoke clears the Sistine chapel, it is obvious the papacy, and the world, will never be the same.
>
> The new pope, James I, shatters long-held positions and the accepted image of the Bishop of Rome. Not everyone is hap-

py. Cardinal Manoles Sicoli, a fundamental doctrinaire who has long had his eyes on the Papacy, fears James is the Antichrist. And he will stop at nothing to end James's reign.

ForeWord Clarion Reviews gave *Conclave Conspiracy* 5 stars saying, "This thriller is a must-read for anyone with an interest in the Vatican and its role in the modern world." Kirkus Reviews wrote, "This story of a provocative new pope questioning tradition is both poignant and probing." The last I looked, it had 4.8 stars on Amazon.

I wrote this novel because, like other Catholics, I wondered throughout my adult life how my church could be more meaningful and relevant to the day-to-day lives of Christians, including my own. To me, the Catholic Church seemed out of touch. Its positions on social issues were sometimes contradictory, if not irrelevant. The priest sex scandal had caused consternation, shame, and sadness to Catholics worldwide, including our family.

Your mom was raised Catholic, but she left the church due to the hierarchy's protection and cover-up of priests who had so significantly damaged the lives of so many. Abusers seemed to be everywhere. A priest abused someone I know well.

I've struggled with the church's apparent inability to adequately rectify this tragic situation, as well as its lack of commitment to the poor and emphasis on pomp, ceremony, and the inconsequential. I still sometimes wonder why I remain in the church.

On Easter Sunday, 2008, while on a road trip with two of you, I listened to the pope's homily from St. Peter's Basilica on our car's satellite radio. I was particularly struck by the lack of substance in the Pope's message.

"The Pope spoke for 15 minutes, but said nothing," I later told a priest friend, Greg Skrpeck. Greg asked me what I had hoped the Pope might say? What should he have said? What would I have said if I had the opportunity to speak to a worldwide audience of Catholics? Those questions were the start of *Conclave Conspiracy*.

Upon reflection, I concluded that the Pope was just saying what popes always say. Further, any man educated in and formed by the church's politics would be an unlikely candidate to say what I thought needed to be stated. It was simply not possible for a Cardinal of the Catholic Church to propose the changes I discerned were necessary to restore the church's relevance and Christian leadership role. I decided that a layperson could make such changes. But a layman Pope? That, I was told, was science-fiction. And that is the reason I told this story as fiction.

I started to write *Conclave Conspiracy* in late spring of 2008. Grandma Gran died the previous December. As part of your mother's grieving process, she traveled a great deal that year, leading Global Volunteers international service programs, meeting with our community partners around the world, climbing Mount Kilimanjaro, and scuba diving the Great Barrier Reef. While she traveled, I wrote.

Throughout the summer and fall, I researched what I considered the pressing theological and social issues—birth control, married priests, female ordination, the church's responsibility to the poor. Those questions provoked additional inquiry—what if anything she was doing in support of unifying Christian denominations, the basis for the church's stance on homosexuality, the church's role in war and peace, and what she taught about forgiveness of sins and repentance. These were all challenging issues, and I found intriguing and compelling arguments on both sides of many.

Now I needed a layman Pope. The character, Jimmy Flahvin/Pope James, emerged as I wrote, as did the other people in this book. A few events in Jimmy Flahvin's life are similar to those in mine, but most are taken from the lives of others I know or are pure fiction. This is also true of the other characters. For example, Father Greg Keegan, a key player in the story, is a composite of several Catholic priests and a Presbyterian minister I knew well.

The story also emerged. I decided at the beginning that the first layman Pope in 1,000 years would be a lawyer, primarily because I know something about lawyers. I also envisioned how the story would end. But everything in between just emerged.

I wrote about places I have visited. And if I hadn't been someplace that needed to be included in the story, I traveled there. For example, I walked the streets of Winnetka, Illinois, and worshiped at the local Catholic and Presbyterian churches on a Sunday morning. I drove from Winnetka to Chicago via freeway and the more scenic route along Lake Michigan's shore. I took the elevator to the top of the Willis Tower and peered out the window from the North East side, visualizing what Jimmy Flahvin would see every day from his law office. I toured the Sistine Chapel, prayed in St. Peter's Basilica, and was granted an unusual visit to the Swiss Guard barracks in Vatican City. I had dinner at the Italian restaurant where Jimmy would eat the night before becoming pope and drank in the bars where Jimmy would drink. And all the while, I wrote in time carved out of an otherwise arduous schedule.

In January 2009, the story was complete. The draft was titled *The First American Pope*. I learned; however, that the writing was far from done. I asked several friends to read the first draft, and they offered comments and suggestions. All their input was constructive, but it sent me back to the writing-table. I sent the second draft to a few other friends, and they too provided significant insights, all of which required additional changes and edits. Your mom was most helpful—she read both the first and second versions offering invaluable suggestions and advice. I registered a copy of this "final" version of the book with the US copyright office in March 2009 while I was in Washington DC meeting with officials at the US Department of Agriculture about the possibility of my taking the job as Deputy Undersecretary.

I was privileged to serve at USDA, but that caused me to put this novel on hold. I didn't do anything until spring 2011 when I was back at Global Volunteers and finally found some time to devote to it. Then we discovered there was another novel entitled, *The American Pope*, and so I changed the title to *The Book of James*.

While attending a new authors session at The Loft in Minneapolis, I met Ashley Shelby, a novelist and inspiring editor. Ashley worked with me for several months, as I wrote and rewrote. By fall 2012, it was "finished" again. Or so I thought.

I submitted excerpts, summaries, and synopsis to 30 agents Ashley recommended. Then I impatiently waited for their responses. A few agents sent me individual notes, but most mailed or emailed their standard impersonal rejection letter. One rejection letter was a fuzzy off-center photocopy that I presumed had been sent to hundreds, perhaps thousands, of other aspiring authors. That was discouraging. But I understood it was part of the process.

I finally considered the possibility of self-publishing but had no idea how to go about doing that. On a business trip to Phoenix, I met one of our volunteers who had self-published. The purpose of our meeting had nothing to do with publishing books, but during our conversation, she told me that she was publishing her book through Create Space, an Amazon company. After investigating their services, I decided to submit my book to them. Nearly immediately after making this decision, Pope Benedict XVI resigned. It was clear it would be prudent to wait until I could include his successor's name in the novel to enhance currency and authenticity.

Then the College of Cardinals elected Pope Francis. This man was different from previous popes; I needed to include more than just his name. Jim Berry, who had read an early draft, called and said, "I think Francis is a whole lot like your Pope." Another friend told me, "I think Pope Francis takes a lot of steam out of the underlying story of Pope James." I decided to wait to see if Francis walked his talk.

That was the spring of 2013. I waited until March 2014 and then incorporated Pope Francis into this story as I believed appropriate. Shortly after that, I discovered another author had recently published a novel with the title, *The Book of James*. Although the topics and storylines are entirely different, it did not seem wise to retain the title. So, I renamed it *In the Shadow of My Lord's Brother*, based upon a reference made in Galatians. In May, I started working with Create Space. I have nothing but accolades and kudos for the talented people at this company. They were professional, creative, and extraordinarily helpful.

During this time, I mentioned to Bob Hudnut, my mentor and author friend who had read the first draft, my quandary over the title and the decision to rename it *In the Shadow of My Lord's Brother*. He was not impressed. He told me, "No one will read a book with that title. It's too long and too convoluted." I was back to the drawing boards.

I explained to your mom the criticism of the title, and she concurred that I needed to do better. She said, "The entire book revolves around the conclave— it needs to reflect that in the title."

A few nights later, we were lying in bed watching Saturday Night Live on TV and discussing possible titles during the commercials. After kicking around a couple of ideas, she said, "the primary element is a conspiracy. It should include the words 'conclave' and 'conspiracy.'"

Now, as the saying goes, you know the story behind the story.

The Lesson: I enjoyed every aspect of creating *Conclave Conspiracy*—researching issues and church processes; learning about the Catholic Church and the arguments offered for and against vital issues; recording old memories; traveling to places where I previously had not been; tying all the pieces together;

making stuff up out of whole cloth—but nothing that affected the authenticity of church processes or issue positions.

The Lesson: The best part about writing a novel is you get to think about your story all the time. As the story unravels in your mind, you can enjoy it throughout the day, day-after-day.

The Lesson: What I enjoyed the most surprised me the most. I thoroughly enjoyed editing and polishing the story—selecting descriptive words, ensuring the grammar was correct, checking the research, toning the arguments, and making detailed corrections to ensure everything hung together. That's what I've enjoyed about this book as well.

What do you have in mind?

"Our goal is to influence history instead of
merely observing it."

~ John F. Kennedy, Author and 35th President of United States

Tom Vilsack and I first met during his inauguration as governor of Iowa; although, we had visited by phone during his campaign when he called for a financial contribution. I met Tom's wife, Christie Bell Vilsack, years before when she and her brother, my dear friend Tom Bell, helped us renovate Global Volunteers corporate offices in Little Canada.

Today, Tom and Christie, and their boys are multi-time Global Volunteers and good friends. We have been to their home in Mount Pleasant, Iowa, and have stayed at the governor's residence in Des Moines. Tom and Christie and the five of us volunteered together in West Liberty, Iowa, during the week between Christmas and New Year's 1999–2000 on Global Volunteers' Millennium Service Project. And Tom and Christie spoke at the 20th Anniversary Gala Celebration dinner in St. Paul in 2004.

After Barack Obama was elected president in November 2008, CNN reported that the president-elect appointed Tom Secretary of Agriculture. I called to congratulate him, and I could tell he was thrilled about this opportunity. During our brief conversation, I mentioned that if there was any way I could help, he should let me know.

"What do you have in mind?" Tom asked.

I didn't have anything in mind; I hadn't given it any thought. My offer was more of a throwaway line that you would tell any friend who was on the cusp of a significant opportunity. So, I just repeated myself, "I don't have anything in mind, but if there's some way I can be helpful, let me know."

He responded by encouraging me to propose something I might do at USDA, although it was clear he was not offering me a job. And I did not need a job. As CEO of Global Volunteers, I had the best job in the world. But his words intrigued me. Barack Obama's would be a historic presidency, and to be even a small part of that would be extraordinary.

I investigated what USDA did and discovered that the department was engaged in an enormous array of essential activities and managed significant programs that affected nearly every aspect of American life—nutrition, school feeding, food safety, forestry, agricultural trade, rural development, agricultural research, farming, and so much more. It also played a substantial role in international food security. Now, that was something in which I was interested.

The Foreign Agricultural Service (FAS), with a staff of more than 1,000 employees, managed food assistance and food aid programs, in addition to agricultural trade. The FAS Administrator directed those programs in countries all over the world. I informed Secretary-designate Vilsack that I could be of assistance to him as the FAS Administrator.

But I knew there had to be more to the process than merely telling the Secretary-designate that I was interested in a particular position. I called former US Congressman Bill Luther, my longtime friend I served with in the Minnesota House and the Best Man at our wedding. Bill was incredibly supportive and encouraged me to contact Congressman Collin Peterson, who was Chair of the House Committee on Agriculture. I had known Colin for more than 20 years, having met him when he was a state senator when I was at DNR. Later I volunteered on his congressional election recount. Colin gave me the contact information for Marshall Matz, a Washington, DC lawyer whom he believed understood the political appointment process.

When Matz returned my phone call, I explained that Tom Vilsack was a good friend and encouraged me to apply. Marshall then shared something vitally important. He advised that I get eight to 12 letters of reference from prominent people recommending me for the FAS Administrator position. He said, "these letters are not intended to convince Vilsack. Rather, they are for Vilsack to share with others when he needs to convince them." Made sense to me.

Now I was getting charged up about this opportunity. I was in the hunt. I asked ten people to write letters of recommendation—former and current members of Congress, Humphrey School professors, corporate executives, Minnesota state officials, and other notables I knew. Everyone I asked helped; each provided me with a letter of recommendation.

Sometime in February 2009, I had dinner with Secretary Vilsack in Washington, DC. He inferred that the FAS Administrator position was no longer open, but there were other opportunities. We discussed several possibilities, and I gave Tom a folder containing the ten recommendations and my résumé.

I was disappointed that the FAS Administrator position had been filled. That seemed to be the perfect job. Furthermore, the other functions we discussed either did not sound interesting or didn't pay enough to make it worth my while to take a sabbatical from Global Volunteers.

Nearly a month later, I got a call from the White House liaison for USDA. He asked me if I would consider Deputy Undersecretary for Farm and Foreign Agricultural Services (FFAS). I asked him, "How does that position relate to the FAS Administrator position?"

"The FAS Administrator reports to the Deputy Undersecretary," he responded.

That's all I needed to know. I spoke with your mom, and we agreed this would be a good thing for me to do. I called the White House liaison the following day to tell him I would accept the position. I started a few weeks later.

My first day on the job was April 6, 2009, at the International Food Aid Conference coordinated by USAID and USDA in Kansas City, Missouri. That morning, I was in my hotel bathroom, getting ready for the day, when the phone rang. I put a towel around my waist to answer the phone. It was a USDA official who needed to administer the oath of office before I started work. Every new federal employee is required by law to take an oath to support and defend the Constitution, and the oath is generally administered on the first day of employment. When she asked me to raise my right hand and repeat the words after her, the towel fell to the floor. There I was, telephone in my left-hand with my right hand raised, ready to repeat the oath as she read it, stark naked. Not the prettiest of pictures.

Later, during a private conversation with Secretary Vilsack, I asked how my appointment as Deputy Undersecretary for FFAS came about. He told me, "The White House and USDA staff assigned to recommending political appointments were working late one night when I walked into the conference room to see how they were doing. They had a lot of positions to fill and were struggling. I took the folder you gave me and set it on the conference room table. I suggested they look at your material. The next day they told me they were recommending you for Deputy Undersecretary."

The Lesson: When you're in the hunt, get as much advice from as many people as you can. Then follow the advice that makes sense to you.

The Lesson: If you ask people for a reference, advice, or assistance, they quite often will offer it.

The Car will be on the Apron

"It's still magic even if you know how it's done."

~ Terry Pratchett, an English humorist, satirist, and author

USDA's Washington DC administrative offices are situated in the Jamie Whitten building on the Capital Mall, not far from the Washington Monument. It is a stately Beaux-Arts style government building, the only cabinet-level department on the Mall, and the only building on the Mall not open to the public. I had visited the Jamie Whitten building twice before I started working there, once with Bill Norris and Ralph Thompson, when I worked for Rural Ventures, and earlier in 2009 for an interview.

On my first day of work in DC, I was informed that I had a meeting at the White House at 1 PM. That took me by surprise. I asked how long it would take to get there by taxi, and my scheduler advised, "The car will be on the apron at 12:40."

I had no idea what an "apron" was but was told to go downstairs and out the front door; the driver would take me to the White House. As it turned out, the meeting was not actually in the White House. It was in the Old Executive Office Building, which is part of the White House complex, all of which is considered the White House. Nevertheless, it was quite a thrill to be in such proximity to the Oval Office and critical government players.

I remember expressing to one of the more seasoned political appointees at the meeting that my children would be impressed their dad had a meeting at the

White House. She looked at me with downright disdain. She did not say the words, but her face spoke that I showed naïveté at being so struck by the surroundings.

I visited the White House campus on numerous occasions while I served at USDA. Still, I never lost the remarkable feeling of amazement and never stopped marveling that I was in these hallowed buildings collaborating on vitally important policy issues. I felt sorry for the woman I met that first day. She seemed to have lost that sense of wonder; it had all become routine for her.

Serving the American people should never become routine. It is an honor to serve. It is an honor that others have put their faith and trust in you.

The Lesson: Don't let the genuinely remarkable ever become routine because it never is routine and always short-lived.

The Lesson: The trappings of government office are insignificant compared to the honor and responsibility of serving the American people.

Dead Silence

"Words do two major things: They provide food for the mind
and create light for understanding and awareness."

~ Jim Rohn, an American entrepreneur, author, and motivational speaker

My first of many international trips as USDA Deputy Undersecretary was to the World Food Programme (WFP) Executive Board meeting in Rome in April 2009. WFP is a part of the United Nations and the world's largest humanitarian agency fighting hunger. Its vision is a "world in which every man, woman, and child has access at all times to the food needed for an active and healthy life." WFP works in concert with the Food and Agriculture Organization (FAO) and the International Fund for Agricultural Development (IFAD), also UN agencies with central offices in Rome.

The Executive Board is WFP's supreme governing body. Comprised of representatives from 36 States—all UN Members—the board provides intergovernmental support, policy direction, and supervision of WFP's activities. The US Ambassador to the UN food agencies had not yet been appointed, so I was the head of the delegation to this meeting. My primary purpose was to deliver a speech describing the Obama administration's focus on food security.

The board meeting room is an impressively large space with a massive oval-shaped table around which representatives of the member states sit. Behind every representative are several chairs for each country's key lieutenants, and behind them are numerous chairs for other members of the delegations.

Resting on the table in front of each member is a ten-inch long dark brown wooden placard identifying its country. When a nation wants to be recognized by the chair, its representative removes the placard from its horizontal position and holds it vertically until the board's president acknowledges the country's desire to speak. Seasoned US government staff advised me that the US generally speaks after six or so other countries have spoken, so I should raise the placard accordingly.

I had thoroughly prepared for this speech. USDA staff wrote the initial draft. I made substantial edits to make it feel as my own. Someone unknown to me at the State Department reviewed and approved the final version. And even though I was expected to read it, I had virtually committed it to memory.

While the first several countries' representatives spoke, there was considerable background noise—lots of people talking, many not paying attention. At times, the noise was so loud that it was difficult to hear what the representatives were saying save for the headsets. When it was my turn, the WFP executive board president said, "the United States of America is recognized."

I'm a confident speaker. I have a strong, clear voice. I have given perhaps a thousand speeches over the years. I know how to deliver a speech. Further, I knew this was an informative and even entertaining speech. And I suspected the audience wanted to hear what I had to say. While I was not overly nervous, I was moved by the emotion of the moment, knowing that I was representing the country I so dearly love.

Then, as I began to speak, I heard dead silence.

All the background noise stopped. No one was speaking. The hundreds of people in the room were all looking in my direction.

I was taken aback.

Then, I looked down in front of me and saw the placard that read, "The United States of America."

At that moment, I realized that I was representing the United States and the President of the United States. All these folks in the room wanted to hear this new US administration's food security policy positions—President Barack Obama's administration positions. They were not interested in me; they wanted to listen to what the United States of America had to say.

The Lesson: Other countries look to the United States for many things, but perhaps most importantly, they look to the US for leadership. When the United States speaks, the rest of the world wants to listen.

The Lesson: Government officials who hold power do so only because they represent the people they serve.

$4.3 Million

"So. Tell me. What do you think? Which is better? To take ac-
tion and perhaps make a fatal mistake—or to take no action
and die slowly anyway?"

~ Ahdaf Soueif, an Egyptian novelist

My office at USDA was large by any standard. Overlooking the Washington Mall, the furnishings included an oversized executive desk, a conference room table that sat 10, a leather couch, a coffee table, several comfortable sitting chairs situated around the coffee table and opposite the sofa, a small refrigerator, a flat-screen television, some glass-doored shelving cabinets, a photo of President Obama, a photo of Secretary Vilsack, a United States flag, a USDA flag, pictures of you and your mother, and some other personal wall hangings.

I didn't understand why I needed such a large workspace until my first meeting when ten people showed up. We all barely fit around the conference room table.

At one of those early meetings, Ron Croushorn, a FAS executive responsible for food assistance, briefed me on a section of the 2008 Farm Bill that authorized a study of local and regional procurement (LRP) of food for international food aid programs. At that time, virtually all US food aid was purchased from US farmers and shipped around the world on US merchant ships to food-insecure areas. From a purely cost perspective, this was an inefficient process. US food was expensive, and shipping containers of food on the high seas increased the cost significantly. However, this made good political sense because the program was supported by members of Congress who represented farm states and those who represented the shipping industry. Food assistance programs might not be approved without the support from those members of Congress.

Nevertheless, there was a provision in the 2008 Farm Bill that allowed for LRP to be studied. $60 million was allocated for a four-year program—$5 million in year one to develop a study for a pilot program, $50 million for years' two and three to implement the pilot program, and $5 million in year four to evaluate the program.

When the briefing concluded, I expressed my surprise that it would cost $5 million to develop a study. Global Volunteers' total annual budget in the previous year was $5 million, and I couldn't imagine how anyone could spend $5 million just to develop a study.

Five months later, Ron Croushorn returned to brief me on the status of the LRP program. He explained that they had decided to conduct the study in-house rather than contract it out and was pleased to report that they had spent only $700,000 on the study. I told him that was terrific. "Congratulations!"

But that was not the end of the story. Now we had $4.3 million FAS didn't know what to do with, and they wanted me to decide. My first inclination was to return the money to the treasury. After all, the government was racking up another significant deficit that fiscal year. But I was dissuaded by the argument that this money was intended to help feed hungry children, and there were more malnourished children on the planet in August 2009 than ever before.

We decided to figure out how to effectively and legally spend this $4.3 million on behalf of hungry children. It was mid-August, and the money had to be committed before September 30. After several long meetings, one of which included seven lawyers in addition to me, we devised a plan where the money legally could be allocated to WFP for the benefit of children. Secretary Vilsack was on board with the plan; WFP's Executive Director, Josette Sheeran, was pleased; we had consulted with USAID as required by the statute; the lawyers said we were on solid legal footing. I said, "Let's do it."

And then someone said, "Now, four other agencies have to sign off on this decision."

I couldn't believe it. I knew the government was slow and bureaucratic, but four other agencies?

I instructed my staff to hand-carry the paperwork to each of the four decision-makers required to sign off to ensure the documents did not end up at the bottom of someone's inbox. They did it, and we beat the September 30 deadline.

The law and protocol required that USDA inform the Senate and House agricultural committees of what we were doing. When we met with Senate staff and explained how we saved $4.3 million that would now be used to feed hungry children, some of the staff became apoplectic. They recognized that we had the authority to implement the plan as I described it, but they made it clear that they did not want us to do it. And if we did do it, they emphasized that USDA, and FAS in particular, would suffer during the next Farm Bill. We were not dissuaded, but I was shocked.

I don't know why the Senate staff were so opposed to this plan; it was a thoughtful and responsible use of the money on the merits. However, one of our team mused that the Senate staffers might have been concerned about being embarrassed. It was they who had signed off on a $5 million study that cost $700,000, and some might have thought that information could damage their credibility and careers. In any event, they were overwrought.

This conversation was more than a bit perplexing to me. I have a bachelor's degree in political science, a master's in public affairs, and law practice focused on government law. I served in the Minnesota House of Representatives, was an Assistant Commissioner for the Minnesota Department of Natural Resources, and had run for governor of Minnesota. One would think that I knew something about government and politics. But it was days like these when I realized I didn't know much of anything when it came to the US government.

The Lesson: No matter how much you think you know, life is full of surprises. The human condition makes much of life unpredictable.

The Lesson: Whenever you get a chance to feed a hungry child, do whatever it takes.

The Practical

Sometimes, work can be easier and more productive if you simply employ some fundamental, even simple procedures and methods. These are not philosophical or spiritual; they are just practical. I have learned these over the years, and you may find some helpful. In previous chapters, I have alluded to or discussed some of these and expound on others in subsequent chapters. But that's okay because repetition in a learning environment can be useful. Some of these things I learned on my own; others I was taught by my parents, teachers, or mentors and confirmed their reliability.

The Lessons:

1. **Create To-Do lists:** Make a daily list of what you need to accomplish; then execute from your list. This offers at least three benefits. First, it helps you remember what you need to do. Few people can remember all the things they want/need to accomplish without writing them down. Second, it can help you prioritize what you want/need to do. This is especially valuable as external events creep in and alter your day. Third, if you cannot complete everything on your list today, you don't have to remember to write it down again tomorrow. Phone apps are available that make all this relatively easy; when you enter them once, they stay there until you click it as completed.

2. **Number what you put your pockets:** Far too often, I would leave home without something I needed later in the day—keys, reading glasses, hand sanitizer, credit cards, money, etc. I finally made a list of what I needed to take with me every morning in my iPhone notes section. For a while, I physically checked off the list before I left home. Later, I mentally reviewed the list. Now, I mentally review the ten things to put in my pockets every morning—(1) reading glasses, (2) microfiber cleaning cloths for my reading glasses; (3) cell phone, (4) air pod case, (5) watch, (6) credit cards, (7) money clip, (8) three cough drops, (9) hand sanitizer, and (10) car keys. If I count only nine, I know I'm missing something and consult the written list. Bottom line: I no longer leave home without it.

3. **Sleep 7 to 9 hours:** It still amazes me how much better I feel and how much more productive I am after a good night's sleep. All the health books confirm this. For most people, between seven and nine hours are required every night. Learn the number you need and then do what's necessary to get that amount of sleep. I need a minimum of 7.5. Anything less dulls my day. Again, several useful phone apps can help you achieve this.

4. **Get an annual health checkup:** As mentioned previously, I go to the Mayo Clinic every year for a comprehensive exam. All my good numbers have gone up over the years, and the bad numbers have gone down. A high-quality annual checkup also increases the odds of detecting bad things early when more can be done to address the condition. And you will feel better knowing that you are better.

5. **Establish a routine:** To lessen the time it takes to get ready in the morning, prepare for a meeting, or grocery shop, develop a pattern. Do the same things in the same order, and you will have time to spare.

6. **Minimize alcohol:** A glass of wine or a cold beer after work or with dinner is lovely. Four glasses of wine or four beers—not so much. Too much alcohol messes with your attitude, your driving, and your sleep, and leaves you hanging over the next morning

7. **Exercise daily:** This was hard for me in the beginning. I knew the benefits of daily exercise, but seldom did it. Then in my fifties, I was at the home of a friend who was in his early 70's. When it was time for dinner, he struggled to get up and walk from the living room couch to the dining room table. He wasn't ill or obese; he was just way out of shape. I committed that would not happen to me. I started walking every day, at least five miles six days a week. And it felt good. When I injured my foot and couldn't walk, I bought a quality exercise bike and rode it for an hour every day. I listen to audiobooks as I walk or ride, which offers a double benefit.

8. **Take your meds:** As you get older, you will likely be prescribed medications for many common health issues. Take them as prescribed. Drug stores sell small day pill reminders in which you can put all your morning and evening meds and vitamins for each day of the week. This helps you stay on top of them and not miss any doses.

9. **Eat healthy:** Your mother told you to eat your fruits and vegetables, as did mine; so does the USDA. Five to eight servings of fruits and vegetables every day will help keep you healthy. Also, limit the red meat and enjoy an occasional dish of your favorite ice cream.

10. **Read:** Be curious and continue learning. One of my sister's husband once told me that he did not read anything. When I asked him why, he said, "I already know everything I need to know." I was stunned. You never know what you don't know until you know it. God's creation is amazing, there is so much to learn about it, and life is never long enough to embrace at all.

11. **Vote:** Government plays a significant role in our family and work lives. One of the best ways to ensure that your voice is heard is by voting. Sometimes, you may feel like politicians don't listen, or there's no real difference between the candidates. Vote anyway. From years of experience in and out of government, I guarantee you elected officials listen to those who vote, and there are always differences between the candidates. However, politicians do not listen to those who do not vote. So, vote in every election.

Global Volunteers

"There are children raised in sorrow on a scorched and barren plain. There are children raised beneath a golden sun. There are children of the water, children of the sand, and they cry out through the universe, their voices raised as one. 'I want to live; I want to grow; I want to see; I want to know. I want to share what I can give; I want to be; I want to live.'"

~John Denver, an American poet and singer-songwriter

Global Volunteers' story will be chronicled in a separate tome. The following brief synopsis is a simple acknowledgment that Global Volunteers played a vital role in the lessons I have learned. Likewise, most of the lessons I learned while at USDA during the first Obama administration are not addressed in this volume. The lessons from that experience have become so fundamental to Global Volunteers' history that they must be included as a part of that story.

Although business law was lucrative and challenging, it was not sufficiently fulfilling or rewarding. Ten months after opening my private law practice, we incorporated Global Volunteers on January 26, 1984. Your mother, Sam Hanson, Milo Cutter, and I comprised the initial board of directors.

From the beginning, we decided to run this nonprofit enterprise like a for-profit business—we offered people the opportunity to volunteer in a developing community for a tax-deductible fee. Many asked, "you want me to pay to volunteer?" Our answer, "this costs money; the local people are too poor to cover the cost. Governments and faith-based organizations have their objectives and agendas, and local people must be in charge. So, if not you, who?" It was tough sledding in the beginning. But over time, the number of volunteers grew. Now, more than 37,000 volunteers have served hundreds of communities in 36 countries on six continents. In 2008 alone, nearly 2,500 people volunteered.

I was the unpaid CEO at Global Volunteers for ten years; your mom volunteered for the first six years, and many others volunteered long hours to make this effort work. We initially ran Global Volunteers out of the law office. The staff grew too large, and my partners decided they would rather not work in a law office where folks wore blue jeans and sweatshirts.

In 1990, your mother and I bought the convent from St. John's Catholic parish in Little Canada. With many others' help, we renovated it as office space, moved my law practice there, and I became a solo practitioner once again. In May, we relocated Global Volunteers to Little Canada. Then in 1994, I shut down the practice to devote full time to Global Volunteers.

In 1990, six years after we founded Global Volunteers, I practiced law to pay the household bills and help fund Global Volunteers. My time was stretched. Your mother offered to become a full-time Global Volunteers employee to promote the effort and provide some staff structure. That made all the difference. She has directed the marketing efforts from the beginning and has led nearly 60 Global Volunteers teams to communities throughout the US and worldwide. And volunteers and community partners love her. She continues to receive among the highest evaluation numbers from volunteers.

In 2009, I was offered the opportunity to serve in President Obama's administration, and your mom stepped in as CEO. My experience as a senior federal government executive introduced me to numerous contacts and presented tremendous lessons. All of that helped us transform Global Volunteers into the comprehensive human and economic development organization first envisioned in 1984. All we have accomplished through Global Volunteers' Reaching Children's Potential (RCP) Program was initiated by the people I met and the time I spent at USDA.

There have been huge ups and downs over the past nearly four decades and massive challenges—pandemics, tsunamis, wars, 911, the Great Recession—some of which generated fears of bankruptcy. But the rewards of growing Global Volunteers, serving local people, and making a significant difference in children's and volunteers' lives far outweigh the financial or other rewards of practicing law.

But as stated, this book is not about Global Volunteers; that book is still in process. The lessons learned from that endeavor are vast and hopefully will have a wider audience.

The Lesson: We are all given wonderful opportunities, talents, gifts, and insight. I believe each of us is obligated to use those in service to others. Global Volunteers has allowed me to focus my service on waging peace, promoting justice, and creating an environment where all children can realize the fullness of their God-given potential.

Retyremint

"My candle burns at both ends; it will not last the night; but
ah, my foes, and oh, my friends—
it gives a lovely light!"

~ Edna St. Vincent Millay, an American poet and playwright

Throughout my life, I've enjoyed 's work, although I haven't enjoyed every job. I started working relatively young while still in grade school. And I have seldom been satisfied with doing just one thing at a time.

The summer after I graduated from high school, I worked four different jobs. While a full-time undergraduate at the University of Minnesota, I was also a full-time employee at Sperry Univac. I went to graduate school while I served in the Minnesota House and later as DNR Assistant Commissioner. We started Global Volunteers during my first-year practicing law.

When I ran for governor, I spent two years planning and one-year campaigning while continuing to lead Global Volunteers. But campaigning was more than a full-time job—as demonstrated by the 135 house parties all over the state in 12 months—and that made it difficult for me to keep up with all my responsibilities. But the challenge was thrilling.

I wrote my first novel, *Conclave Conspiracy*, while also working full-time for Global Volunteers, and wrote this book the same way.

I enjoy being challenged in a variety of ways simultaneously. Finding the time and the creativity to write this book while managing Global Volunteers was not burdensome. Doing those two things simultaneously was my way of enjoying life and contributing to the greater good.

Some of my friends think I retired when I closed my law practice to lead Global Volunteers full-time. They suggest that running a nonprofit was something I wanted to do; it wasn't "real" work. Others think that when a Minnesotan spends eight months out of the year in Florida, he must be retired. What else is he doing? Of course, leading an international nonprofit is a lot of work, albeit meaningful work. And, given modern technology, a person can work full-time from anywhere, even in Florida.

I suppose that's why I don't know how to spell retyremint, and I hope I never have to experience it. I thoroughly enjoy meaningful work and cannot imagine what I would do if I did not work.

The Lesson: Work is good for the soul, not just the pocketbook.

The Lesson: Work for the common good and secure a meaningful life.

The Lesson: Write a book about the history of Global Volunteers. That is next on my list.

On WAR

"Every gun that is made, every warship launched, every rocket fired signifies in the final sense, a theft from those who hunger and are not fed, those who are cold and are not clothed."

~ Dwight D. Eisenhower, an American 5-star army general
and 34th President of the United States

War has had an enormous effect on my life; although, I never fought in any battle. World War II ended a year before I was born; I'm a member of the first year of baby boomers, those born immediately following WWII. The Korean War started when I was four years old and ended in 1953. The Vietnam War lasted for 20 years (1955 to 1975). The Gulf War (1990-1991); the Bosnian War (1992-1995); the Kosovo War (1998-1999); the war in Afghanistan (2001-present); the Iraq War (2003-2011); the intervention in Syria (2014-present); the Yemeni Civil War (2015-present); and other conflicts in which the US has been engaged, all affected my life. The US has been at war or in military conflict somewhere in the world for nearly two-thirds of my 74 years. And I have been involved because friends died, my taxes helped pay for the violence, and my world is less safe now than ever.

War is said to be a failure of diplomacy. The inability of politicians to resolve differences. But it is much more than a simple human failure.

War is the utter ruination of life, the destruction of hopes and dreams, the collapse of civilization. A mother who loses her son, a husband who loses his wife, children who lose their parents are among the hundreds of millions who have suffered the greatest of tragedies. And for what?

Some argue that war protects civilization. That is a false promise; it doesn't. Every war creates a callousness toward violence, a desire to develop ever more lethal weapons, and a commitment to engage those arsenals in the name of peace. Many scientists who worked on the Manhattan Project in Los Alamos developing the atomic bomb, believed their nuclear weapon would end all wars because countries would fear its devastating destruction. Not to be.

The US has been at war for most of the years since the bombs were dropped on Nagasaki and Hiroshima in 1945. Nuclear weapons have proliferated. The world continues to live in constant fear that someone will use a nuclear device, and the aftermath will destroy the planet.

Civilization founded on war begets war. History attests to this reality. Countries that engage in violence are destroyed by violence.

But families and communities bear the greatest suffering—physical, emotional, economic, spiritual. And they never fully recover. War begets war; violence produces violence; the cycle of pain and suffering recycles.

There are occasions when a country or a people must defend themselves from imminent attack. But the response to attack must be defensive only. As soon as a government decides to take preemptory offensive measures against a potential invader, war is in full force, and the results are always the same.

In the United States, the occasions requiring defensive military measures have been rare. WWII is an example of an external attack that required defensive action. However, the wars fought in Vietnam, Kosovo, Iraq, and Syria cannot be justified based on defending the American homeland.

Moreover, a defensive response to an attack must be proportional to the attack itself. And the answer must be directed toward those who perpetrated the atrocity. Vietnam and Iraq were not defensive wars. Neither the governments nor the people of those countries were involved in any attack on the United States.

Afghanistan may be a bit different. Al Qaeda was responsible for the vicious and tragic attack on New York on 9/11. The United States had a responsibility to defend itself from future similar attacks. And so, it is arguable that the US had an obligation to eliminate Al Qaeda. The Afghanistan government protected Al Qaeda, so it was necessary to go after Al Qaeda on Afghan soil.

But the US response to Al Qaeda was not proportional. Upwards to 200,000 have died—civilians, soldiers, and militants—but mostly civilians. Moreover, the Afghan war continues well beyond the decimation of Al Qaeda's leadership.

US Senator Mark Hatfield, a Republican from Oregon, offered this about modern war. "We stand by as children starve by the millions because we lack the will to end hunger. But we have found the will to develop nuclear missiles capable of flying over the polar cap and landing within a few hundred feet of their target. This is not innovation. It is a profound distortion of humanity's purpose on earth."

With that said, the military tragedy that personally impacted me was the Vietnam War. The US government drafted me to fight in that war.

Vietnam: 1968-1972

"They shall beat their swords into plowshare, and their spears into pruning hooks; nations shall not lift up sword against nation, neither shall they learn war anymore."

~ Isaiah 2:4

US engagement in the Vietnam conflict had waged on for years before I had to decide how or if I would participate personally. In my junior year at the University of Minnesota, Phil Ricker, my good friend and grade school and high school classmate, and I decided to enlist in a US Army ROTC program that allowed "buddies" to train and serve together as officers. In the mid-1960s, every young man knew he was subject to the draft upon graduation from high school or college, and it seemed prudent to go through the process of becoming an officer rather than serving as a draftee. Phil and I had been accepted to this program, but the days immediately before we signed the papers, I had second, third, and fourth thoughts.

I concluded America's involvement in the Vietnam War was morally wrong. The Vietnamese had never threatened the United States, and the US had no right to interfere in another country's internal strife. Moreover, I could not justify killing others, except in self-defense or the defense of my country. I told Phil that I couldn't join the ROTC program with him. It was a terrible thing to do to a friend, especially at the last minute. But I felt I had no choice.

For those who fought in the Vietnam war, protested against this war, or resisted the draft that supplied the US soldiers for this war, Vietnam was not known as a country. The word "Vietnam" was a noun that meant war.

Division and dissension were rampant in the US. Hundreds of thousands of young men and women all over the country opposed this war. For several years, there were almost daily massive and sometimes riotous protests in multiple cities. Many were televised on the nightly news sandwiched between reports and video of combat on the ground in Vietnam. Often, the scenes of protests and battles were gruesome and saddening. Tens of thousands of Americans were killed in the fight, but some were also killed during protests; Kent State being the most appalling.

I was not much of a protester. In fact, throughout all the years of my opposition to the Vietnam War, I participated in one antiwar protest, and that was because I wanted to date a woman who told me she was going to join the march the following day. It was 1965, and we were both students at the University of Minnesota. There was an armory on campus for ROTC students, and this was to be a silent protest of students walking around the Armory for an hour in silence. I joined her. But every time I tried to say something to her, she would say, "Shh. No talking."

A network of organizations helped young men who wanted to resist the draft by getting them into the National Guard to avoid fighting in Vietnam, moving to Canada which offered refuge to draft resisters, or applying for CO status. I considered all three options, but only CO status made sense for me. I even traveled to Winnipeg, Manitoba with a friend for a couple of days to see if that might be an option, but concluded it wasn't in me to run away.

In 1968, I filed the necessary paperwork to be granted conscientious objector (CO) status so that I would not have to fight in that ghastly war. I knew this was a stretch; I was not opposed to all war, only wars of aggression and those that did not meet the Just War Theory. My local draft board denied my application for CO status. Several organizations offered advice to those who denied CO status, and I followed their advice. I appealed.

At my appeal hearing, I asked the men sitting around the table to explain why they concluded that I did not qualify for conscientious objector status.

The draft board chairman responded to the effect that "each member's reasons are individual and personal. Each of us looked at your file individually, and our reasons for denying your claim were of a personal nature." He didn't say anything more.

I asked, "Did you conclude that my objections to the Vietnam War are not religious in nature?" The chairman refused to answer.

"Do you think I'm not sincere?" I asked.

"We have nothing more to say about this matter," the chairman said. And that was the end of the conversation.

I had been advised to write everything down immediately after the hearing, which I did. When my local draft board denied my appeal, I appealed to the national draft board, but that appeal was rejected as well. I then submitted the paperwork to appeal to the President of the United States, but that was also denied.

On December 1, 1969, the Selective Service System conducted a lottery to determine who would be drafted to serve in Vietnam from that point forward. The objective was to address perceived inequities in the draft system and to increase the number of draftees. My number was relatively low, which virtually assured I would be drafted.

In the summer of 1970, I received my draft papers—an Order to Report for Induction into the Armed Services of the United States. The initial induction notice was postponed due to my candidacy for the Minnesota House of Representatives that fall. Immediately after the election, I received another notification.

I reported to the Federal Office Building in downtown Minneapolis on the designated November morning as required. When the officer in charge began filling out my paperwork, I advised him that I would cooperate fully in all pre-induction activities but intended to refuse induction.

The officer stopped writing and looked up. "That's a very serious decision that could result in grave consequences. Are you sure you really want to do this, son?" he asked.

"Yes, I'm sure."

After a full day of tests and a complete physical, government personnel escorted all the inductees into a spacious, ornate room with soft brown walnut paneling and multicolored flags of the United States and all the armed services. About 30 of us lined up in a single row facing an Army colonel in dress blues. His job was to administer the oath of service.

The standard procedure called for each inductee to take one-step forward to demonstrate his willingness to serve. The colonel instructed the men to take a step forward. When they did, I stood still. The colonel had been advised of my decision not to comply, so when I did not move, he said simply, "Mr. Philbrook, you may go home."

All the other young men turned and looked at me incredulously. I suspect some wondered if that was all they had to do to avoid going to Vietnam—just not take that step.

Draft resistance was a federal felony, and I knew the government would eventually arrest me. In November 1971, the grand jury indicted me, and shortly after, the FBI showed up at Sperry Univac while I was at work. I got a call from the receptionist that there were some men in dark suits in the lobby asking for me. I knew it was time. I told my boss, Lewie Rydeen, that they had come, put on my dark blue plaid sport coat, and walked down to the lobby.

They arrested me, and the federal government charged me with failure to comply with the draft board's induction order. I was fingerprinted, processed, and placed in a vacant cell in Hennepin County Jail. The rules permitted a phone call. I called the draft resistance office, and they bailed me out later that day.

During my 1970 campaign for the Minnesota House of Representatives, I met Don Heffernan, a St. Paul attorney who had represented several draft resisters in federal court. I hired Don to represent me; although, his fee was remarkably low—almost pro bono.

Edward Devitt was a conservative federal judge assigned to my case. Don advised me that Devitt convicted virtually all "draft dodgers" who showed up in his courtroom and sentenced them to the maximum penalty—five years in federal prison. My odds for an acquittal were one in a million, at best.

"If you go through with this trial, you should be prepared to go to prison," Don advised. "And with Devitt as the trial judge, you should plan on five years in Sandstone."

FCI Sandstone was a low-security prison for male offenders, about 100 miles north of St. Paul in Sandstone, Minnesota. The good thing about Sandstone was that it was close to home, so my family could visit. But it was still five years!

Other than a trial, my options were limited—enlist in the Army, try to get into the National Guard, or flee to Canada. I had already decided that trial was my only real option.

One thing gave me strength during this time—knowing that we are all bound by our conscience. As a Catholic, I learned we had no choice but to follow our conscience. The Second Vatican Council wrote the Constitution on the Church in the Modern World. One paragraph was especially relevant.

"In the depths of his conscience, man detects a law which he does not impose upon himself, but which holds him to obedience. Always summoning him to love good and avoid evil, the voice of conscience, when necessary, speaks to his heart: do this, shun that. For man has in his heart a law written by God: to obey it is the very dignity of man; according to it he will be judged. Conscience is the most secret core and sanctuary of man. There he is alone with God, whose voice echoes in his depths. In a wonderful manner, conscience reveals that law which is fulfilled by love of God and neighbor. In fidelity to conscience, Christians are joined with the rest of men in the search for truth, and for the genuine solution to the numerous problems which arise in the life of individuals and from social relationships. Hence, the more right conscience holds sway, the more persons and groups turn aside from blind choice and strive to be guided by the objective norms of morality."

These words spoke to me. I was not permitted to participate in the Vietnam War because it was contrary to my conscience.

At trial, Heffernan argued that I had presented a prima facie case for CO status. Because the draft board refused to respond to why they denied my CO claim, their decision was invalid, and therefore, the induction notice was invalid. They had violated specific rights afforded every American in the United States Constitution. It was a straightforward argument: no one could effectively appeal a government decision if they did not know why the government made its decision. It was impossible to argue against government rationale when the government refused to explain their reasoning.

Further, Heffernan contended the court could not adjudicate whether the draft board acted properly because the board refused to advise the court of their reasoning as well. The panel provided no basis for their decision in their record, thus denying the court the necessary information to determine if they acted appropriately.

Don Heffernan was not just my lawyer; he was a brilliant lawyer.

On February 10, 1972, the court informed Heffernan that I was acquitted. I was in Duluth campaigning with Senator McCarthy on that winter day when Don called to advise me of the court's decision. The judge found me not guilty because the local draft board failed to explain why they denied my request for classification as a conscientious objector. This constitutional argument of denial of due process had been used as a basis for acquittals in other jurisdictions across the country, but not in Minnesota.

I was astounded and overwhelmed. It was amazing! I had fully expected to spend five years in Sandstone Federal Prison.

Judge Devitt had previously served in the US Congress as a Republican, and he knew I was a Democrat. But he also knew that the law was nonpartisan. Devitt supported the Constitution of the United States and followed the rule of law. He acquitted me not because he believed in my position; he acquitted me because he believed in the rule of law.

Years later, I was admitted to the federal bar. Judge Devitt presided over the swearing-in ceremony in his courtroom. After the formalities, I went to his chambers to thank him. When I reminded him of our past, he said, "I remember you. Congratulations on your admittance to the federal bar."

Judge Devitt was a conservative judge. He sent a lot of young men to federal prison, enforcing the maximum penalty for draft resistance. But he was a good man and, in my case, an honorable judge.

All those who served in the military in Vietnam or other posts during the war because they believed they were answering a legitimate call to duty are without question patriots. They stood up for what they believed.

But now there is broad consensus that the Vietnam War was morally wrong, unnecessary, and a terrible waste of human life and national treasure. It did not meet the minimum standards for waging a just war and wrought untold devastation on our country and Vietnam.

Those who refused to serve in Vietnam because they believed the war was morally reprehensible and contrary to fundamental American values are also patriots. We, too, stood up for what we believe.

Resisting the draft was not a refusal to serve my country. It was a refusal to kill Vietnamese for no good reason. I was more than willing to serve my country through community service, homeland security, or as an international volunteer. Those options might postpone, but they would not keep me out of the war. Had there been genuine alternatives to military service, I would have gladly served.

Phil Ricker joined the ROTC program and upon graduation from the U of M was commissioned an officer in the US Army. He was stationed in Germany and then joined the Army Reserves. He never served in Vietnam. I often prayed that Phil not be assigned to Vietnam out of fear he'd come home in a body bag. When the war ended, I thanked God that he never had to fight there.

The Lesson: Do the right thing—it's better in the end. And sometimes things work out better than expected.

The Lesson: The judicial system is not always just and fair, but it can be. Judges who honor the rule of law enhance the possibility of obtaining justice.

The Lesson: It may be challenging to live by our conscience day-to-day, especially on the little things. But when it comes to big decisions, those that affect life and death, we must follow our conscience, regardless of the potential consequences. There is no choice.

Vietnam: 1994

*"Returning violence for violence multiplies violence, adding
deeper darkness to a night already devoid of stars."*

~ Dr. Martin Luther King, Jr., an American Baptist minister
and civil rights leader

The United States and Vietnam have had a tortured history. The US government supported the French occupation of Vietnam until the French were defeated by the Vietnamese in 1954. Then the US refused to validate the results of the 1956 country-wide elections in Vietnam. After fighting for the south from 1964 to 1973 during Vietnam's civil war, extensively bombing the north, including its capital city of Hanoi, and killing upwards of several million Vietnamese, the US imposed a devastating trade embargo on Vietnam from 1973 until 1994.

I first traveled to Vietnam in 1994, immediately following President Clinton's lifting of the trade embargo. I visited Ho Chi Minh City and several communities in the Mekong Delta. My reflections, written during that trip, follow:

> Beautiful, petite, slender, young women in striking single-colored floor-length gowns glide by as if floating on a thin film of air. Old women, permanently stooped over from years in the rice paddies, go about their daily labor. Smiling, ragged street children sell postcards and stamps to all foreigners sympathetic to a toothy grin. Aggressive young men push

through the crowded streets picking pockets of the unexpected. Three-year-old bare-foot toddlers with forlorn stares beg on the sidewalks, patting their mouth and then their stomach, mouth then stomach, mouth then stomach, in hopes of being given something—anything. Mothers with peachy clean babies in strollers and decorated sailor outfits stroll for a Sunday walk. Sad-eyed mothers hold hollow-eyed babies in one arm while the other outstretched pleads for alms. Youthful and serious-looking olive-drab clad militia check foreigners' documents, asking a series of straightforward questions.

The open markets offer hand butchered, uncooked, and uncovered beef, pork, fish, and poultry lingering on card-board trays for purchase. Fish-heads in a clay pot are a choice menu item in an elegant restaurant. White rice in small bowls held directly below the lower lip is scooped into the mouth with chopsticks. Green bananas, green oranges, red and green mangos, brown coconuts, pink dragon fruit, yellow papaya, red rambutan all adorn abundant fruit trays. Street vendors sell everything from home-roasted cashews to pork chops prepared on a tiny side-walk grill—while you wait. Fragrances of every variety entertain the nostrils while the sounds of every pitch bludgeon the ears.

Thousands of bicycles, scooters, motorcycles, cycloes, pedestrians, ox-drawn carts, trucks, cars, and vans fill the roadway simultaneously moving—moving— moving. No one stops, but all give way. At first, it appears chaotic. Then there is order in the throngs, although the road rules are not readily apparent. Just keep moving.

Vietnam is economically devastated. The abject poor are everywhere. The innocent, vulnerable children and elderly, as always, are the most adversely affected. They are at the most significant risk for disease, starvation, and deadly accidents.

These are the images of Vietnam in 1994. Twenty years earlier, some of the images were probably the same. But the images Americans my age remember are those of a young Vietnamese girl running stark naked down a rural road fleeing a napalm attack; a restrained Vietnamese man executed at point-blank range by a South Vietnamese military officer; flag-draped coffins being escorted out of the rear of US military aircraft; and helicopters lifting off the roof of the American Embassy with people grabbing on as our country fled a war-ravaged land.

For some Vietnam Vets, the war continues to affect their lives. For the rest of Americans, the Vietnam War is ancient history. Memories of the war have faded, and our support for, or opposition to, this war is covered over by decades of day-to-day life. POW's and MIA's virtually reduced to white letters on black flags flying over baseball stadiums. The plight of impoverished Vietnamese people not even a blip on our personal radar screens.

But my travel to Vietnam uncovered those memories and reopened the debate. Issues that had not been examined for 20 years or more reappeared. Feelings long-repressed gushed out and overwhelmed. Explain again, I ask:

- Why did we fight this war?
- How did we get bogged down for so many years?
- How could we justify the massive killings?

- What was the purpose of sending American boys into this Asian civil conflict?

- What was so important to warrant the deaths of 58,000 of our loved ones, their names now permanently carved in black granite in Washington DC?

- Why did our government oppose the 1956 country-wide elections, which history now identifies as one of the key events that initiated the civil war?

- Was our stated goal really to "bomb them back to the stone-age"?

- Did our sons, brothers, husbands, lovers, and fathers really napalm the rain forest and intentionally set aflame entire villages?

- Were some of our soldiers guilty of war crimes?

- Did they really rape women, slaughter children, behead the enemy?

- How did we allow this to continue for so long?

The Vietnamese refer to this time as the "American war." The American War Crimes Museum in Ho Chi Minh City is an unassuming assortment of grounds and buildings displaying captured US military equipment, enlarged black & white photographs of alleged atrocities, charts identifying the types and tonnage of bombs dropped, the billions of dollars spent, the number of Vietnamese killed, wounded and maimed. Presidents Eisenhower, Kennedy, Johnson, Nixon, and Ford are individually pictured, each in serious contemplation. The unstated implication is that they are co-conspirators in the alleged crimes of war depicted in the museum. The My Lia massacre of old men, pregnant women, and little children is prominently displayed. Most Americans will be deeply embarrassed and profoundly saddened by this exhibit.

While it is doubtful that all the images or the various allegations are authentic, if even a small percentage are what they are said to be, these actions are incomprehensible to those who strongly believe that our troops don't do those things.

Very few museum visitors will be untouched by this awesome display of man's inhumanity to man. Regardless of all the despicable acts the North Vietnamese brought upon their southern brothers and sisters, regardless of the terrible suffering endured by American troops at the unclean hands of the Vietcong, regardless of the known brutality of war, most Americans would be overwhelmed by this exhibition. Our strong belief is that our country fights just wars, and when we go into battle, we fight fairly. This exhibit depicts American GIs as torturers, rapists, napalmers, and fraggers, and our nation as "Imperialist."

How could any American be a part of this? is the first question. How can I say, "we are sorry"? is the second.

Many, if not most, Americans now agree that the Vietnam War was a war that should not have been fought. It had a devastating effect on all participants. The United States lost 58,000 men and women and hundreds of thousands more seriously wounded—physically, emotionally, mentally, and spiritually. Billions of dollars wasted. Trust in our government strained to the limit. An entire generation torn apart as no generation before.

And the Vietnam government estimates that three million of their soldiers and civilians were killed. Their already impoverished country set back decades, if not centuries.

When I returned home from that first trip to Vietnam, I wrote:

> Now we have a chance to heal some of the wounds of the Vietnam War. With the lifting of the US trade embargo, Americans can now lend a hand to help rebuild Vietnam and, at the same time, help mend our own lives, which were ripped apart by the events of those war years. Global Volunteers offers that opportunity. We provide the chance to help reconstruct that which we helped destroy and to say, "we're sorry" for what we did or for what we failed to do.

The Lesson: "War is not healthy for children and other living things." (Lorraine Schneider wrote this profound statement on a poster she created in 1967 which became an ubiquitous anti-Vietnam War icon.)

Vietnam: 2017

"History teaches that wars begin when governments believe the price of aggression is cheap."

~ Ronald Regan, an American actor and
40th President of the United States

I have returned to Vietnam numerous times since my first visit in 1994, and my impressions of this beautiful country continue. The people are incredibly friendly as they express their admiration for and love of Americans; nearly 80 percent of its 97 million were born after the war. The economy continues to improve, and the government continues to reach out to the west.

Hanoi is exceptionally charming, with several lakes bordered by parks and walking paths, almost unlimited restaurants, comfortable hotels, crafts and art shops galore, a large Catholic cathedral, and several Buddhist Pagodas. The Old Quarter is a particularly fascinating and a lovely place to enjoy the Vietnamese culture. It is safe to walk in the city in daylight, and there are abundant taxis to get around by night.

With an ever-increasing number of Americans visiting Hanoi, it's important to note that this capital city could well be the world's motorbike capital—they are omnipresent and create breathtaking situations for the uninitiated attempting to walk across a street. Signal lights are not on every corner, and pedestrians crossing the street is quite tricky. You must do it with great care and determination. The motorbikes, rickshaws, buses, and cars will make way for pedestrians, provided you walk at a slow but steady pace. Once you start, you cannot lose your nerve—you must keep walking as you focus your vision intently on the vehicles coming directly at you. The traffic density determines the speed at which you walk—the greater the number of vehicles, the slower you walk. Crossing a street in Hanoi or Ho Chi Minh City is not for the faint-hearted. Just keep moving—moving—moving.

Shortly after lifting the US trade embargo, the Vietnamese government decided to reach out to and embrace the West. Tourism flourished, and economic opportunities grew. In 2008, the government-initiated Project 2020, a mega English language education effort with the goal of English becoming the language of instruction in all schools by 2020. They decided this to compete in the world marketplace. Although Vietnamese computer engineers have excellent math and computer science skills, they could not compete for international jobs if their engineers' English skills were insufficient. Further, international tourism expanded rapidly throughout the country and became a significant source of jobs and income. Consequently, hotel clerks, taxi drivers, restaurant workers, etc., needed to speak reasonably acceptable English.

In 2017, I met with Prof. Dr. Bui Tat Thang, a delightful man, and president of the Vietnam Institute for Development Strategies (VIDS). VIDS is a central government agency within the Ministry of Planning. Many of its 150 employees are young and bright researchers tasked with developing long-term strategies for their future. VIDS recently published *Vietnam 2035*, a joint undertaking by Vietnamese and World Bank experts, evaluating Vietnam's opportunities and challenges over the next 20 plus years. The subtitle of this report is *Toward Prosperity, Creativity, Equity, and Democracy*.

"Democracy"?! I suspect that would surprise some former US government leaders who decided to engage our country in the Vietnam War and bomb them back to the Stone Age.

The Lesson: War creates more questions than answers. 58,000 Americans and millions of Vietnamese killed—for what? Forty-five years later, what evidence shows that the Vietnamese people would be better off had the North lost the war? Might the Vietnamese government have reached out to the west or decided to compete in the global marketplace sooner if the trade embargo had not been put in place or lifted earlier?

The Lesson: All of this begs the question; is a non-defensive war ever worth the cost? My answer, "No!"

9/11

"Even the smallest act of service, the simplest act of kindness,
is a way to honor those we lost, a way to reclaim that spirit of
unity that followed 9/11."

~ Barack Obama, an American lawyer
and 44th President of the United States

I was running late for a meeting at the United Nations in New York City. As I dressed, CNN showed smoke spewing out of one of the Twin Towers in lower Manhattan. I looked out the window from the hotel's 32nd floor and saw the tall building and dark grey smoke.

The reporters weren't sure of the cause of the fire, initially reporting that a small private aircraft might have struck the side of the 110-story skyscraper. Fifteen minutes later, I witnessed the second plane crash into the South Tower. The commercial airliner enveloped into the building; it sliced straight through. To this day, I don't know if I saw the second plane from the hotel window or watched it on television. But it doesn't matter; it was a horrifying event. In less than two hours, both buildings collapsed; the final death toll was nearly 2800.

The Monday night before, I considered going to the Windows on the World for breakfast the following day. One of New York's favorite tourist destinations, this restaurant was located at the top of the North Tower of the World Trade Center and offered spectacular views of the city and waterways. Thankfully for me, I stayed up too late watching some dumb TV shows and didn't have time in the morning.

After the planes struck, I spoke at length with Col. Warren Williams (Ret.), a dear friend I first met during one of my early visits to Vietnam when he volunteered with Global Volunteers. Our first thoughts were that tens of thousands of people might have been killed given the total destruction of the buildings and that nearly 50,000 people could have been in their offices that day. As it turns out, less than 18,000 were in the towers when they were attacked; nevertheless, it is nothing short of miraculous that thousands more did not die.

I decided to give blood at a local hospital, as was suggested by the media. As I hiked south on Park Avenue, hundreds of people covered head-to-toe in gray ash walked north, away from the World Trade Center. It was a scene out of a horror film, except this was no movie. When I got to the hospital, the staff told me I was not needed; too few survivors required blood.

The next day, I rented a car and left the city in the afternoon, arriving at Global Volunteers' Little Canada office mid-day Friday. Throughout those three days, I was alone with countless hours to contemplate this vicious and senseless attack on fellow human beings and our country.

It remains incomprehensible to me what could provoke someone to kill themselves and simultaneously thousands of others. War in is an anathema to me, but 9/11 was beyond war. To indiscriminately kill thousands of innocent civilians to make some kind of economic, political, or religious statement must be outside the imagination of even the sickest of minds.

We pray for all those who died that day and their families!

The Lesson: I'll never understand the taking of another's life, except in self-defense or defense of country in imminent danger.

The Lesson: Life has "fork-in-the-road" moments. Deliberate decisions cause some, others are the result of simple dilly-dallying. We can only imagine where life might have led had we taken the road not taken.

The Lesson: Sometimes, watching dumb TV shows reaps inexplicable outcomes.

On WISDOM

"The older I get, the better I was."

~ Author unknown; inscribed on an "Old Men Rule" T-shirt

It has long been said that wisdom comes with age. At least, we should hope it does. Some are wise beyond their years, while others struggle throughout life to gain minimal good common sense, judgment, or prudence. Earlier in this book, I wrote that this is not intended to be a book of wisdom, and it is not. But I have learned some things that have enhanced my wisdom. This chapter includes some of those lessons. (BTW: your mother gave me the "Old Men Rule" T-shirt.)

Failure: A Most Effective Teacher

"Success is not final; failure is not fatal:
it is the courage to continue that counts."

~ Winston Churchill, a British politician

During the time the University of Minnesota suspended me because I had failed three classes the term immediately before graduation, I applied for and was accepted in a US government program called Volunteers in Service to America (VISTA). This agency was a national effort to fight poverty in the US and later became a part of the Corporation for National and Community Service. I had considered joining the Peace Corps and even filled out the application paperwork but decided to serve at home in the US instead. Had I not joined Vista, I would have been drafted by the US Army to fight in Vietnam. It was the winter of 1969; I was 22.

Approximately 60 of us twenty-somethings were trained in Washington DC. After six weeks of instruction, the process called for a small group of us to be elected by all trainees to make recommendations about each trainee's suitability to serve. I was elected the leader. I didn't campaign for this role but was flattered when nominated, and the vote was near-unanimous. I fulfilled my job well, and shortly after, we all went off to our assignments throughout the US.

I was assigned to Mantua, an impoverished black community in the western part of Philadelphia, Pennsylvania. I enjoyed getting to know and working with the local people, but it turned out that I was not well suited for this program. I failed miserably. Being a white minority in an all-black community; observing tremendous economic poverty where people had no available exit; encountering gang violence on virtually every street corner; witnessing poisonous drugs being sold by teenagers to teenagers; watching rats scamper along the walls of my sleeping room; living amid constant fear and deprivation were all too much.

I had grown up poor in Minnesota, but Mantua was a wholly different universe. The economic poverty my family faced in suburban St. Paul did not compare in magnitude or consequence to that suffered by virtually every family in Mantua.

I wrote letters home to my parents, which my mother kept for me. Part of one of those letters describes the situation:

February 1969

Mantua has the highest crime rate of any other community in the crime-ridden city of Philadelphia. There are eight gangs of about 100 members, mostly teenagers and guys in their early 20s.

Cops are detested and with some good reason. This morning, we were told that there was a car chase last night—police pursuing a carload of gang members. The guys drove into an alley, jumped out, and started running. The cops got out of their car and yelled at them to stop. The last guy to get out of the car did stop and turned around. One of the police shot him through the head. They told us he was unarmed. This morning he died.

There are a lot of rats in Mantua. It was estimated last year that there were 176,000 rats in the 84 blocks of Mantua. That's eight rats to every resident. The human population has grown very little; the rats continue to multiply. Each female produces about 50 pups a year, and young females begin reproducing at 2 ½ months. And these are big, well-fed rats, and as filthy as they come. The city of Philadelphia allocated 2.5 million dollars for rat control—Mantua got $600.

Mantua is like a battleground where no one walks alone at night, and women don't go out on the street unless accompanied by a man. In Mantua, people starve because they don't have enough to eat—barely 12 blocks from some of the finest restaurants in the world in downtown Philly. In Mantua, people live in ignorance with the University of Pennsylvania, Drexel Institute of Technology, and three other colleges that comprise University City five blocks away. In Mantua, people live in rundown buildings—no heat, no yards, no parks— while five minutes away is one of the most beautiful parks and zoos in the city.

But all is not dim. Our sponsor, the Mantua Community Planners, is a young progressive organization whose elected leaders and staff are all ex-gang members. They run a mini-school, a vector control project to control the rats, a health clinic, and a community center, and they work on housing and welfare rights.

Another trainee and I are living with an elderly black woman and her sister in their home. We pay her $20 a week for room and board. There is little, if any, heat. She has rags stuck in the windows—no storm windows or anything like that. Most of the doors don't close, but it doesn't matter because there are no doorknobs. The stairs just don't creek; they sound as if they are crying out for their very life. In short, we live in what is typically called substandard or poor housing—nice terms that allow us to turn the other way.

We only have to live here for a few weeks. But Mrs. Jones and her sister live here year-round and will live here until they die—of pneumonia or some other illness caused by unlivable living conditions. Mrs. Jones is a nice old lady, active in the community, and a dreamer. Her dream is to fix up her house and make a place for old veterans to give them a homey atmosphere. She will die with her dream, but for now, her dream gives her life.

Tonight, I am cold—very cold. I will sleep in my long underwear, pajamas, and bathrobe. I won't get sick; I'm taking good care of myself.

Living in Mantua was the most challenging thing I'd done in my young life, and the challenge was overwhelming. After a six-week probationary period in-community, all trainees returned to DC for a week of evaluation. It was clear to me, and my youthful supervisors, that I had performed poorly. I was overcome by the tragic circumstances in which the people of Mantua lived day to day. I was incapable of helping them because I could not get beyond the paralysis caused by their tragic circumstances. I had failed. I quit. If I had not quit, I am quite sure I would have been summarily dismissed.

For several years that followed, I reflected on those days in Mantua and my abysmal failure. I realized that I was utterly unprepared for the experience. Other young men and women did fine; however, that did not matter to me. I did not do fine.

My failure in Mantua was among the first foundational building blocks for the rest of my life of service. In Mantua, I learned some of what I needed to know to co-found Global Volunteers.

The Lesson: If I were ever to make a positive difference in impoverished people's lives, I needed to toughen up. I needed to better understand severe economic poverty and its effects on crime, education, health, order, family, and community.

The Lesson: One option to failure is to simply accept it, move on, and not look back. A preferable alternative is to learn from failure, decide to do better, and then do better.

Be the Change

"Live as if you were to die tomorrow. Learn as if you were to live forever."

~ Mohandas Gandhi, lawyer, anti-colonial nationalist,
political ethicist, and father of the Indian nation

Frederic Lewis Donaldson was an Anglican priest and Archdeacon of Westminster from 1937 to 1946, the year I was born. In 1925, he gave a sermon where he identified the seven deadly social sins. Somewhere along the way, I was introduced to these seven sins. They made an indelible mark on me as these traits are spiritually perilous to humanity.

1. Wealth without Work
2. Pleasure without Conscience
3. Knowledge without Character
4. Commerce without Morality
5. Science without Humanity
6. Religion without Sacrifice
7. Politics without Principle

The Lesson: All are embedded in the words; no more needs to be said.

10 Cups of Coffee

"Candy is dandy, but liquor is quicker."

~ Ogden Nash, an American poet

"Everything in moderation" has been a struggle for me. Moderation is an admirable quality. But . . . .

I used to buy family-sized bags of miniature snicker bars with the intent of having chocolate candy available for a couple of weeks. Then I would eat the entire bag in one sitting. The solution was to stop buying chocolate by the bag.

I had a similar issue with coffee and Diet Coke. One morning while at my law office, I counted that I had drunk 10 cups of coffee before noon. I tried cutting back, but a week later, I was back to 10. So, I quit drinking coffee altogether in 1989 and have not had any coffee since. But then I took up Diet Coke and soon after was drinking a six-pack a day. Years later, my physician explained the physical damage caffeine does to the body and suggested I cut back on the Diet Coke. I knew that for me, it was an all or nothing decision. I decided to stop drinking Diet Coke. And I did stop for several years. Then, I started having one Diet Coke after breakfast in the morning—didn't need any more for the rest of the day. But that didn't last. Now I'm at two to four cans a day; more on a long road trip.

I had the same issue with hard alcohol. I'm not an alcoholic, but as a young man, I drank too much. When I was 35, I started having repeated heart attack symptoms—chest pains, tingling in the arm, lightheadedness. It took several trips to the ER and an overnight in the hospital to discover I was allergic to beer and hard alcohol. The reaction caused the heart attack symptoms. It was merely an allergy, but it was troubling and scary. I stopped drinking alcohol—cold turkey.

For ten years, I did not have any alcohol. Then, when closing a Global Volunteers deal in Moscow, one of our community partners poured me a shot of vodka, explaining that we needed to consummate the agreement with Russians' preferred beverage. I explained that I couldn't drink alcohol due to a heart condition. That was an unacceptable explanation.

"Either we close the deal with vodka, or there is no deal," he said emphatically.

I protested.

Finally, one of the women present proposed that I drink champagne while the others toasted with vodka. I knew that some Russians think of champagne as we might look at water, so I succumbed. And to my pleasant surprise, there were no adverse side effects from the champagne; although, I worried about it all night. I did not want to go to a Russian hospital with heart attack symptoms.

When I returned home, I had an experimental glass of white wine, again, no adverse effects. Then I tried red wine, which I much prefer, and still no side effects. So now I drink red wine, but I haven't had any hard liquor or beer since I was 35.

Cigarettes were another challenge. I smoked two to three packs a day for nearly ten years—from age 16 to 26. After five years, I did not want to smoke anymore, but I was addicted to nicotine. It was hard to quit. One year I stopped 19 times. I counted because I knew I had unsuccessfully tried to quit so many times the previous year.

Then on a Saturday morning at work, I told my friend and coworker, Lenny Painchaub, that I'd quit once again—"this time for good!"

"I'll bet you hundred bucks you can't quit smoking for a month," Lenny said.

"You're on," I replied, assuming $100—which is about $700 in 2020 as compared to 1970—would provide additional motivation to quit.

Later that day, we went out for lunch. Typically, we wouldn't have a beer at lunch, but this was a Saturday and therefore an exception. After we had our burgers and beer, Lenny opened his pack of Lucky Strikes, put one in his mouth, and lit it. I smelled the alluring aroma. Without saying a word, he offered me a cigarette. Without thinking, I took one. It was merely a force of habit. He gave me a light. I took a drag, enjoying the sensation that a cigarette offers after a spicy meal and a cold beer.

As I exhaled, my 'friend' said, "You owe me 100 bucks."

I tried umpteen times to stop smoking over the ensuing years but to no avail. Then, while in my mid-20s, I had a date with a beautiful woman I had asked out several times before she finally accepted. We had a wonderful evening. At the doorstep of her apartment, as I moved close intending to kiss her good night, she put her hand in front of my mouth and said, "I don't kiss men who smoke."

That was February 12, 1972. I have not had a cigarette since.

The Lesson: If you find yourself eating a whole bag of miniature snicker bars in one sitting, STOP! And don't buy chocolate candy bars by the bag.

The Lesson: Don't throw money away on bets you're probably going to lose.

The Lesson: The power of a kiss can trump the power of addiction. Provided, of course, you really want to overcome the addiction.

Set Your Sails

While in Sile, Turkey, in 1996, I spoke with a young woman about where she was educated. In addition to being a student at Istanbul University, she studied in the United States and a university in France. I asked her if she had any plans to go abroad in the future. She told me that she would like to return to France and America, but she had no plans to do so.

I asked her why not. She responded that her plans never happened as she hoped, and therefore, she did not make plans any longer. "Making plans," she said, "was a waste of time."

I told her that I did not know much about life, but this I do know.

To plan is to envision what life will be. This is a critical human endeavor. Even though we may be certain that the plans made will not come to fruition as we might hope, in the absence of envisioning, we have little influence over our lives.

The winds of the sea, as they unexpectedly catch our sails, will blow us off course. But if we have not set a course, if we have not envisioned the future, it is better never to leave the harbor. Without a prepared course, when the wind catches our sails and blows our ship at its will—and it will—we will not know how to adjust the rigging to set ourselves straight because we won't know where we're going.

Thus, we will be blown across the sea of life without purpose, landing where the wind chooses to put us. Eventually, she will choose to put us on the rocks where we will sail no more.

But if we have set a course, when the wind blows us off our course, we can adjust our sails, find the course again, and continue toward our destination. The journey may be different than what we had planned, but our vision of what life will be, will be.

The young women listened intently. She thanked me and told me that she would always remember these words. And upon hearing that, I wrote them down so that I too would remember them.

The Lesson: Set your sails. Make plans. When your plans do not come to fruition, you can still adjust your course.

The Lesson: Keep track of your ideas, good and bad. Write them down; put them in your phone or on the back of an envelope. Periodically, look at them to see if your thinking has changed or matured. When you get older, you can include them in a book for your children.

Midnight Cowboy

"The two natural items to sustain life are sunlight and coco-
nut milk. Did you know that?"

~ Enrico "Ratso" Rizzo, a character in Midnight Cowboy

In the 1969-70 school year, I was asked to teach religious education to Catholic kids attending public schools. It was a one-hour class on Wednesday nights, like children's Sunday school in Protestant congregations. I don't remember why I was asked, but I agreed to do it. There were several volunteer teachers for the various grades; my assignment was high school seniors.

There's nothing particularly significant about the students or my teaching that year—the only year I ever taught religious instruction. However, a valuable bit of wisdom was gleaned from my arranging for the students to see the movie *Midnight Cowboy*. The movie, starring John Voight and Dustin Hoffman, was about a genuine friendship between two young men who first met in midtown Manhattan under less than laudable circumstances. Voight plays a naïve prostitute, and Hoffman is Enrico "Ratso" Rizzo, an ailing con man. When I first saw the movie, I realized the story offered meaningful lessons about friendship and the Christian value of caring for others when they are down and out.

The movie was rated R, which at the time was for those 16 and older, and I knew all my students were at least 17. I invited a Catholic nun, teaching religion to another high school senior class, to join me and bring her students along. She agreed.

Unbeknownst to me, the movie was not rated R; it was rated X. Initially, the movie was an R, but the film rating staff at the Motion Picture Association of America (MPAA) acquiesced to the advice of psychologists. They recommended it be X rated because Voight's character was homosexual and offered "possible influence upon youngsters." Moreover, movies or books about gays were unacceptable to the Catholic Church at that time.

In any event, on a Friday night, we all went to the Midtown Family Theater, where I had previously worked, and David Levy, the owner, had offered me free tickets for all the students. Everyone appeared to enjoy the film; however, as might be expected, some of the students told their parents.

When the Catholic parish council learned that I had arranged for high school seniors to see an X rated movie, they became enraged. They demanded that the nun and I attend a parish council meeting to defend our actions. After a conversation with Jack Murray, a parish council member and a friend of my parents, it was clear that this would not be an opportunity to defend anything; rather, it would be an inquisition—an occasion for the council to rake us over the coals. I declined to attend.

In retrospect, it was cowardly of me to allow the young nun to go to that meeting without me. She was required to be there. She had no choice because she was an employee of the church. While she was being skewered, I was someplace else. I have regretted that decision ever since.

Midnight Cowboy was a notable film. It won three Academy Awards—Best Picture, Best Director, and Best Adapted Screenplay. It's among the top 50 greatest American movies of all time, as listed by the American Film Institute. It was the first "Best Picture" of a gay-related film and was the only X-rated film to win Best Picture; although in 1971, it was reissued and rated R. In 1994, the Library of Congress declared *Midnight Cowboy* "culturally, historically or aesthetically significant."

Several years later, I got a late-night call from Jack, the friend who served on the parish council at the time of this brouhaha. He told me he and his wife had watched *Midnight Cowboy* that evening and exclaimed what a delightful film it was. He said, "now I understand why you took those high school seniors to see this movie."

Years later, as I had a drink with Ron Kensey in a Beverly Hills Hotel lobby bar, I saw Dustin Hoffman. I spoke with him briefly, telling him how much I enjoyed his work, especially *Midnight Cowboy*. When I told him this story, he said, "well, of course, the Catholic Church would be pissed. *Midnight Cowboy* was rated X." That's when I first became aware this film was not R-rated.

The Lesson: Show up. When someone accuses you of doing something wrong, show up, and defend your actions. If you need to apologize, do so. If you do not believe you have done anything wrong, explain why you did what you did and why you believe you were right to do so. But do not take the cowards way out. And never let someone else take the heat in your absence. Show up!

Stuff

"Take care to guard against all greed, for though one may be rich, one's life does not consist of possessions."

~ Luke 12:15

I took my first international trip outside North America in 1975, shortly after my 29th birthday. I traveled with the Institute of Cultural Affairs (ICA)—an international NGO located in Chicago with offices around the US—the same organization that facilitated our honeymoon in Guatemala four years later. The ICA was conducting human and economic development programs in countries all over the world in 1975. About a year after being elected to the Minnesota House, Minneapolis ICA leaders, Sam Hanson and Sue Laxdal, invited me to participate in a village human development program in India. The community was Maliwada, a small rural village several hundred miles northeast of Bombay (now Mumbai). However, when I agreed to go, I was not aware that I had to pay my way.

With my income limited to my modest legislative salary, I couldn't cover the airfare and other trip expenses. I decided to do some fundraising. Sam Hanson and I met with former Minnesota Governor Elmer Anderson, whom I knew from when he was chairman of the Board of Regents at the University of Minnesota and I worked for MPIRG. Governor Anderson was a Republican, and I was a Democrat, but he immediately agreed to help. The governor's only requirement was I speak to the St. Paul Rotary Club about my trip when I returned home. Done deal! Through his and Sam's efforts, I secured the money to make the trip.

I have wonderful memories of that first international experience, even though it was so long ago, and I returned home seriously sick from water-borne parasites. The docs believed they were probably imbedded in the ice used for my scotch on the rocks. But the unforgettable memory is seeing a mother rock her baby in her arms in front of her small hut. I didn't think anything of it at first. However, as I walked by several times during the day, I wondered. In the evening, when I saw that she was still sitting there rocking her baby, I asked an Indian woman who was part of our group why this mother sat holding her baby all day.

"The child died last night," she told me. The mother was in deep grief; she couldn't let go. Her family and the community let her rock her baby boy until it was time to bury him.

I felt a deep sadness for her. Knowing the loss of a child, I empathized with her horrendous pain.

One of the things that struck me in Maliwada was that the people had no things—no electricity, no running water, no health clinic, no TVs, no cars, no anything. But they appeared satisfied and happy. I have since witnessed the same phenomenon in economically impoverished communities all over the world.

I remember thinking that US advertisers barrage us with messages about buying stuff to be happy. And, if you have stuff but still are not happy, then buy more stuff. "Buy stuff—be happy" was and still is the predominant advertising message.

That message misses the whole point of a meaningful and rewarding life. Our goal should be to improve the quality of life, not quantity. As soon as we believe we need more stuff to be happy, and we are not content because we do not have enough stuff—that is when we find ourselves looking into the abyss.

Politicians, government agencies, universities, faith-based organizations, and professional associations should strive to create an environment where life can be meaningful to its fullest. Without question, everyone needs a certain amount of sustainable income. But once that level is achieved, it is contradictory to happiness to try to get more. The question must never be simply, "How do we increase people's incomes"? The question must be, "What can we do to serve others so that they can enjoy a meaningful life?"

A meaningful life is not about more stuff, things, material, money. Efforts to acquire material wealth will rob you of your life's most significant treasure—happiness—like a thief in the night. Economic wealth will not sustain you. Meaningful life is about relationships and service. Those are what brings happiness.

What is Happiness?

Happiness is experienced when we are kind to others, when we look out for others, when we serve others. A simple smile; helping a stranger in need; being present in a time of tragedy; teaching a child—there are a multitude of examples, each of which can bring happiness to ourselves and joy to others.

Happiness is found in meaningful relationships—family, friends, and colleagues. Joy is experienced in sharing who we are with those we love. Contentment is offering a needed word of encouragement or an acknowledgment that you care. Happiness is being present to another in need.

Feed your soul through service to others; you will be enriched.

The Lesson: Don't believe those who declare that others value life less than we do. Every culture values human life, and every parent grieves the loss of their child.

The Lesson: We <u>help others achieve</u> happiness by serving them. <u>We achieve</u> happiness by serving others.

The Lesson: Meaningful life is not about stuff, things, material, or money. Meaningful life is about meaningful relationships. And meaningful relationships are founded in the love of and service to others.

God is not to Blame

"Everyone has a thousand wishes before a tragedy,
but just one afterward."

~ Fredrik Backman, a Swedish columnist, blogger, and writer

Tragedy strikes all around us; none of us are immune—devastating weather, mass shootings, suicide, pandemics, war, and the devastation of war—and we do not know why. The greatest tragedies, and the most difficult to deal with, are when we lose a loved one—a son at birth, a 27-year-old daughter, a 99-year-old mother.

But God's hands are not present in any of these tragedies. God is not to blame. God's hands bring us yellow daffodils, green spinach, white snow, red wine, blue skies, bright sunshine, dazzling stars, deep seas, rugged mountains, elegant deer, smiling babies, sex, and love—all of creation in its finest.

Tragedies come large and small. Many are man-made; others are natural disasters. Our planet endures enormous catastrophes—war, earthquakes, tsunamis, drought, hurricanes, stunted children, pandemics, and terrorism. Every individual suffers tragedy—a debilitating illness; the breakup of a marriage; conviction of a crime, especially when innocent; an estranged family member; loss of a job; bankruptcy; and failure to be all that you can be. Throughout history, tragedy has been a significant ingredient of the human condition.

Yet, some tragedies are without explanation—a child who dies in her sleep, leukemia in a healthy parent, Alzheimer's at any age, a mosquito that infects a pregnant woman, a baby who dies in childbirth. Some day we may know why these things happen.

Tragedy is a part of the human condition. What is disconcerting is human hands often bring on tragedies. Humans are responsible, whether by omission or commission, for climate change and all its consequences, untreated mental illness, hungry children, traffic accidents, nuclear weapons, children separated from their parents, murder, unemployment, poverty, and the obscene abundance of wealth amidst profound poverty.

However, it is not the heartbreak in and of itself that should cause us to shudder. We should tremble when we do not do all we can to help those who experience tragedy.

The Lesson: It is in the midst of tragedy that we can provide the most generous assistance to others—to love our neighbor and help heal their pain.

The Lesson: Tragedy offers the opportunity to serve and express selfless love.

The Lesson: Tragedy allows us to demonstrate our values and live our faith—to walk our talk.

Fear of Sharing

"You pray for the hungry. Then you feed them.
That's how prayer works."

~ Pope Francis, a leader of the Catholic Church

Tom Vilsack, my friend, former governor of Iowa, former US Secretary of Agriculture, and multi-time Global Volunteer, told the following compelling story at a conference I attended in 2009. It is relevant to all we do today.

"I was in church not too long ago when the priest from my faith came out and decided to explain the gospel he was going to read during the church service to the children who were in the congregation. I must say that I perked up when he said that because oftentimes, I don't understand his sermons, and so I thought this might be an opportunity for me to better understand what he was saying.

"He came out, and he told the wonderful story of the loaves and fishes. Regardless of your faith tradition, it is a wonderful story. It is a story of Jesus speaking to the multitudes, and he sees that they are hungry. He says to his disciples, 'Go feed the people,' and the disciples looked around, and they saw five loaves of bread and a couple of fish. They said to themselves, 'We can't possibly feed the multitude with such a meager amount.'

"Jesus, recognizing their hesitation, basically said to them, 'Have faith. Pass the baskets.'

"Indeed, they did pass the baskets. All 5,000 were fed. When they brought the baskets back, they actually had more food than when they started.

"The priest explained it this way. He said, 'What Jesus did in that story is he removed the fear of sharing.' I would suggest to you that that is what community does, whether it is a small community in a small town or a sense of community in a nation or an international sense of community, that what we can do together collectively with small acts is create a sense of community that removes for all of us a fear of sharing.

"And when that fear is removed, we become more generous with what we have. As we become more generous with what we have, we actually receive more than what we give.

"This is a powerful story at this point in time when the world faces an economic crisis, and in a land of plenty, in a land where there is so much potential, it is appropriate for us to lead this effort, to remove that fear of sharing, to create a greater sense of connection and community, to allow all of those billion people who are hungry today, the knowledge and the hope that there are people who care and people who are working each and every day to try to reduce that number."

The Lesson: There is plenty to go around. When we all share the plenty we have, there will no longer be anyone in need. But first, we must overcome the fear of sharing.

Lava Soap

"We must learn to live together as brothers
or perish together as fools."

~ Dr. Martin Luther King, Jr., an American Baptist minister
and civil rights leader

When I was growing up in Roseville, Minnesota, in the 1950s and 1960s, there was little opportunity to get to know people of color. There were no African Americans, Asians, or Latinos in my neighborhood or our church. Although I learned about the horrors of slavery and the equality of all people, the suburban Catholic grade school I attended was all white. In my urban Catholic boys' high school, there was one African American in our class of several hundred and one black teacher in the entire school—a Christian Brother.

Moreover, society portrayed whites as better than blacks, and African Americans were considered by many as inferior to European Americans. Television, radio, movies, plays, newspapers, magazines, even black radio shows, all depicted whites as superior to blacks. There were "Whites Only" signs in southern states that designated what and where people of color could do and go. In some states, there were miscegenation laws that prohibited interracial marriage and criminalized sex between people of different races.

Society simply taught white was better than black. Society taught racism, and much of society was segregated.

However, racism was never practiced or tolerated in our home. My father and mother abhorred any disrespect directed toward any person, especially people of color. My mother would wash my mouth out with Lava soap if I used disrespectful words to describe anyone. She'd stick a wet bar of soap in my mouth, wiping it against my tongue. If you don't know what Lava soap tastes like, trust me, it's bad—really bad!

Segregation inflicted enormous harm on people of color. Segregated education resulted in inferior education. Segregated healthcare resulted in inadequate healthcare. Segregated housing resulted in substandard housing. Segregation meant lower-paying jobs, less nutritious food, and increased poverty.

But African Americans did not sit idly by. Throughout the 1950s and 60s, they fought for equal civil rights. Led by Dr. Martin Luther King, Jr., they brought attention to the injustice of segregated education, segregated restaurants, the poll tax which denied the right to vote, and so much more.

This protest peaked coincidentally on my 17th birthday, August 28, 1963, when more than 200,000 people of all races joined together at the Lincoln Memorial to push the US government to abolish segregation and racial discrimination. It was at this event where Dr. King gave his insightful and inspiring "I Have a Dream" speech. Less than a year later, Congress passed, and the president signed the Civil Rights Act of 1964. This law banned discrimination based on a person's race, color, national origin, religious beliefs, or sex and defended every American citizen's right to use public facilities, get a job, and vote.

However, neither the Civil Rights Act nor subsequent civil rights legislation could ban racism. Racism is embodied in the heart, well beyond the purview of government edicts.

Over the years, I realized that, regardless of my mother's teaching, societal training had sunk in. It had indelibly stained my inner being. One day I came to the gut-wrenching conclusion that I too harbored prejudice in my heart. This was dreadfully difficult for me to admit, even to myself. But it was true!

As a young adult, I questioned whether a black doctor was as good as a white doctor. I've chosen to sit next to a white person rather than a black at McDonalds. I've felt fear when coming across African American teenagers on the street—fear that I didn't experience when I encountered white teens.

During a speech in New York City in my mid-40s, I explained that I struggled with this issue. After my presentation, a woman came up and admonished me; she took offense at my implication that all in the audience were racists.

"There aren't any racists in New York," she exclaimed.

I apologized and explained that I did not intend to imply that she or anyone else was a racist. Then I told her that I was surprised that she thought racism was not an issue in New York City. Earlier that day, I needed to get a taxi to go to Harlem for a newspaper interview. I relayed to her, "Three taxis stopped, but when I told them where I was going, no one would drive me there."

"Of course not," she said. "No white person's going to take you to Harlem."

During President Clinton's administration, Henry Cisneros, the Secretary of Housing and Urban Development, warned that racism is a disease that had crept into every social issue. If it continued, we would all suffer.

Unfortunately, not enough has changed in the past several decades.

Racism persists as cancer, eating away at our social fabric. It is manifested in many ways, most tragically when white police officers kill unarmed black men. Perhaps the most egregious and grotesque was the murder of George Floyd in 2020 by Minneapolis police on a street corner less than 10 miles from our Maplewood home.

A law client, a black Baptist pastor, once said to me, "We all harbor bias in our hearts." I was surprised by this. I naïvely thought only white folks were prejudiced. He told me this knowing that neither he nor I felt any bias toward the other. We had become friends as we worked together on a joint project.

Today, I know that a person's color—black, brown, or white—has nothing to do with the quality of their character, the capacity of their intelligence, or the dignity of their being. Crisscrossing this planet, I have learned that we all are so much alike that the differences between us are cause for celebration rather than apprehension, fear, or distrust. It is in this discovery where friendships can be found, and bigotry can be overcome. The Creator designed such a wide variety of races and colors—from the blackest of blacks to the whitest of whites and all the browns in between. We should celebrate that.

Years ago, I got a call from the mayor of Arcola, MS. Cliff Harris explained that he had recently attended the Mississippi Black Mayors Conference and had a conversation with the mayor of another small town where Global Volunteers served. He asked if Global Volunteers might be willing to come to his community. We spoke about that for a while, and during the conversation, I said to him, "Mr. Mayor, you must know that I've struggled with racism in my life."

After I explained what I meant, he said, "Now I really want you to come to my town. You're the first honest white guy I've ever talked to." The mayor understood that racism and bias are learned and that we can all recover from it.

The Lesson: Just as clean alcoholics who are in recovery must first acknowledge that they are an alcoholic to start their journey to recovery, so too must those of us who choose to recover from racism.

The Lesson: Friendship is the therapy that cures all racism. The more friends we have of people of other races, the less racism there will be.

The Lesson: As writer Kelly Hayes says, "There is no shame in admitting that you were previously speaking from a less informed place." We all have permission to amend our thinking and our ways.

No Planet B

In my early twenties, I saw myself as a dedicated environmentalist. Then one evening, on the way to a movie with a lovely woman to whom I was engaged to be married, I threw a gum wrapper out my car window. She called me out, "You can't do that! You say you're an environmentalist, yet you pollute right in front of me." I had never thought about it that way, but Jeannie was right.

And it wasn't merely gum wrappers. I didn't recycle; I drove a gas-guzzling Mustang Mach 1, polluted the air with cigarette smoke, and ate a lot of beef, all of which contributed to the destruction of the environment. I was an environmentalist wannabe; I may have cared about the environment theoretically, but I did not walk my talk.

Some could argue that I was simply a product of my time. Perhaps so, but that may be why Planet Earth is in so much trouble today. We rationalize that everyone behaves that way, it's the way it's always been, or my little bit isn't going to do any harm. But there is no Planet B. Earth is the only planet we have. If we all do not take care of her, our grandchildren will suffer incalculably

I decided to do something constructive. I worked for the McCarthy and Mc-Govern presidential campaigns because both supported strong environmental policies and opposed the war in Vietnam. While at MPIRG, we fought to protect the pristine Boundary Waters Canoe Area. I continued that fight as a member of the Minnesota House and as Assistant Commissioner at the Department of Natural Resources. I supported "Ban the Can," an effort to eliminate or at least recycle soda and beer cans. Governor Perpich appointed me to a Mississippi River task force charged with cleaning up this magnificent river, which had become a dumping site for all sorts of contaminated waste. Your mother and I started recycling all paper, plastic, aluminum, and other waste at our home from the time we were first married. We bought fuel-efficient cars and purchased recycled products for my law office and Global Volunteers. When I ran for Governor of Minnesota, the environment was one of the three main pillars of my 3Es campaign—protecting the Environment, improving Education, and enhancing the Economy. Now we recycle everything, conserve wherever we can, buy energy-efficient products, and plant trees and shrubs. But we all must do more.

As a global society, we must cut greenhouse gases to protect our planet. Alternative renewable energies like solar, geothermal, wind, and plant-based fuels will help. Substantial reductions in fossil fuels will help. Growing massive numbers of trees will help; everyone merely planting a tree for each flight they take or contributing to a tree planting NGO could have a significant impact on sinking CO_2. There are so many ways individuals, small towns, and cities can help. We do not need to wait for the US or Chinese governments or the United Nations to act. Everyone can help; everyone can contribute; everyone can make a difference.

The Lesson: Walk your talk. Talk is cheap; living your talk is what counts.

The Lesson: Don't through gum wrappers or anything else out the car window.

Ageism

"It's not loving a man that makes life harder for gay guys, it's homophobia. It's not the color of their skin that makes life harder for people of color; it's racism. It's not having vaginas that makes life harder for women, it's sexism. And it's ageism, far more than the passage of time, that makes growing older harder for all of us."

~ Ashton Applewhite, an American writer and activist

I was 24 when I was first on the ballot for state elective office and 28 when elected to the Minnesota House of Representatives in 1974. I was a kid. I had a lot going for me—smarts, lots of energy, solid work ethic, focus, and dedication to public service. But I didn't have much wisdom. I didn't know how the world worked.

I've thought a lot about that over the years. I have come to realize that I was probably too young to serve in the legislature. If it were today, I don't think I would vote for me. The idea that at 28, I had sufficient life experience to make significant public policy decisions for others seems a bit of a stretch.

Wisdom comes with age. As we experience life, we become wiser in the ways of life. Every year I find that I've grown and matured, often in ways that I did not anticipate. I not only know more each year; I understand more. I am more realistic in what is doable and less critical of others who disagree with me. I am still an idealist, but my perspective has tempered. I see more clearly.

I listened to the first democratic presidential primary debate in 2019 on satellite radio. I didn't always know who was speaking, but at times I was proud to be a democrat, and at other moments I was embarrassed and outraged. Some of the younger politicians suggested that it was time to move on to the next generation and elect younger people. The implication was clear—the older candidates were not as capable, were not current with the times, did not represent the new.

These candidates rightly deride racism—the belief that "one race is superior to another, and that all members of a particular race possess characteristics or abilities specific to that race, especially to distinguish it as inferior or superior to another race or races." Racism is an abomination that often results in discrimination and prejudice towards others simply because of the color of skin. It is unjust, irrational, and immoral.

Ageism is like racism. The older or the younger believe that they are superior to the other. Ageism concludes that all members of a certain age bracket possess characteristics or abilities/inabilities specific to that age to distinguish it as superior or inferior.

Unacceptable in any society—at any time!

Ageism is the stereotyping, prejudice, and discrimination against people based on their age. Ageism is widespread and an insidious practice that negatively affects older adults' health and is bad for society. For older people, ageism is an everyday challenge. Overlooked for employment, restricted from social services, and stereotyped in the media, ageism marginalizes and excludes seniors in their communities.

Ageism is everywhere, yet it is the most socially "normalized" of any prejudice. Moreover, it is not widely countered—like racism or sexism. Ageism negatively impacts health and well-being and leads to the marginalization of older folks.

Moreover, ageism is nonsensical. Young people, some still in their teens, can accomplish amazing things and make tremendous contributions to society. So too, folks in their 80's, 90's, and 100's can also accomplish incredible things and make significant contributions to society.

Many cultures hold dear the value that elders play in society. Those cultures honor the wisdom that age and experience bring. Among them are the lessons gained from mistakes. The older we are, the more mistakes we've made. The more mistakes, the greater the learning and the greater the opportunity for wisdom.

It is a national tragedy that we "retire" older folks—those who have learned so much from so many years of mistakes and errors. I appreciate the desire to retire and enjoy life during one's final years. However, today people can live 25 to 30 years or more after they've retired. The result is that society too often is deprived of wisdom-filled years.

Public service could be the beneficiary of this tremendous resource. And elective office might be a good place—school boards, town and city councils, state legislatures, even Congress and the presidency. If you want wise public leaders, don't overlook the older person.

The Lesson: Society needs to keep people fully engaged long after they have "retired."

The Lesson: Discriminating against anyone based on any characteristic over which a person has no control significantly diminishes both the discriminated and the discriminator. Further, it poses a dangerous threat to society because it attempts to reduce the positive influence individuals can contribute.

On SPIRIT LIFE

"What you are is God's gift to you,
what you become is your gift to God."

~ Hans Urs von Balthasar, a Swiss theologian and Catholic priest

The stories, essays, and vignettes in the previous chapters convey important lessons, but not the most important. I have saved the most important for this final chapter.

Faith

"Faith is the realization of what is hoped for,
and evidence of things not seen."

~ Hebrews 11: 1–2

My mother and father taught me Christianity in the Catholic tradition. They took me to mass every Sunday; ensured that I learned about and received the sacraments; sent me to Catholic grade school; encouraged me to attend a Catholic high school; emphasized the importance of loving God and serving others. My grade school teachers taught me the catechism, and my high school teachers taught me about Scripture. At my father's suggestion, I began reading Scripture aloud to the church congregation at Sunday mass when I was 16. I had 13 years of formal religious education in one form or another and enjoyed many theological conversations with Catholic priests and lay ministers.

All my friends were Catholic; I didn't have a non-Catholic girlfriend until I was 19. Even in college, I spent a lot of time at the Newman Center, the primary Catholic gathering facility on campus. All these experiences profoundly impacted my faith journey. And I was proud of my Catholic heritage.

As I wrote earlier in The Foundation, I do not require faith to believe in God. God reveals Itself to me every day in the wonders of creation. However, faith is essential to my belief in life and that Jesus the Christ is the Son of God.

Faith is necessary to believe that "God so loved the world that He gave His only begotten Son." And without faith, it is impossible to comprehend the Holy

Trinity. Three persons in one God? What's that about? And it gets more complicated; Father is the Creator; Jesus is the Creator; the Spirit is the Creator? How is it possible to get your arms around that? There is no doubt; <u>faith is essential to my religious beliefs</u>.

Faith is necessary to comprehend why an all-powerful God would send his son (Itself) into the world as a human being to suffer an excruciating death on a cross at the hands of ignorant mortals whom It created. Faith is required to have any hope of understanding why an all-loving God would create intelligent human beings who end up in poverty and despair amidst war, suffering, and desolation. Faith is essential because there are no rational answers to the Son of Man having nails pounded into his wrists to bleed to death or billions of people suffering from deprivation. It is simply beyond our intellectual capacity to conceive rational reasons for these things. All of this requires faith because they are not empirically, scientifically, or logically apparent.

Faith is a gift granted by the Creator to each of us. "For by grace you have been saved through faith, and this is not from you; it is the gift of God; it is not from works, so no one may boast." Ephesians 8-9.

But faith is a use it or lose it gift. You must exercise it. You must exhibit it. You must live it. You must walk it. Or you risk losing it.

With all that said, I do not now and never have worn my faith on my sleeve. I've tried to live the gospel's teachings but suspect I have failed more than I have succeeded. My most profound belief is that God is merciful, and my hope and prayer are for mercy.

The Lesson: Without faith, it is impossible to embrace Jesus the Christ as the only-begotten Son of the Father.

The Lesson: Without faith, it is impossible to comprehend that "God so loved the world that He gave His only-begotten Son, so that all who believe in him may not perish, but may have eternal life." John 3:16

An Aspiring Christian

Scripture reports that God inspired prophets and saints to help us learn how to live. God knows, as we all know, the human condition is fraught with the negative. Left to our own devises, without the guidance of prophets and saints, humankind would likely self-destruct.

Our human propensity appears to be intent on annihilating our enemies and destroying our planet. That may sound harsh, but why else would so many countries have nuclear weapons that can obliterate entire cities and every living thing in them. What other explanation is there for the US, Russia, and China possessing more nuclear weapons than required to destroy planet earth multiple times over? Why else would we continue to pollute the atmosphere knowing from our personal experience the serious damaging effects of climate change?

Man's self-destructiveness and inhumanity to man knows no bounds. From the earliest days of Cain and Able to crucifixions; to the Inquisition; to Egyptian, Ghanaian, and American slavery; to firing squads; to public lynching; to the electric chair; to the Baton Death March; to Nagasaki and Hiroshima; to wars in Korea and Vietnam; to the twin towers; to wars in Iraq, Afghanistan, and Syria; to mass killings—we continue to perfect our ability to denigrate, disparage, and kill others while we diminish ourselves in the process.

Further, we have elevated greed at the expense of everything and everyone else. Society encourages us to accumulate wealth, buy stuff, consume energy, live for today—all regardless of others—and then society honors those who are the most efficient at acquiring wealth at the expense of others. Governments enact laws to protect wealth and property, beat down movements to conserve natural resources and safeguard creation, and statutorily create entitlements for which future generations must pay—all so we can fulfill our desire to have more stuff today. Society promotes the pleasures of life—sex, food, technology—but does not require they be enjoyed responsibly.

We know all of this is self-destructive and antithetical to enriching our spiritual being.

That is why Jesus is so important.

Scripture explains who Jesus was, how he lived and died, and why he rose from human death. But most importantly, Jesus teaches us how to live life without destroying ourselves in the process. "Be merciful, just as your Father is also merciful. Do not judge, and you will not be judged. Do not condemn, and you will not be condemned. Forgive, and you will be forgiven. Give, and it will be given to you." Luke 6:36-38. And Jesus assures us that whoever perseveres until the end shall be saved.

Throughout his time on earth, Jesus taught us how to live life through his words and his actions. In the Sermon on the Mount, he summarized his teachings. He taught that those who are poor in spirit, the meek, those who mourn, those who hunger and thirst for justice, the merciful, the pure in heart, the peacemakers, those who endure persecution for the sake of justice, and those who are slandered and persecuted in his name, are all blessed. They are the salt of the earth and the light of the world. Matthew 5:2-14. He reminded us that we should not murder but also urged that we not become angry with our brother or sister. He admonished that we not call others "idiot" or "worthless" and encouraged that we reconcile disputes and disagreements with our sisters and brothers. Matthew 5:21-25.

He warned that we neither commit adultery nor have lust in our hearts. Matthew 5:27-28. He told us to keep our word and ensure that when we speak, "Yes" should mean "Yes," and "No" should mean "No." Matthew 5:37. He amended the law of "an eye for an eye, and a tooth for a tooth" by encouraging us not to resist one who is evil but to turn the other cheek. Matthew 5:38-39. If someone asks you to give to him or borrow from you, we should not turn that person away. Further, we should love our enemies, do good to those who hate us, and pray for those who persecute and slander us. Luke 6:27-28.

Jesus also warned that we should not make a public deal out of helping others. He said, "when you give alms, do not choose to sound a trumpet before you, as the hypocrites do in the synagogues and in the towns, so that they may be honored by man. When you give alms, do not let your left hand know what your right hand is doing, so that your almsgiving may be in secret, and your Father, who sees in secret, will repay you." Matthew 6:2-4.

He taught that we should pray in secret, "do not choose many words," and offered the Lord's Prayer as an example of how to pray. One part of this prayer that he emphasized was forgiving others. "For if you forgive men their sins, your heavenly Father also will forgive you your offenses. But if you will not forgive men, neither will your Father forgive you your sins." Matthew 6:5-15.

He explained that there is no value in storing up treasures for ourselves on earth. "For where your treasure is, there also is your heart." And later, "you cannot serve God and wealth." So, he suggests that we not be anxious about life, what we will eat, what we will drink, or what we will wear because life is much more than food and clothing. And he recommends that we not be anxious about tomorrow; "for the future date will be anxious for itself." Matthew 6:19-34.

Jesus advises that we not judge others so that we may not be judged. John 8:1-8. He tells us if we ask, it shall be given; if we seek, we shall find; and if we knock, it shall be opened. "And exactly as you would want people to treat you, treat them also the same." Luke 6:31

Throughout the gospels, Jesus encourages us to share who we are and what we have, to help the poor, feed the hungry, welcome the stranger, clothe the naked, visit the sick and imprisoned, and love our neighbor and our enemy alike. And there is more that is not included here. Some of these teachings may require the interpretation of a learned theologian; however, many of these instructions are clear on their face.

Jesus inspired his followers 2,000 plus years ago and continues to inspire us today. But he never coerced people into following him or forced them to comply with his words. He merely spoke truth with total conviction. And Jesus does not coerce or force anyone today. He does not require governments to legislate or enforce his teachings. Jesus does not demand that governments ban war, feed the hungry, or prohibit abortion. Jesus simply teaches us how to live our human experience so we can fully embrace our spiritual existence. It is up to us if we want to engage in war, help the destitute, or abort our child.

I believe in Jesus the Christ because his teachings are necessary for human creation to have the opportunity to fully live, and to live life fully.

I believe in Jesus the Christ because he shows us how to become genuine spiritual beings.

I believe in Jesus the Christ because he affirmed, "I am the Way, and the Truth, and the Life. No one comes to the Father except through me." John 14:6.

I believe in Jesus, but I too often fail to walk my beliefs. I aspire to walk in the light of the Christ, but I stumble more often than not. I hope someday to be a Christian and am comforted knowing that hope springs eternal.

I believe in the Eucharist—the spiritual food Jesus gave us for our spiritual journey. Scripture records that, "Jesus took bread. And blessing it, he broke it and gave it to them, saying, 'Take. This is my body.' And having taken the cup, giving thanks, he gave it to them. And they all drank from it. And he said to them: 'This is my blood of the new covenant, which shall be shed for many.'" Mark 14:22-24.

However, in the absence of faith, it is impossible to believe in Jesus or the Eucharist. A man-God? Human and divine? Transubstantiation? Eating the body and blood of a fellow human being? How does any of that work?

But if you do believe, Jesus will lead the way. If you believe, then the Eucharist becomes a beautiful gift, one of which we should partake. St. Ambrose wrote, "I must receive (the Eucharist) always, so that it may always forgive my sins. If I sin continually, I must always have a remedy." Pope Francis said the Eucharist "is not a prize for the perfect but a powerful medicine and nourishment for the weak." A spiritual journey without spiritual food and medicine makes the journey more difficult.

I believe in the Spirit, the Lord, the giver of life. Scripture is the method through which God speaks to us. The Spirit inspires Scripture—the word of God. The Spirit has been with us from before the dawn of human creation.

When Jesus died and ascended into heaven, it continued to be necessary for God to live among us to constantly inspire those who choose to love and follow his teaching. Prophets and saints—they too are inspired by the Spirit to live good lives, and they help show us the way of Jesus as we prepare for our spiritual eternity. And God—the Father, the Son, and the Spirit—is with us every day. "For wherever two or three are gathered in my name, there am I, in their midst." Matthew 18:20.

But faith is essential to grasp the tremendous significance of the Spirit.

Jesus was clear on the importance of the Spirit: "But when He, the Spirit of truth, comes, He will guide you into all the truth... He will glorify Me because it is from Me that He will receive what He will make known to you." John 16:13-14. "The fruit of the Spirit is love, joy, peace, forbearance, kindness, goodness, faithfulness, gentleness and self-control. Against such things there is no law.... Since we live by the Spirit, let us keep in step with the Spirit." Galatians 5:22-23, 25.

I believe Jesus founded the Christian church during his lifetime and that all Christians are part of his church. Over the centuries, Christians developed different denominations that allow for an array of faith expressions, worship services, and religious experiences. However, no denomination, sect, or faith community has a lock on the truth or the one or only way to worship, love, or serve the Christ. The human condition simply does not allow that luxury. We are all creatures prone to error. Further, non-Christian faith traditions that recognize and honor the Creator and teach the responsibility to love our neighbor and our enemies, also support and enable their believers on their faith journey. For, as Matthew recorded, "Not all who say to me, 'Lord, Lord,' will enter into the kingdom of heaven. But whoever does the will of my Father, who is in heaven, the same shall enter into the kingdom of heaven." Matthew 7:21

With all that being said, I still have many more questions. Even with faith, I share doubts. I struggle with both the seen and the unseen.

Christian theologians teach that higher intelligence—beings who are self-aware—is the essence of being ensouled. All humans are ensouled; each of us is a spiritual being. That makes sense to me.

However, if God created self-aware beings of higher intelligence on other planets, how does Jesus the Christ relate to them?

With 100 billion galaxies and perhaps 1,700,000,000,000,000,000,000 planets in the observable Universe, it lacks credibility to argue there can be no other habitable planets with intelligent life—those who are ensouled. So, we ask: was Jesus' incarnation solely for humans on planet Earth? Or did Jesus live and die for all ensouled life throughout the universe? If so, why was Earth the only planet chosen? Or is it the only chosen planet?

Is sinfulness inherent to intelligent life? Or are humans the only ensouled beings who separated from the Creator through sin? Are we the only sinners—the lost sheep—the ones who need saving? Does Jesus teach and save all ensouled life or just humans?

If other ensouled beings are also sinners or need to learn how to become spiritual beings, could there have been multiple Incarnations?

Is Jesus the only begotten son of the Father, or is he one of many sons and daughters, all of whom serve our extraterrestrial brothers and sisters?

The Lesson: Questions abound. Answers are too often too few and too obscure. Faith is the only solution.

The Lesson: I have never been comfortable calling myself a Christian; although, I aspire to become one. Someday, I may grow in sufficient faith and virtue to be called a Christian. In the meantime, I must be content with the aspiration of becoming a Christian.

The Lesson: Each of us is a work in progress. As scripture implies, God is not done with any of us yet. Philippians 1:6

Spiritual Beings

"The function of prayer is not to influence God, but rather to change the nature of the one who prays."

~ Soren Kierkegaard, a Danish philosopher, theologian,
poet, social critic, and religious author

As I've pondered my personal existence, I've realized that I am much more than my body. I am much more than limbs, organs, and a brain. There is something about me that is beyond the physical—beyond body and mind. Something that exists independent of my body and mind.

Because of that, I can't contemplate my existence ending when my heart stops beating and my brain stops functioning. Existential death is outside my realm of imagination—I simply cannot imagine not existing. Some define this eternal existence as the soul. If that is the case, then I am my soul; my soul defines who I am.

I believe my life is eternal, and yours is too. Once we are conceived, our souls live forever—for all eternity. Although, what that existence might be like is unknown. Belief in an eternal soul requires faith; it is not empirically or scientifically evident because of the Creator's presence.

However, my faith in eternal life is based on rational thought.

Pierre Teilhard de Chardin, a 20th-century French author, philosopher, paleontologist, geologist, and Catholic Jesuit priest, taught, "We are not human beings in search of a spiritual experience. We are spiritual beings immersed in a human experience."

I subscribe to Teilhard's teaching.

Assuming life exists beyond human death, and assuming life is eternal, our human life lasts for a nanosecond compared to eternity. Given that relationship, it is rational to conclude that we are spiritual beings who are currently having a human experience.

Reflect on that possibility for a moment.

For me, it puts everything into a logical perspective.

I believe Teilhard accurately describes our common existence. That is why there is no reason to fear human death.

But then I ask, "If we are spiritual beings, what is the purpose of human life?"

"Why are we here?"

"What does it all mean?"

These are questions that have been asked throughout the millennia.

Scripture teaches that we are to love God above all things and to love our neighbor as ourselves. A compelling description of love is a combination of service and sacrifice. St. Francis of Assisi said it well, "when you leave this earth, you can take with you nothing that you have received, only what you have given—a full heart, enriched by honest service, love, sacrifice, and courage."

These are the purposes of life; the answers to why we are here: Service to others— God's creation—is the purpose. Protecting God's creation—our neighbors, our neighborhoods, our planet, and the universe—is the purpose. Loving our enemies—and thereby not destroying God's creation—is the purpose. It is through these activities that we become enriched and enlightened spiritual beings.

Scripture attempts to explain some things through stories. One story is about Adam and Eve, an apple, a serpent, and the resulting "original sin." A man and a woman sin, and that sin forced them and all humans out of the utopian Garden of Eden. This sin was so egregious, so terrible, so heinous that it could not be forgiven, save heavenly intervention—Jesus dying on the cross.

This is an interesting story; one easily remembered and easily told. But this story of original sin and punishment lacks credibility if God is all-loving and all-merciful—both today and when Adam and Eve allegedly ate the apple.

I suspect the apple story was recounted because some explanation needed to be passed along the generations to rationalize human life's pain and suffering. In the absence of the story of original sin—man dissing his creator—God would likely be perceived as an "unloving being" given the enormous struggles of daily life. Why create humans to have them suffer so and then die. Original sin explains this away. Humans committed the original sin—it was man-made. All of life's struggles are a result of this one sin. Thus, all of life's pain and suffering are man-made.

So that gets God off the hook. God is not "unloving." God is simply "just." Man disobeyed God, and God punished. That is rational by human standards.

But God is not merely all-powerful. God is also all-loving, and love requires mercy. God sends his only son to account for man's grievous sin. God demonstrates his universal and eternal love and offers forgiveness through the cross.

But how could an all-loving and merciful God exile all humanity for the sinful act of a single man and woman? If God is love and merciful today, why was God not love and forgiving at the time of Adam? And if God was all-powerful and all-loving when Adam and Eve ate the forbidden fruit, how could God exile them from the garden? Where was mercy? Where was love? And why was it necessary for God to submit his son to the cross to atone for Adam's and

Eve's sin? How could that one sin be so terrible that God had to bleed-out on a cross?

A possible alternative explanation for why God sent his Son to earth is to teach humans how to live life and become enriched spiritual beings. Jesus repeatedly tells us that he is a teacher. His teachings explain how to live with each other in harmony. He shows us how to live in communion with all creation and the Creator. He instructs us how to prepare for eternal life. He encourages us to follow him and says, "I am the way, the truth, and the life." John 14:6. And it is our belief in Jesus that guides us on our journey as we follow him and learn to become spiritual beings.

I'm not declaring this explanation is the actual reason God sent his Son to earth, but it may help those who struggle with the Apple story.

The Lesson: Our spiritual life is more important than anything else.

The Lesson: The purpose of life is to love God and serve others, and in the process, learn how to become a spiritual being. Everything else does not matter much.

The Lesson: Life's a blur, until it turns totally dark. Then you see light.

Audacity of Belief

"The desolate and impassable land will rejoice, the place of solitude will exult, and it will flourish like the lily. It will spring up and blossom, and it will exult with rejoicing and praising."

Isaiah 35:1-2

Given how small and insignificant planet Earth and humans are in the universe, I've often wondered: doesn't God have better things to do than to worry about or pay attention to each of us?

Given the billions upon billions of potentially inhabitable planets and the tens of quadrillions of potentially ensouled beings inhabiting those planets, is it not extraordinarily audacious to believe that the all-powerful, all-mighty, all-loving, and all-merciful Creator spends any time at all thinking about you or me?

Given the Creator's transcendence, how can we possibly believe It expends any time considering our prayers for insignificant asks or pleas for forgiveness of repetitious sins?

How arrogant are we to believe that the Creator focuses such attention on us, either collectively or individually?

God sent His only Son to save us and instruct us how to be spiritual beings—really?

Yet, that is what Christians believe.

It may be audacious to believe that the Creator knows even the number of hairs on our head, but that is what Jesus infers. "But even the very hairs of your head have all been numbered. Therefore, do not be afraid." Luke 12:7

Christianity is an audacious faith.

The Lesson: One or more sextillion of potentially inhabitable planets and billions of sextillions of ensouled beings created lends enormous credence to the belief that an all-powerful and all-knowing Creator could be aware of and attentive to each of us individually. The mere magnitude of creation affirms the unimaginable and incalculable capability of God to do all things and all things simultaneously.

The Lesson: We may not be able to understand or even imagine the magnitude of creation, but that's okay. Believing that which cannot be understood or imagined is the essence of faith. *"No mind has imagined the things that God has prepared for those who love him." 1 Corinthians 2:9.*

Use It or Lose It

"To the world you might be one person, but to one person you just might be the world."

Claudia Minden Weisz, an American poet and writer

I remember meeting a man on a Chicago street when I was in the city on business. As I walked by, he asked, "Is there a church nearby?"

Without breaking stride, I told him, "I'm not from here. I don't know where anything is."

"You're the first person who's spoken to me today," he called out.

I slowed, then stopped, turned around, looked at the man, and finally asked, "How can I be helpful?"

His eyes filled with tears. James told me he was out of work. He had recently burned his hand in a fire. The scars were fresh. He had two kids—a six-year-old boy and a four-month-old girl. They had no food. That morning he had hiked three miles on foot to the city welfare office; he didn't have money for the bus. The government worker could not help him today. There were forms to fill out. Time periods to wait. His kids needed help now.

I asked him what he needed to get through the day.

"Some food and diapers for my baby," he said, "that's all I need. There's a Walgreens right up the street."

"Well, let's go then," I said.

As we walked into Walgreens, I was unsure what I'd gotten myself into. James moved quickly, as if he needed to get this done before I changed my mind.

I kept the receipt from that day to remember what James selected from the shelves because it surprised me so. He got two boxes of cereal, two half-gallons of milk, a loaf of white bread, a jar of peanut butter, a twenty-four count of disposable diapers, baby wash, a container of soft soap, two boxes of laundry detergent, a package of bar soap, and some Vaseline for his burnt hand.

As we left the store, James turned to me and said, "I've gotta ask for one more thing."

"What's that?"

"Could you give me some money to put me on the bus?"

I gave him some money and said, "This will get you a ride home and a meal for today." James stood staring at me for a moment, then broke into a huge smile. We embraced, and he said, "Thank you, brother."

"You're welcome."

James began walking toward the bus stop and then turned back and said, "I guess I did find the church today. God bless you."

I don't tell this story out of any sense of virtuousness. My actions were not an enormous kindness; this was a simple act of service we are all called to exhibit—every day.

Jesus taught us, "Whoever asks of you, give to him." Matthew 5:42; Luke 6:30. In Proverbs, we are told, "Whoever gives to the poor, shall not be in need. Whoever despises his petition will suffer scarcity." Proverbs 28:27. Again, "Let us not love in words only, but in works and in truth." 1 John 3:18. Scripture is replete with instructions that we care for the poor and love one another through service—every day.

It's not productive to ask yourself if the guy begging on the freeway off-ramp or the homeless woman on the street will use the money to buy booze rather than food. If you ask that question, you're likely not to give them anything out of concern that you might be enabling their addiction, or it's a con, or they'll waste the money anyway.

You give to the beggar because you don't know if he has a four-month-old baby at home. You don't know if she has a burnt hand. You don't know if he's sought help from the government, but his family can't wait for all the forms to clear. You don't know if she knows how to seek help from the government or fill out the forms.

You'll probably never know what the money will be used for because the odds are that you don't have the time to find out. But that's not the point. The objective is not to know how she will use the money; the objective is to love her. Moreover, the money in your pocket is not yours anyway. It all belongs to God. We are simply stewards of Its creation.

We exercise our faith when we give to those who ask; help others in need; intervene when others are in danger or are being bullied or persecuted; when we speak up about and try to root out injustice; when we wage peace; and when we love our neighbors and our enemies. We risk losing faith when we are callous toward others. When we are suspicious of the beggar. When we discount another due to their religious beliefs. When we harbor bias in our hearts because of another's skin color, race, ethnicity, gender, or sexual orientation. And when we hate our enemy. Like many things in life, faith must be exercised. It is not unlike body muscle. When you fail to exercise it, you risk losing it.

The Lesson: You give $20 to the guy asking for money on the freeway off-ramp for two reasons. First, to help ease his misery. Second, to help you keep your faith because faith is a use it or lose it gift.

The Lesson: We share who we are by sharing what we have.

God said, "No"

~ Mother Theresa, an Albanian-Indian Roman Catholic
nun and missionary

One day after school at St. John's Catholic School, one of you told me about your religion class that day. Your teacher was explaining prayer, and she used an example of her praying for a parking spot, which God found for her. She told your class that you can pray for anything, even a parking spot at the shopping mall, when you can't find one. Or that's how you explained it to me. You asked if that was true.

I don't remember what I said then, but it reminds me of a joke I heard later. A guy prayed to God to find him a parking spot so he wouldn't be late for an important meeting. Immediately after that, he rounded a row in a parking lot and saw an open place. He said, "Never mind, God. I just found one."

Prayer is an integral part of our spiritual journey. Jesus prayed to the Father often, suggesting that we too ought to pray often. Jesus also taught us how to pray. He said:

> "When you pray, enter into your room, and having shut the door, pray to your father in secret, and your father, who sees in secret, will repay you. And when praying, do not choose many words, as the pagans do. For they think that by their ex-

cess of words they might be heeded. Therefore, do not choose to imitate them. For your father knows what your needs may be, even before you ask him. Therefore, you shall pray in this way: Our Father, who is in heaven: May your name be kept holy. May your kingdom come. May your will be done, as in heaven, so also on earth. Give us this day our life-sustaining bread. And forgive us our debts, as we also forgive our debtors. And lead us not into temptation. But free us from evil. Amen." Matthew 6:6-13

Much has been written about prayer and what we can and should pray for. Three statements about prayer influence me. The first is from the New Testament, 1 John 5:14. "And this is the confidence which we have toward God: that no matter what we shall request, in accord with his will, he hears us." Of course, the keywords are "in accord with his will."

The second is from Kierkegaard, the prominent 19th-century Lutheran theologian whom I quoted previously, "The function of prayer is not to influence God, but rather to change the nature of the one who prays."

The third is an example of a prayer offered by Pope Francis. He said, "You pray for the hungry. Then you feed them. That's how prayer works."

For decades, I have prayed for wisdom, so I might know what I am to do with my life. I've prayed for strength so that I could do that which I am supposed to do. And I pray for grace, so that I may do well that which I am to do.

I also pray for others that they might withstand the pain from ill health, that they can deal constructively when calamity or disaster strikes, and that they are comforted upon the death of a loved one.

Recently, I found a piece of poetry that reflects my understanding of prayer. *God said, 'No'* was written by Claudia Minden Weisz.

"I asked God to take away my pride.

God said, 'No.' He said it was not for him to take away, but for me to give up.

"I asked God to make my handicapped child whole. **God said, 'No.'** He said her spirit is whole, and her body is only temporary.

"I asked God to grant me patience. **God said, 'No.'** He said patience is a by-product of tribulation. It isn't granted; it is earned.

"I asked God to give me happiness. **God said, 'No.'** He said He gives blessings. Happiness is up to me.

"I asked God to spare me pain. **God said, 'No.'** He said suffering draws us apart from worldly cares and brings us closer to Him.

"I asked God to make my spirit grow. **God said, 'No.'** He said I must grow on my own. But He will prune me to make me fruitful.

"I asked God for all things that I might enjoy life. **God said, 'No.'** He said he will give me life so that I may enjoy all things.

"I ask God to help me love others, as much as He loves me. **God said... 'Ahhhh, finally you have the idea.'"**

The Lesson: Prayer is important.

The Lesson: Most important is what we pray for.

Why I Worship in Church

"The Christian does not think God will love us because we are good, but that God will make us good because He loves us."

~ C.S. Lewis, a British writer and lay theologian

I attend Sunday mass at two different parishes, Espiritu Santo in Safety Harbor, Florida, and St. Odilia in Shoreview, Minnesota. I have been a member of both communities for several years and lector at both, something I've been doing since I was 16 when my father and I were invited to read Scripture during mass at St. Rose of Lima in Roseville.

I don't agree with everything the Catholic Church teaches, proclaims, or requires. And I completely understand those who might have been raised Catholic and have left the church because of the sex abuse scandal or other issues.

Given my Irish heritage, I consider myself an Irish Catholic rather than a Roman Catholic. I define an Irish Catholic as one who expects the church to be correct 60 or 70 percent of the time and subscribes to 60 to 70 percent of what the church demands. That makes remaining a Catholic easier.

But I try to attend mass on Sundays where I am spiritually fulfilled by the opportunity to:

- Worship the Creator in a formal setting.
- Pray in a structured manner.

- Be nourished by the Eucharist.
- Learn from talented homilists.
- Participate in community—community for me is like a plant-growing medium.
- Listen to scripture.
- Read scripture to the congregation.
- Enjoy the music.
- Appreciate the quiet time and the occasion for reflection and meditation.

Following is an article I was asked to write for the *St. Odilia Messenger*—the parish newsletter—a few years ago. I share it with you so you can better understand why I worship in church on Sundays.

I've attended mass at hundreds of churches in the metropolitan area, throughout the US, and around the world. I've been a registered member at four Catholic parishes during the past 65 years, an experience that can best be described as rocky. I served on the parish council at one—that caused me to question my faith. We sent our kids to catholic schools in compliance with how my wife and I were educated, but that too turned out to challenge my faith rather than enhance it. Then my wife left the Catholic Church due to the hierarchy's mishandling of the priest sex scandal. All those events put me in a tumble that was difficult to navigate.

I wasn't willing to leave the Catholic Church, nor was I going to let the church adversely interfere with my spiritual life. I decided to continue attending mass and receiving the Eucharist—two activities essential for my well-being—but I vowed I would never again become a parish member or get involved with church politics.

I found a little parish not far from our home that permitted me to worship the Creator and reflect on Holy Scripture without dealing with all the garbage. I became friends with the pastor, Greg Skrpeck—an excellent homilist—and some parishioners. All was well for several years—until the archdiocese shut down this little church. "Merger" was the euphemistic term used to describe the destruction of a community of people who joined together to worship God and enjoy a common faith and spiritual journey.

I was devastated.

I went from church to church for a while but did not find comfort. Then I stopped attending altogether. After several months, the spiritual emptiness was overwhelming. My sister, Claudette, told me that the pastor at St. Odilia gave excellent homilies and suggested I give it a try. I was reluctant. We had been members at St. O's before—before and during the pedophile mess. But I was so hungry that I was willing to do anything.

I went to Sunday mass one summer morning and was awed by the homily and delighted by the music, which I'd come to enjoy years before. Perhaps my sister was onto something. I went back the next Sunday in hopes that I might hear the same priest, and I lucked out. As it turned out, Father Rask preached for six weeks in a row that summer because his assistant was in Mexico studying Spanish. Every Sunday, the clarity and depth of his scriptural message fed my soul and inspired my heart. The music enriched my being, and visiting after mass with friends from long ago offered great joy.

I've worshiped at St. Odilia every Sunday I've been in town for the past four years. This year, in violation of my vow, I even became an official member. Although I have no intention of getting involved with anything that looks like church politics, I've offered to lector—something I started when I was still in my teens but haven't done for many years—and I've attended a bible class.

It is sometimes important to remind ourselves of our good fortune. That is the purpose of this message. Phil Rask and Doug Pierce are outstanding preachers—grounded in scripture, remarkably relevant, and consistently inspiring. Dan Perry and his choirs lift our spirits—clearly among the best in the country. And all the volunteers who help every Sunday—servers, Eucharistic ministers, lectors, greeters, mass coordinators, and our wonderful Deacons—they so enrich the service. We have the whole package. All who worship at St. Odilia are genuinely blest.

I could write something similar about Espiritu Santo in Safety Harbor. It is a welcoming community, the pastor, Len Piotrowski, is a terrific homilist, and the opportunity for prayerful meditation is present. I am blessed to be able to be a member of two wonderful Catholic parishes.

The Lesson: It is spiritually beneficial to have a regular and reliable place to worship the Creator, listen to Scripture, reflect on the meaning of life, and be a part of a Christian community.

The Lesson: When your expectations of an institution are low, it is easier to accept serious wrongdoing when the leaders of the institution inevitably fail to conduct themselves consistent with its stated purpose.

Mortality

"I shall pass through this world but once. Any good, therefore, that I can show to any human being, let me do it now. Let me not defer nor neglect it, for I shall not pass this way again."

~ Stephen Grellet, a prominent Quaker missionary

As a young man, I did not spend much time thinking about death or my mortality. However, in my late 20's, I wondered what my father thought about his mortality. He was in his mid-60's, and although death certainly was not imminent, I was curious whether he ever thought about dying and how he felt about it.

I never asked him, although I thought about how I might approach the subject on several occasions. My curiosity was eclipsed by my stronger desire not to cause him any suffering or pain. I assumed he feared death and that he simply put it out of his mind.

When I turned 60, I concluded I was probably wrong about my father. If he was anything like me, and I'm told we have many things in common, he thought about his death, his human mortality, and the meaning and purpose of life. Although death is by no means foremost on my mind, as I get older and more of my friends and extended family die (15 died before their 60th birthday), I think of death more often and focus more intently on making a positive difference with my life.

I do not doubt that death is final. It is the end of our human existence. Death is defined as "the cessation of all biological functions that sustain a living organism." And death causes enormous sadness and a deep sense of loss for those left behind. I know my death will cause grief among my family and friends. Even with all my faults and peculiarities, they will miss me. Some will cry; some will feel an emptiness in their being. For some, the sorrow will be relatively brief; for others, grief will linger. Nearly 30 years later, I still mourn for my father. I think about my mother often too. And I pray for all my friends who died before their time. I miss them all.

Moreover, I have known death as close and personal as is possible; my first son died in childbirth when I was 20 years old. Although he and I never embraced or spoke a word, he touched my heart forever. The pain of his death and the loss of what might have been are never-ending.

With that said, I do not fear my death. Upon reflection, I now suspect my father did not fear his death either. My father and I believe in the Almighty Creator, who made all that is seen and unseen. Moreover, we believe the Creator made us to spend eternity in Its presence.

Now eternity is a really long time—it goes on forever and ever and ever. When comparing our lives to the course of eternity, we live on earth but for an instant —it is extremely short. While on her death bed, after 92 years of a full life, my mother said to me, "Life is so short." I concur.

One morning in 2018, after doing my back-stretching exercises, I experienced excruciating pain in my mid-back. The soreness came unannounced. It was intermittent, but at times breathtaking, paralyzing my entire body—a 10 on a 10-point pain scale.

Saron recommended that I go to urgent care, and I took her advice. Jake drove me. By then, the pain was radiating to my chest. Urgent care referred me to the ER at the nearby hospital. My pulse was 35, and my blood pressure was

220 over 95. The ER docs told me that I might be having a heart attack. Their faces and actions conveyed serious concern. And I too became concerned and frightened.

The docs needed to do some tests. An orderly rolled me on a gurney from the ER to the MRI. As I lay on my back and watched the white ceiling tiles and lights pass overhead, I contemplated death—my death.

I had said that I had no fear of death, but those were mere words. This was different—this was the first-time my death had crept up in close proximity. Now, it appeared as if death could be a real possibility.

As I pondered that final eventuality, I thought about what death might be like. And a calm enveloped me. There was clarity, but no fear. I felt anticipation. Death offered a new spiritual adventure. I recalled the scripture words, "The eye has not seen, and the ear has not heard, nor has it entered into the heart of man, what God has prepared for those who love him." 1 Corinthians 2:9

I've been a sinner all my life; albeit, in a constant struggle to do what is right. I've repented, asking forgiveness, and vowing to amend my ways, even though I broke my pledge over and over. But I love my Creator and have tried to keep my commitment to sin no more.

I know God loves me. So, I looked at this thing called death as a beautiful opportunity—the next step in my spiritual existence—what a wonderful, peaceful embrace.

As it turned out, there was nothing wrong with my heart. After a night in the hospital, all the tests proved negative—"no heart event." The doctors did not know what caused the back pain, but they prescribed a couple of over-the-counter pain meds and sent me home.

But this "near-death" experience was a gift. I had often thought that I did not fear death, but I really did not know. Now I knew. I could embrace death.

Death had no hold on me. Death was not something I needed to fear; it was the next great adventure—something everyone will eventually experience.

However, I do fear judgment. Christian theology teaches that each of us will be held accountable for how we lived our human existence.

But I have tremendous hope. Jesus said, "Whoever hears my word, and believes in him who sent me, has eternal life, and he does not go into judgment, but instead he crosses from death into life." John 5:24.

The Lesson: Death is not to be feared; it is merely the passing of this life to another.

The Lesson: When you free yourself from the fear of death, life opens up. You can embrace the ecstasy of living to its fullest without fear of anything.

The Lesson: Mourn me when I am gone, but more importantly, carry on the vital work we have started together.

Funerals

Funerals are such sad times. The loss of a loved one is the most difficult of life's experiences. Attending funerals is difficult, too—what to say? How to comfort?

When my dearest friend, Bob Hudnut, died after a long and difficult hospitalization, I learned he had decided not to have a funeral, and he so instructed his family. He didn't want people to make a big deal out of either his life or death.

Bob was my boss when I worked for MPIRG in 1973; he was on sabbatical at the time from his role as a Presbyterian pastor. He became my mentor, and we were great friends for 45 years. Rev. Robert Hudnut wrote multiple religious books, one of which was *Practical Grace - How to Find God in the Everyday*. Among the profound experiences in my life was when he gave me a copy of *Practical Grace* over lunch one day and suggested I look at the dedication. He had dedicated his book to me. He wrote: "For Bud Philbrook, exemplar of grace." I was blown away!

On another occasion, I confided in Bob that I had a tough decision to make and sought his counsel. He told me to "pray long and hard."

I asked him, "Why do I need to pray long? Doesn't God hear me right away?"

"Yes," he said. "God hears you immediately. You pray long and hard for you to hear God."

Bob and I had lunch nearly every month for 20 plus years—assuming we were both in town—and we talked about virtually everything, but he never told me or even suggested that he might not have a funeral.

I was pissed when I learned this. Bob denied me the opportunity to say goodbye.

Friends need to say goodbye to you. Friends want to tell others why you were friends; why they loved you; what they admired about you; the great and silly things you did together. Friends want to hear others' stories about you—perhaps a perspective of which they were unaware. Friends need to comfort each other. Friends need closure.

Bob was an extremely generous and thoughtful man. He would never intentionally hurt anyone, especially a friend—especially me. I understand he decided not to have a public funeral because he didn't want to burden his family and friends. He didn't want anyone to make a fuss over him. He was simply trying to be respectful.

Bob was wrong! Funerals are not a burden. Funerals do not cost too much money or take up too much time. Funerals allow people to grieve and to say goodbye so they can get on with their lives.

The Lesson: Funerals are for the living, not the deceased.

The Lesson: Comfort the living by telling them you are sorry for their loss and that their loved one lives in the love of the Creator.

The Lesson: I hope all my family, friends, colleagues, and coworkers from around the world can attend my funeral so they can celebrate, mourn, enjoy each other's company, comfort each other, tell stories—the good, the bad, and the ugly—and say goodbye. And then go back to work and get on with your lives.

Our Journey Home

"Joy is the infallible sign of the presence of God."

~ Pierre Teilhard de Chardin

At a younger age, life is merely another day. But as you get older, you know that each day is one day less.

Less of what? Why are we concerned about one more day?

If we believe life is eternal; if we believe life eternal is spent in the presence of God; if we believe "The eye has not seen, and the ear has not heard, nor has it entered into the heart of man, what God has prepared for those who love him;" why do we want to live this human life as long as possible?

My dear friend, Rev. Bob Hudnut, fought death until the end. I asked him about this years before he became ill, and he told me something to the effect that "people want to live long lives because life is good."

I've often wondered about this. I have known men and women of faith who feared dying. Men and women who believed that they would experience a spiritual life well beyond their imagination, yet they wanted to live this human life as long as possible.

Did they simply fear death? If so, why?

Perhaps we want to live a long life because, while we hope life is eternal, deep down, we are skeptical.

Perhaps we fear that everything may end when it all goes dark.

I do not share that fear.

To my core, I know there is a Creator who reveals Itself us every day through the Universe, through the complexity of all creation, and through friendships and joy life brings, even amidst its hardships. I know that the Creator is all-intelligent, all-meaningful, and all-loving. It would not have created me, or you, for no purpose. While I fear the physical pain that may precede death, I embrace my death as a part of my life. I welcome it because I know I am a spiritual being, and through death, I am going home.

Fear is such a debilitating emotion. Where there is Faith, there is little fear. Faith overcomes fear. When there is no death to fear, there is no fear. Franklin Roosevelt taught us that "the only thing to fear is fear itself." There is wisdom in those words.

The Lesson: I shall never die. My body will die—it will rot away—"from dust to dust." But that which is me—my soul, my spirit, my essence—will never die. And neither will you!

The Lesson: Life, as we know it, is a temporary stop where we spend time in human form simply to get ready for eternity. Our human experience is merely the preparation stage for our eternal spiritual existence, a space where we learn how to become a spiritual being.

Getting Ready to Go

"Life is like a roll of toilet paper.
The closer it gets to the end, the faster it goes."

Andy Rooney, an American radio and television writer and humorist

The Boy Scouts motto is "Be prepared." I was taught this at a young age. In my later years, it has occurred to me that part of being prepared is getting ready to go. Although none of us know the day or the hour, I will embark on my new journey at some point in the next 20 hours, 20 days, or 20 years. In many ways, I have been preparing for this journey for most of my life. But now, I need to start packing my bags.

St. Augustine wrote, "Live in such a way that when you die, you don't die." I think he means that we should always be preparing for death by living a good life according to our conscience and the tenants of scripture. Others have offered that we "seize the moment to do good while you can." Both are excellent advice.

But I feel the urge to prepare for something more. I have tried to live a good and worthy life, and although my sins are many, I know God forgives me. My life today is full of body, mind, and soul, but not in their final balance. Today my life is mostly about body and mind. They require food, feel pain, need exercise, desire comfort, ingest medicines, seek entertainment, become sad, stimulate creativity, enjoy the wonder, imagine the future, remember the past, encourage others, pursue justice, wage peace, and support children. The demands and desires of my body and mind consume every hour.

Now, I must contemplate living without my body and mind. Or, more precisely, living life fully as a spiritual being. This is not a mere intellectual or emotional exercise. I need to actively prepare for the moment when breath will no longer be necessary to live—I need to prepare for an exclusive spiritual existence.

In part, writing this book has helped me "pack my bags." Throughout these pages, I have reexamined my days, what I think my life has been about, and who I believe I have become. This examination has forced me to think about and focus on my spiritual being. I am deeply grateful to each of you for inspiring me to write this book because it has helped me get ready to go.

The Lesson: I know I must do more to get my bags packed, even though I am unsure of all that will fully entail. However, knowing that I must get ready in a more thorough way is a beautiful realization and excites my awareness of life to come.

The Lesson: Writing this book has offered me a deep sense of gratitude for all the people I have known and the experiences I have enjoyed. Those, too, are an integral part of getting ready to go.

Immortality

"How body from spirit slowly does unwind,
until we are pure spirit at the end."

~ Theodore Roethke, an American poet

An Lin was the beautiful, smart, and loving daughter of your mother and my dear friends, An Wei and Mary An. She worked for several years with our volunteers who served in Xi'an, China. Then, An Lin had the opportunity to study in Michigan. While there, she learned how to drive a car, took her driver's test, and got her license. One November day, on her way to school, An Lin died in a car accident. Her mother and father were devastated.

Due to An Lin's love for America and her parents' commitment to promoting Sino-American relations, they had her funeral service and burial in St. Paul, Minnesota. An Wei asked me to offer the eulogy for An Lin, which I concluded with the following piece of poetry written by Henry Van Dyke.

Gone From My Sight

"I am standing upon the seashore.

A ship at my side spreads her white sails to the morning breeze and starts for the blue ocean.

She is an object of beauty and strength, and I stand and watch until at last, she hangs like a speck of white cloud just where the sun and the sky come down to mingle with each other.

Then someone at my side says, 'There she goes!'

Gone where?

Gone from my sight—that is all. She is just as large in mast and hull and spar as she was when she left my side and just as able to bear her load of freight to the places of destination.

Her diminished size is in me, not in her.

And just at the moment when someone at my side says, 'There she goes!', there are other eyes watching her coming and other voices ready to take up the glad shout, 'Here she comes!'"

The Lesson: We are indeed spiritual beings who are currently having a human experience.

Citizens of Heaven

*"The eye has not seen, and the ear has not heard, nor has it
entered into the heart of man, what God has prepared for
those who love him."*

~ 1 Corinthians 2:9

If we are spiritual beings who live for eternity, it is reasonable to ask, "where do
we live eternally?" Christian theologians submit that after our body dies, our
soul resides in either heaven or hell—heaven if we have been faithful and done
good, and hell if we've failed to believe and done bad.

Of course, no one knows what heaven is or even if it's a place, or if there is a
hell. Scripture teaches that heaven is beyond our imagination.

However, it can be helpful to embrace the poetry of a place called heaven, and
I do so here.

There's an old story about heaven and hell. In hell, everyone is emaciated—
literally starving. Not starving to death; they are already dead—but suffering
the severe excruciating pains that extended hunger brings. In the midst of this
anguish, there are humongous bowls of sweet-smelling fresh soup containing
all the delightful and flavorful nutritious and filling food you could imagine.
But they cannot eat the soup. The extended stretched handles on their heavy
wooden spoons are too long and onerous to get the soup to their mouths. So,
they starve.

In heaven, there are the same giant bowls of sweet-smelling nutritious soup. And they have the same long-stretched wooden-handled spoons. But everyone in heaven is well fed, happy, and healthy. What is the difference? In heaven, they use the long-handled spoons to feed each other.

If there is a heaven or hell, this story clearly depicts in which place I'd rather be.

I do not know if there is a heaven or hell. However, I do think that if there is a heaven, it is not a reward for a life well-led. I don't think "doing good" adds points to our score that determines our heavenly reward, and conversely, "doing bad" does not subtract points.

Believing is all that is necessary. Scripture teaches this well: "For God so loved the world that he gave his only-begotten Son; so that all who believe in him may not perish, but may have eternal life." John 3:16. Jesus tells us, "Whoever believes in me has eternal life." John 6:47.

With that said, acts of service condition our spiritual being, much like exercise conditions our human body. The more good we do and the less selfish we are, the more spiritually healthy we become. Each time we care for another, give of ourselves, extend a hand, or embrace our enemy, we enrich our spiritual being. The stronger our spiritual life, the stronger our faith. And faith is essential to eternal life.

Conversely, when we take more than we give, idly observe the suffering of others, inflict pain on others, do not stand up against injustice, try to destroy our enemy, do not help others in need, deny the community what belongs to the community, or do not protect God's creation, then we denigrate our spiritual being. Jesus said, "As you did it for one of these, the least of my brethren, you did it for me." Matthew 25:40.

I don't think God cares about all the bad things we've done in the past. I believe God cares about where our heart is today. God is always open to us—to our becoming new. We just need to repent.

Read the parable of the prodigal son, Luke 15:11–32. Jesus describes the process of repentance and the role of the merciful father. The son leaves his father and squanders his inheritance. Later, he acknowledges that he messed up. He returns home and expresses sorrow to his father for messing up, committing to do his best not to mess up again. He experiences a change of heart that results in new behavior. That is repentance. The father forgives him and serves a feast.

Initially, the son appears to be the focus of this story. But it is the father who is the center of this parable. The father shows mercy, forgiveness, and joy. The son represents sinners—all of us. The father symbolizes the Creator—the merciful, forgiving, and joyful God.

Our human experience is the time when we prepare ourselves for eternal life with the Creator. Life is full of occasions when we can experience a change of heart that results in new behavior. Life offers repeated opportunities to repent. We can change how and what we do anytime we sufficiently desire.

How repentant we are at the time our body dies may determine where we spend eternity, but more importantly, how we spend eternity. Given the eternity we will spend in "heaven," and the relatively short time we spend on earth, our "heavenly citizenship" is immeasurably more important than anything we do on earth, especially the money we make, the citizenship of the country to which we belong, or the flag we salute.

We must be wary of overemphasizing our loyalty to worldly things, dreams of a better life, an earthly flag, our ancestry, or our geographical country, at risk of underemphasizing devotion to the Creator. We must not be overly loyal to things that can separate us—money, country, flag, race, ethnicity, gender, language, even religion—you get the picture.

We can be loyal to and honor different things, provided we keep them in proper perspective and priority as we fully embrace our genuine purposes on earth—

to love our neighbors as ourselves, to love our enemies, and to love God above all. That will prepare us well for becoming a "citizen of heaven."

Read the following poem. It may bring a smile.

Heaven's Surprise, by Rod Hemphill

"I was shocked, confused, bewildered
as I entered Heaven's door,

Not by the beauty of it all, nor the lights or its decor.

But it was the folks in Heaven
who made me sputter and gasp—

The thieves, the liars, the sinners,
the alcoholics, and the trash.

There stood the kid from seventh grade
who swiped my lunch money twice.

Next to him was my old neighbor,
who never said anything nice.

Herb, who I always thought was rotting away in hell,

Was sitting pretty on cloud nine, looking incredibly well.

I nudged Jesus, 'What's the deal? I would love
to hear your take.

'How'd all these sinners get up here?
God must've made a mistake.

'And why's everyone so quiet, so somber—give me a clue.

'Child,' He said, 'they're all in shock.
They never thought they'd be seeing you!'"

The Lesson: If your priority is to be a respectable "citizen of heaven," you are on a good track.

The Lesson: The magnitude of the universe informs us of the Creator's existence. Jesus the Christ teaches the purpose of life and how to live life fully. Our inner being confirms existence extends beyond body and mind. Faith embraces life eternal.

The Lesson: Fear not; love God, love your neighbor, love your enemy, do good to others, read scripture, follow your heart and your conscience, and live in the presence of the Almighty.

The Lesson: God blesses you every day. Share that blessing with everyone you know and meet.

Epilogue

"There are no true solo acts. If someone tells you they got where they are all by themselves, they're lying. Don't believe them, and don't buy what they're selling."

Sam Davidson, an English poet and author

I have been blessed by hundreds of people who have advised and guided me throughout my life. My parents and your mother were, by far, the most important and influential. My parents taught me the values of service, kindness, and integrity. Your mother has loved me, supported me, encouraged me, counseled me, consoled me, and put up with me for decades. She always hasn't been easy on me, but she has always cared for me.

Of the hundreds of others, I identify here a few so that you might get a glimpse of the magnitude of support I've received. Some of the people mentioned you know; others you may recognize by name; some will be new to you. But they are all important to me. Of course, it is precarious when making a list of people in any regard. Someone will inevitably be left off; no list will ever be complete. This list of 100 does not capture all individuals who have been influential in my life but offers a sample.

The following are in alphabetical order because it is not possible to rank them any other way.

Daniel Abebe: Professor and Dean at Metropolitan State University. As an immigrant from Ethiopia, Daniel offered me tremendous insights into East African cultures. Daniel served on Global Volunteers Board of Directors for five years and led our second team of volunteers to Tanzania on short notice after the scheduled team leader was unable. He later led teams to Jamaica and Western Samoa. He also brought to the board and staff a first-hand understanding of living in a developing country. Daniel is a good friend and Nick's godfather.

Judy Ambor: Teacher and Philanthropist. Judy volunteered on six Global Volunteers service programs. After one of the later programs, she donated a substantial amount of money to help construct a community building. Shortly before her death, she agreed that her donation should fund the guest house in Ipalamwa. In the absence of this guesthouse, Global Volunteers could not engage volunteers in the Reaching Children's Potential (RCP) Demonstration Program because there is no other place to stay in this remote rural village. Judy literally laid the foundation for the RCP Program and our efforts to eliminate stunting.

An Wei: President of the Sino American Society and Author. An Wei invited Global Volunteers to Xi'an, China in 1995, and Global Volunteers engaged volunteers in China for 25 years. An Wei has been the primary force behind our partnerships with Chinese communities, facilitated Global Volunteers' involvement in the construction of Project Peace, and arranged for tremendous honors in celebration of Team 50 and Team 100. He was a leading member of Global Volunteers International Advisory Committee and is a dear friend.

Elmer Anderson: Business Owner, Entrepreneur, and Governor of Minnesota. Governor Anderson raised money so I could travel to India with the Institute of Cultural Affairs (ICA) in 1975 when I was both a full-time legislator and graduate student and could not otherwise afford to go. He was a Republican; I was a Democrat. That did not matter to him. The experience serving in Maliwada, India, changed everything. When I returned, I added international development as a focus of my education at the Humphrey School. It was out of the experience in India that Global Volunteers was eventually born, and the RCP Program followed. Governor Anderson made a difference in many peoples' lives and a huge difference in mine.

Janet Arney: Engineer and Senior Program Manager. Janet and I first met in Poland during the spring of 1992. She was there as a volunteer on an around-the-world year-long journey, and I was on a community visit. Later that year, we served together in Indonesia. Shortly after, she came to work for Global Volunteers. These were challenging times. Earlier that year, we encountered significant staff disruptions, and Global Volunteers was growing rapidly. Janet brought considerable leadership and a wealth of knowledge and organizational discipline to our effort. During her tenure, we established policies, procedures, and processes foundational to the company we are today. Janet is among Global Volunteers all-time top five staff.

Tom Bell: Attorney and Legal Staff on the House Watergate Committee. Tom served on Global Volunteers Board of Directors for eight years, up until his untimely death at age 50. He first served in Conacaste, Guatemala in 1988, became a team leader, joined me on the Tonga Exploratory Visit, and led the first team to Tonga. Tom was a consistent source of wise advice and support and a dear friend. He introduced me to Christie (his sister) and Tom Vilsack. Those introductions resulted in my later serving at USDA, which offered insights that have dramatically focused the work of Global Volunteers today.

Jim Berry: Sergeant Major of the Army (Ret), Hennepin County Government Executive, and High School Religion Teacher. Jim and I attended Cretin High School together; although, we did not know each other well. Years later, our families connected through a faith-based group that participated in House Church together when you were young. Jim and I formed a strong bond—a lasting friendship. His thoughtful support over many years has meant a great deal to me.

Marek Blachezk: Director at Reymontowka, Siedlce, Poland. Marek has been Global Volunteers long-time community partner in Poland. He served on Global Volunteers International Advisory Committee, introduced us to Poland government officials at the highest levels, and facilitated Global Volunteers Poland program expansion. His friendship and cooperation span more than 30 years. Marek is the glue that keeps the Poland program together.

Raymond Bohen: Salesman. Uncle Ray was my mothers' oldest brother. We always knew how old he was because he was born on December 30, 1899; his age always coincided with the current year. While I was growing up, Uncle Ray lived next door with Granny Bohen and often accompanied our family when we went on long drives, a source of entertainment. Of most import, he offered me advice, sometimes solicited, sometimes not. I distinctly remember telling him I was going to a job interview, and as I was going out the door to my car, he stopped me. "You should wear a tie," he instructed. "If you want to get the job, show the man respect." I put on a tie; I got the job. Just one example of Uncle Ray looking out for me.

Doug Bolick: US Army First Lieutenant (Ret.) and Lawyer. Doug served on Global Volunteers Board of Directors on two separate stints for a total of seven years. He's led several teams of volunteers, volunteered with me on Global Volunteers' first Free Enterprise Institute in Russia, and accompanied me on an exploratory trip to India. His friendship, insight, and wise legal counsel have been critical on numerous occasions and much appreciated.

Nancy Bolick: Educator and school board member. Nancy served on Global Volunteers Board of Directors until her untimely death in 1996. She accompanied me on the exploratory trip to Russia and introduced me to her husband, Doug. Later, she recommended Global Volunteers to the president of Elderhostel when they were looking to partner with international service program providers. We implemented the partnership with Elderhostel at precisely the right time and engaged thousands of older Americans in service to our community partners. She was a good friend.

Claudette Bougie: Customer Service Representative and Receptionist. Claudette is one of my five older sisters. Her support has been vitally important in many ways over the years. She helped me get my first job at Iverson Rexall Drug Store when I was still in grade school. Claudette and I volunteered together on Global Volunteers' second service program in Jamaica. For years, she graciously hosted country manager candidates from around the world at her home during our annual Team Leader Training. She would then report to me her observations and critique of the candidates, which helped inform our decision process as whom to hire. Claudette is Jake's godmother and continues to support Global Volunteers financially.

John Brandl: Deputy Assistant Secretary for the US Department of Education, University Dean, and Minnesota State Senator. John was the Dean of the School of Public Affairs at the University of Minnesota when I first studied there. He was instrumental in my being admitted to graduate school, even though I did not have the necessary undergraduate credentials. John sought my counsel when he decided to run for the Minnesota legislature and remained a friend until his death.

Pat Brinkman: Business Lawyer. Pat rented me an office in his law firm at the American Bank Building in 1983 when I first started my law practice. A year later, he recommended me to some of his clients when he shut down his practice to take on the role of general counsel for his primary client. Many of his clients hired me; his trust allowed me to build my practice quickly, which permitted your mother and me to help finance the startup of Global Volunteers.

Tom Christian: Laicized Catholic Priest, Corrections Executive, and Author. Tom was the assistant pastor at St. Rose of Lima parish during my later teenage years. He became a spiritual advisor and had a profound impact on me during that time. After he was laicized, we continued to stay in touch and do so to this day. Tom and his wife Bernice have served on several Global Volunteers service programs.

Don Clark: US Army Captain (Ret.), High School Counselor, and Professor. Don was one of my high school teachers and counselors. He inspired me to be all that I could be and continued to assist me well after graduation. Don wrote a letter of reference when I was applying for conscientious objector status, even though he was an officer in the US Army Reserve and did not share my opposition to the Vietnam War.

Nick Coleman: Minnesota Senate Majority Leader and Advertising Agency Executive. Nick came to my assistance when the newly appointed DNR Commissioner was intent on firing me. There were no political advantages for the Senate Majority Leader to do this. He simply acted out of the generosity of his heart and his sense of justice and fairness. Nick ran for governor in 1970 and the US Senate in 1978; I worked on both campaigns. He was a good man and a dedicated public servant.

John Connolly: Lawyer and Minnesota District Judge. I met John when he was managing US Senator Eugene McCarthy's 1972 Minnesota campaign for President of the United States. John hired me as a Minnesota congressional field coordinator for the campaign. At 25 years old, that was my first paid political position. John also introduced me to Don Heffernan, who later became my lawyer and kept me out of federal prison.

Carol Conzelman: Sr. Instructor at the University of Colorado Boulder. We met at Global Volunteers Team leader training in San Juan, Texas, in 1995, where among other important things, we shot many games of pool. Carol served on Global Volunteers Board of Directors two separate times for nine years and volunteered as a team leader on numerous service programs. Carol kept the Board true to our philosophy of service, contributing her voice when others may have veered away. She has been a good friend and an inspiration to me.

John Corbid: Minnesota State Representative, Lobbyist, and Entrepreneur. John and I were elected to the Minnesota House in 1974, where we became fast friends. He was a friend to both your mother and me, and at one point tried to help me get us back together before we were married, but she wanted nothing to do with that. John always had my back and was a groomsman in our wedding party. Years later, after law school, John, Dave Velde, and I started a lobbying partnership, CPV and Associates, which helped get my law practice off the ground. John supported my 2006 campaign and has been a dear friend for more than 45 years.

Julie Costa: Global Volunteers 25-year staff person. There are hundreds of people who have worked for Global Volunteers, and most contributed significantly to our work. Julie is among the all-time top five staff; she has contributed well beyond the call. There is no question that in the absence of Julie's dedication, commitment, hard work, and enormous talents, Global Volunteers could not have achieved what we have.

Dan Coughlan: Attorney and Screenplay Writer. Dan served on Global Volunteers Board of Directors in the early years. His counsel helped me steer through choppy waters and challenging times. His friendship never wavered; his commitment to our vision was constant. Dan died way too young. A group of his friends and family gather every Christmas season for lunch to honor him and our mutual friendships.

Annabelle Crosdale: Jamaican Coffee Farmer and Community Organizer. Annabelle was Global Volunteers community host in Woburn Lawn, Jamaica, the first community we served. Small in stature but huge in every other way, she taught me about community organizing at the local level. She farmed coffee on steep mountain hillsides, and I once asked Annabelle how she planted the coffee on such precipitous slopes. She replied, "You plant the seed right in front of your nose." Annabelle was a remarkable woman and a dear friend.

Milo Cutter: School Principal. Milo helped think through the concept of Global Volunteers, was one of four incorporating members of the Board of Directors, and our initial vice president. She volunteered with me on Global Volunteers' first-ever service program in the Blue Mountains of Jamaica in 1984 and served on the board from 1984 through 1990. Milo worked diligently to get Global Volunteers off the ground and moving in the right direction.

Cathy Deal: Law School Professor. Cathy taught me federal tax law and later helped me understand the law's tax deductibility requirements related to service program contributions. That knowledge allowed us to promote Global Volunteers service program fees as being tax-deductible. Many people have been able to serve with Global Volunteers due to the tax deduction's financial benefits.

Philip Farrocco: US Navy Officer and Civil Engineer. On two separate occasions, Philip served on Global Volunteers Board of Directors. He accompanied me on exploratory trips to Rota, Spain and Ostuni, Italy, and was our country manager in Spain and Italy for years. I had two of the best dinners ever with Philip in Rota, Spain. For all practical purposes, he initiated and conducted our service programs in Western Europe. Philip accompanied me on our initial exploratory trip to Cuba; he and Maria then served with me on the first service program in Havana and Ciego de Avila. He subsequently led teams to Cuba. Philip has been a longtime friend.

Jack and Ruth Flood: High School Teacher, Counselor, Deacon, and Homemaker. Jack and Ruth managed my 1976 reelection campaign for the Minnesota House of Representatives. We lost that year, and Jack was never comfortable with the result. Many factors caused that loss, of which Jack or Ruth could not have done anything. Years later, they helped me edit *Conclave Conspiracy*. Jack remained a genuine and good friend until his death; your mother and I continue to enjoy Ruth's company, especially in Irish pubs.

Susanne Forsyth: Accountant and Philanthropist. Susanne volunteered in St. Lucia. She called me when she returned home and offered to donate to the St. Lucia RCP Pilot Project. The following year, she donated the money to pay the RCP caregivers' salaries in Ipalamwa, Tanzania, the staff who make regular home visits to RCP families and encourage parents to embrace new knowledge and adopt relevant technologies that greatly help their children. Over the ensuing years, Susanne and her husband have contributed substantial amounts to Global Volunteers Reaching Children's Potential Program.

Diane Fredrickson: Global Volunteers 23-year staff person. Diane is another of the all-time top five staff who have worked for Global Volunteers. In addition to her commitment and dedication to our work, she also played a significant role in my 2006 Minnesota gubernatorial campaign when she took a leave of absence from Global Volunteers to work on the campaign full-time. Diane arranged house parties for me all over the state, ensuring there were enough attendees. Diane has been a good friend to both your mother and me.

Tom Garvey: Catholic Priest. Tom was an assistant parish priest at St. Rose of Lima when I was in grade school. He was involved in the school's football and baseball teams on which I played, and he taught me about Christian theology and Catholic doctrine. In later years, Tom became a friend and spiritual advisor.

Richard Gerlach, FSC: Christian Brother and High School Principal. Brother Richard was the principal at Cretin High School when I was a student there. He recognized something in me that others at Cretin apparently did not. He offered me the opportunity to participate in a program that allowed high school seniors to take college courses well before AP or other similar programs were options for high school students. Although I didn't take full advantage of that chance, his confidence in me helped steer me in the right direction.

Eduardo González: Baptist Pastor in Ciego de Avila, Cuba, and a Leader in the Cuba Council of Churches. Michele and I met Eduardo at the home of friends in Minneapolis in 2007, where he invited Global Volunteers to serve in Ciego de Avila. It was five years before the political and legal climates were aligned, and I could conduct exploratory trips. Eduardo may not be your typical Baptist pastor, but he is a remarkable community leader and deeply committed to building bridges of friendships between the Cuban and American people. Eduardo is the principal organizer of Global Volunteers program in Cuba and a dear friend.

Sam Hanson: Attorney, ICA Director, and Justice of the Minnesota Supreme Court. Sam and I volunteered together through the ICA in Maliwada, India, in 1975. That was the beginning of a long and meaningful friendship and my work in international human development. Sam was one of the initial four directors on Global Volunteers board, where he served for over 30 years. He conducted the India Exploratory Trip, led a Millennium Service Project team, participated on the first China Lawyers service program, and led the second. On more than one occasion, Sam and his wife Mirja personally guaranteed Global Volunteers bank loans that allowed us to continue operating. He and Mirja have been extremely generous financial donors. I asked Sam for his advice before I started law school, and he told me to learn the language. His counsel made all the difference. Sam's astute and knowledgeable support helps guide Global Volunteers to this day, where he continues to serve as a Trustee.

Jimmy Hartman: Pipefitter and VFW Commander. Jimmy and I were procession partners in 2nd grade when all the boys and girls made our first communion on the same Sunday at St. Rose of Lima. That was 67 years ago. We've done a lot of silly things together over the years and remain good friends to this day. Jimmy is a rock, a stabling force. He has no airs, does not suffer fools lightly, and is a reliable and dependable friend.

Cliff Harris: Businessman and Mayor. Cliff was the Mayor of Arcola, Mississippi, when he invited Global Volunteers to serve in his 95 percent African American community. We became friends, and I visited Arcola multiple times.

I happened to be in this small town of 600 people on the evening when Cliff led his all-black town board to name their most important building, their new town hall, after a white man, the former mayor. Cliff and his fellow board members showed me that there was much for the whole world to learn from them about mutual respect and honoring others for the good they did.

Wally Heath: Professor at Western Washington State College and Non-Profit CEO. Due to Wally's intervention, I was able to stay on at Rural Ventures after I'd been fired for big "D" political reasons. I did not ask him to intervene. I did not tell him the whole story as to why I was leaving Rural Ventures after being fired. He figured it out on his own and decided to help. That was important given that your mother and I were about to get married, and I planned to start law school eight months later. I did not have another job lined up and knew it would be difficult to get any contract for such a short time. Wally's assistance enabled me to attend law school as planned. That was big!

Don Heffernan: Attorney. Don represented me in my 1971 federal trial for draft resistance. In the absence of his astute knowledge of the law and compelling legal arguments, I may have been convicted and incarcerated for five years in federal prison. Those five years, 1972–1976, were pivotal. During that time, I was employed by Senator McCarthy's and Senator McGovern's presidential campaigns, worked for the Minnesota Public Interest Research Group (MPIRG), was elected to and served in the Minnesota House of Representatives, started graduate school, and volunteered in India with the ICA. Everything would have been different had I spent those five years in prison. Of most importance, I probably never would have met your mother! Think about that.

Rosalie Hennessey, OSM: Catholic Nun and Teacher. Sister Rosalie taught me in 1st, 7th, and 8th grades at St. Rose of Lima Catholic Grade School. Later in life, we became good friends, and she supported my work, encouraged me to be more, helped me edit *Conclave Conspiracy*, and offered meaningful advice. She emailed me the day before she died, asking me to pray for her as she was having open-heart surgery the following day. She died on the operating table. I continue to pray for her; although, I'm sure I need her prayers much more than she needs mine.

Gene Hoeschler: Banker and Financial Manager. Gene managed a Minneapolis suburban bank, which loaned Global Volunteers necessary funding in the 1980s. Years later, he volunteered on my 2006 gubernatorial campaign as finance chair. Gene came into the campaign office every day for months to deposit donations, record expenses, and pay staff, ensuring I knew where we were financially and encouraging me to raise more money. He learned the campaign finance regulations, and because of his leadership, I was always confident that our campaign was complying with the finance laws.

Mike Hostage: Corporate Executive and Philanthropist. Mike retired at a relatively young age as CEO of the Marriot Corporation to spend more time with his lovely wife, Dotty, and 11 children. That's when he and Dotty started volunteering with Global Volunteers. We met in Tutova, Romania, in 2003 and became fast friends. Mike was a reliable donor to the vulnerable children's program we served at Tutova. Whenever there was a significant need, I could call Mike, and he would send us a check. He also offered welcomed and helpful advice, which proved extremely valuable over the years.

Hu Di: International Human Development Executive and Intercultural Coach and Trainer. Hu Di offered her volunteer assistance as a translator and coordinator in Xi'an during Global Volunteers China Team 100. Later, we hired her to assist our China Country Manager and then promoted her to China Country Manager when that position opened. Several years later, we hired her again after she moved to the US and completed her master's degree in international development. Hu Di was Global Volunteers Director of International Operations for several years and was instrumental in establishing the RCP Pilot Program in St. Lucia. Hu Di is among Global Volunteers all-time top five staff. If someone were so lucky to engage 100 Hu Di's, they could rule the world.

Bob Hudnut: Presbyterian Pastor and Author. Bob Hudnut was my mentor. He hired me in 1973 as his administrative assistant when he was Executive Director at MPIRG while on sabbatical from the church. Bob promoted me to finance and communications director and introduced me to Governor Elmer Anderson and Congressman Rick Nolan. Years later, Bob pressed me to launch Global Volunteers finally; he chaired my 2006 campaign for governor; and helped me edit *Conclave Conspiracy*. For 45 years, he was a constant source of guidance and inspiration. We had lunch every month whenever we were in the St. Paul area until he died in 2018. A better friend no one can have.

Terri Hudoba: Legislative Page and Indexer. Terri is one of your mother's best friends and Jake's godmother. She was your mom's Maid of Honor and has consistently supported both of us throughout our lives. Terri volunteered with me on Global Volunteers' second service program in Jamaica and served on Global Volunteers Board of Directors for eight years. She has been a faithful financial contributor to Global Volunteers for decades.

Lori Kensey: Paralegal. I hired Lori as my paralegal in 1987. She capably researched legal issues and kept me on task until she helped me close the law practice in 1992. Then Lori joined Global Volunteers staff, something she swore she'd never do, and we worked together until she married Ron Kensey and moved to Wyoming.

Ron Kensey: Business Owner and Entrepreneur. Ron volunteered with me on Global Volunteers first Free Enterprise Institute in Russia in 1993 and joined the Board of Directors six years later, where he served for eight years. He was on the Finance Committee for many of those years, where his business acumen and financial knowledge were crucial to our success. He and Lori served on China Team 100, and they made an extremely generous donation to Global Volunteers for Project Peace in An Shang.

Keith Kresge: Attorney. Keith has volunteered on 28 Global Volunteers service programs, several with your mother. In 2014, he was elected to the Board of Directors, where he continues to advise and lead. He is an incredibly generous financial contributor to Global Volunteers and chairs the Development Committee. His understanding of and commitment to the work we do is of utmost importance to my being able to lead this organization.

Dean Lafrenz: Educator and School Principal. We met Dean and his wife, Carol, when they volunteered with all of us in China on Team 100. Dean chaired the 2006 Gubernatorial Campaign Education Task Force and later served on Global Volunteers Board of Directors. His friendship, steady hand, and thoughtful demeanor served us well.

Dick Lamm: Governor of Colorado, US Presidential Candidate, and Author. Dick was a life-long democrat but became disheartened with both political parties because of their reliance on and control by special interest money. I was also concerned about how both parties were moving further from the center, Democrats to the far left and Republicans to the far right. When the former Governor of Colorado decided to run for the nomination of the Reform Party for president in 1996, I joined his campaign as a political advisor. Later, in the early stages of my gubernatorial campaign, Dick offered helpful advice and support.

Sue Laxdal: Organizational Consultant. Sue and I met at the ICA Minneapolis office in 1974 while I was campaigning for the Minnesota House, and she has been a constant source of wisdom and support all these decades. Sue has served on Global Volunteers Board of Directors for 37 years and was the corporate secretary much of that time. She facilitated most board planning sessions during those years and helped us stay focused on our goals and objectives. Sue has led or served on 17 service programs worldwide and is a vital member of Global Volunteers Board of Trustees. On several occasions in her role as a Trustee, Sue and her husband Stephen personally guaranteed bank loans to help keep Global Volunteers afloat. Sue and Steve have also been extremely generous financial donors to Global Volunteers and are dear friends.

Todd Lefko: International Business Owner and Entrepreneur. Todd and I met in the late 1960s through Ramsey County DFL politics. We became good friends, and he volunteered with me on Global Volunteers' first-ever service program in the Blue Mountains of Jamaica in 1984, where he later led teams. In 1987, Todd joined me on a road trip from Little Canada, Minnesota to Conacaste, Guatemala, where Global Volunteers donated a pickup truck to the community development project. Later he introduced me to his friends in Moscow, participated with me on the Russia Exploratory Trip, served on the Kazakhstan Free Enterprise Institute program, and participated on China Team 100. Todd served on Global Volunteers Board of Directors for more than 30 years and continues as a Trustee. He was a strong supporter of our gubernatorial campaign, and his advice and counsel have been invaluable over all these years.

David Levy: Business Owner and Entrepreneur. David owned and operated several small family movie theaters in the 1960s and '70s. He hired me as the janitor for the Midtown Family Theater in the summer I turned 16. He promoted me to usher and then assistant manager. I worked for David until the spring of my sophomore year at the University of Minnesota when I got the job at Sperry Univac. In the summer of 1969, after my time with VISTA, and before I returned to Sperry Univac, he hired me to manage the Navarre Drive-In Theater. David taught me the basic principles of running a small business.

Jorge Lopez: Foreign Exchange Student and Entrepreneur. During my senior year at Cretin Highschool, Jorge was an exchange student from Guatemala. He lived with my family during our final semester, and we became pals. Jorge taught me about how people from different cultures, who spoke different languages and had different skin color, could become the best of friends. We stayed in touch over the years, and we visited his family in Guatemala City during our honeymoon. Later, his niece lived with us when she was an exchange student.

Mindy Lull: Associate Professor at St. John Fisher College. Mindy serves on Global Volunteers Board of Directors, has led multiple teams of volunteers on the Blackfeet Indian Reservation, and chairs the Reaching Children's Potential Advisory Committee. Mindy, along with her doctoral students and professional colleagues, analyzes and reports the data that shows Global Volunteers RCP Program helps village parents ensure all their children can reach their potential.

Bill Luther: Attorney, Minnesota State Senator, and US Congressman. Bill and I were elected to the Minnesota House in 1974. He was then elected to the Minnesota Senate, where he rose to Assistant Majority Leader, and then to the US House of Representatives. Bill was the Best Man at our wedding and has been a supportive friend all these years. In 2009, Bill encouraged me to apply for a senior position in the Obama Administration at USDA and connected me to key people involved in that process. Serving at USDA was instrumental to our establishing the RCP Program. We've enjoyed a strong friendship for more than 45 years.

Joe Matthews: Methodist Pastor and Co-founder of the ICA. I met Joe in 1975 in Maliwada, India, when he conducted the ICA's Human Development Project Consultation. Joe taught me about the importance of local people being in charge of their own development and how outsiders can help. The Maliwada experience formed the basis of my Plan B at the Humphrey School of Public Affairs. That paper is the foundation of Global Volunteers Philosophy of Service upon which the RCP Program is built.

Eugene McCarthy: US Senator and Poet. Senator McCarty ran for president in 1968 and 1972. I volunteered for him in '68 and was a member of his paid campaign staff in '72. He inspired me to run for public office and was an outstanding example of integrity in public life. I was privileged to work for him and promote his candidacy.

Kay McCarthy: Teacher, Attorney, and Quilter. Kay and I met during our first days at Hamline University School of Law. We were on the same study team, moot court team, and wrote for the law review. She helped center me and made the law school experience doable. Later, Kay hosted an especially successful house party during the 2006 gubernatorial campaign and encouraged others to host house parties. That is how we met Russ Bursch and Lee Mauk, who introduced us to Eduardo Gonzalez, Global Volunteers' partner in Cuba. Kay, her husband Mike, your mother, and I remain good friends to this day.

Betty McCollum: Minnesota State Representative and US Congresswoman. Betty and I have been friends for 30 years. She and her staff have offered ongoing help and support to Global Volunteers throughout her long and successful tenure in the US House of Representatives. She has assisted in getting visas for our international staff, introduced me to foreign embassies in Washington, and offered advice about working with foreign governments and getting federal SBA loans. Betty was also instrumental in my being appointed Deputy Undersecretary at USDA in the Obama Administration.

Owdenberg Mdegella: Lutheran Bishop in Tanzania and Community Organizer. Owden invited Global Volunteers to Tanzania in 1986; we have sent volunteer teams there every year since. Owden led the effort to get Global Volunteers officially registered in Tanzania, ensuring our ability to continue to work there. In 2014, he introduced me to both the Prime Minister and President of Tanzania. Owden asked that we initiate Global Volunteers' Reaching Children's Potential (RCP) Demonstration Program in his home village of Ipalamwa. Bishop Mdegella introduced Global Volunteers to a wide array of government and church leaders over the past three decades, facilitating our work in the Iringa region. The foundation of the RCP Program was built on his extraordinary hard work and passion for and dedication to the people of Tanzania and Global Volunteers.

John Milton: Minnesota State Senator, Health Provider Executive, and Author. John and I first met during the 1970 campaign season when he ran for Ramsey County Commissioner, and I ran for State Representative. Over the years, our professional lives connected at several intersections. John carried the Senate version of the BWCA Protection Act; we worked together when he was at Control Data Corporation, and I was at its subsidiary, Rural Ventures; we worked on several political campaigns together; John served on Global Volunteers board of directors for ten years until I hired him to lead Global Volunteers Millennium Service Project; he helped edit *Conclave Conspiracy*. John has been a long, good, and faithful friend.

Jack Murray: Chiropractic Doctor. Jack and his wife, Maggie, were longtime friends of my parents. In 1970, Jack gave my nominating speech for State Representative at the democratic party endorsing district convention. I was 23. (What was he thinking?) Later, Jack hired me as a PR consultant for the Minnesota Chiropractic Association. We became dear friends and often had lunch together downtown St. Paul. Jack treated me for back pain caused when I was a passenger in an auto accident in 1963. I saw him at his office for a treatment on the day he died.

Art Naftalin: Minneapolis Mayor, Minnesota Commissioner of Administration, and University Professor. Art was my advisor when I studied at the Humphrey School of Public Affairs. He helped me out of a serious situation when a much younger professor gave me a D on a required 3-credit course, thus denying me credit for the course. Art allowed me to conduct a 3-credit independent study on any topic I choose. I decided to learn all I could about international human and economic development in rural villages in developing countries. My report for that independent study morphed into one of my Plan B's, which later became the foundation for Global Volunteers' Philosophy of Service.

Rick Nolan: Minnesota State Representative, US Congressman, and Entrepreneur. I first met Rick when he was running for Congress, and I worked at

MPIRG. We got to know each other better when he served in the US House, and I was in the Minnesota House. When I considered running for an open seat in congress in 1976, Rick counseled me to wait and let more senior democrats vie for the seat. Years later, he helped me think through the philosophy and organizational structure of Global Volunteers and served on the Board of Directors.

Jim Oberstar: Educator and US Congressman. Congressman Oberstar and Governor Perpich both hailed from Minnesota's Iron Range, but they had not always gotten along. In 1977, Oberstar introduced federal legislation affecting the BWCA. Perpich was on one side of the BWCA issue and Oberstar on the other. The governor hired me to work at the Minnesota Department of Natural Resources to represent his position on this bill. In the process, I got to know and respect Congressman Oberstar. Jim and I met on numerous occasions in his DC office. He knew that my job was to get as much of the Governor's thinking included in the bill as possible. Even though our views were sometimes adversarial, Jim listened to what I had to say and treated me with respect. I later volunteered on Jim's US Senate campaign, and he served on Global Volunteers board of directors.

Glenda Otto: Educational Consultant. Glenda and I met while undergraduate students at the University of Minnesota. She served with and introduced me to the ICA and Sam Hanson, Sue Laxdal, Joe Mathews, and many other colleagues. The ICA informed my understanding of human and economic development in significant ways, and Sam and Sue have been vital to the success of Global Volunteers. Glenda and I are dear friends and stay in touch to this day.

Lenny Painchaub: Salesman, Hunter, and Fisherman. Lenny and I first worked together on the night shift at Sperry Univac. Later, after I was promoted to supervisor and assigned to the day shift, Lenny reported to me. At that time, I was 23; he was 28. I'm sure it was difficult for him, and others who were significantly older than me, to take my direction. But Lenny showed me respect, and he encouraged me to do better. After we no longer worked together, Lenny and I were roommates for several years at three different locations, and he was a groomsman at our wedding. Later, he helped your mother and me hire qualified subcontractors when the general contractor scheduled to build 2634 bailed-out due to entering treatment. Lenny died too young at 62, and I've missed him greatly.

Rudy Perpich: Dentist and Governor of Minnesota. Rudy Perpich held a fundraiser to help retire my campaign debt after I lost the Minnesota House election in 1970. We did not know each other well at the time, but I needed help, and he assisted democratic candidates in need. We got to know each other better when I worked on Senator McCarthy's campaign in 1972 and later at MPIRG. In 1975, then Lt. Governor Perpich and I traveled across Minnesota in support of the Boundary Waters Canoe Area Protection Act, which I carried in the House at his request. When I lost reelection in 1976, and he became governor, he hired me to assist him at the Department of Natural Resources. Rudy Perpich picked me up when I had no place to go.

Betty Peterson: Campaign Manager Extraordinaire. Betty managed my 1970 campaign for State Representative. She brought structure to a previously floundering effort. Betty enlisted the wisdom of Bob Goff, Sen Nick Coleman's business partner, when we had to figure out how to handle my US Army Induction Notice several weeks before the general election. Betty taught me a lot about political campaigns that I used when I organized for Senator McCarty and Senator McGovern in 1972 and ran a second time for the house in 1974. Even though I lost in 1970, Betty's efforts allowed me to hold my head high. We had run an honorable and competent campaign.

David Philbrook: Painter, Business Owner, and Entrepreneur. David is my younger brother. He traveled a different road than I did, but he has always backed me and encouraged me. David helped me in my political campaigns, allows me to stay connected to my extended family, and regularly contributes financially to Global Volunteers. He reminds me of the stock from which we both came and the life lessons our parents taught us. David and his wife, Laura, are dear friends.

John Potter: Banker and Financial Manager. John served on Global Volunteers Board of Directors for 11 years. His business acumen and thoughtful guidance helped us excel on numerous occasions and kept us out of financial ruin at other times. More than once, John agreed not to resign from the board due to his age at my encouragement. I repeatedly told him that he was too valuable to think he was too old. John was an extremely generous financial contributor to Global Volunteers.

Marge Prokosch: Campaign Treasurer. Marge managed all the finances for the 1974 and 1976 campaigns for the Minnesota House, which was extraordinary, especially given that in '74, her accountant husband, Tom, performed the same function for my Republican opponent. More importantly, Marge kept me focused. Campaigning is hard work, and it's easy to find things to do that may not contribute to the cause. Marge ensured that I did not dilly dally on things that did not matter.

Craig Rafferty: Architect. Craig, his wife, Kathy, and I went to grade school together at St. Rose. We attended different high schools and different colleges at the University of Minnesota. Still, we stayed in touch over the years and served together on several St. Rose class reunion committees. In 2016, when we decided to construct several buildings in Ipalamwa, Tanzania for the RCP Program, Craig designed the buildings pro bono. He and Kathy are good friends, and Craig continues to help me with the RCP effort.

Philip Rask: Catholic Priest and Biblical Scholar. Phil Rask is the pastor at St. Odilia in Shoreview, Minnesota, a parish where I have attended and read scripture to the congregation for several decades. He is among the finest homilist I've listened to anywhere in the world. His Sunday messages are thoughtful, engaging, and spiritually rich. Father Rask is a source of scriptural understanding that helps me tremendously on my spiritual journey.

Ron Reed: Social Worker and Non-Profit CEO. Ron managed our 2006 gubernatorial campaign as a volunteer after the paid campaign manager resigned. He had never managed a political campaign previously, and he had not been a candidate for office. Still, Ron had a wealth of experience and was an accomplished non-profit manager of people and programs. After I withdrew, he continued to offer valuable advice on managing non-profit corporations. Ron and I had lunch nearly every month until his death.

Ron Reimann: US Navy Commander (Ret), CIA Analyst, US Transportation Department Executive, and Business Owner. Ron volunteered on Global Volunteers Free Enterprise Institute service programs, became a volunteer team leader, joined Global Volunteers Board of Directors (serving on two separate occasions), accompanied me to St. Lucia on two exploratory trips, and became an invaluable source of knowledge and wisdom. He generously contributes financially to Global Volunteers and has encouraged and facilitated his children and grandchildren to become Global Volunteers. Over these years, Ron and I have become good friends.

Phil Ricker: U.S. Army Captain (Ret) and Insurance Executive. Phil and I attended grade school, high school, and college together. I was a groomsman in his wedding; he was a groomsman in our wedding. He and I constructed campaign lawn signs in his garage when I ran for the Minnesota House in 1974. Phil helped me install the antique oak wainscot in our dining room at 2634; that was quite the puzzle. His daughter, Carrie, babysat for you guys when she was a teenager. Phil helped Jake build his racecar when Jake won the Cub Scouts Pinewood Derby. We've collaborated on all St. Rose of Lima class of '60 reunion events. We both drove new Mustang Mach 1's in 1969, and in 2019, Phil found me a 10-year-old black Mustang (looks like the '69) with only

34,000 miles on it—a reminder of my youth. Our politics are not the same, but our deep friendship has never wavered.

Juan Carlos Romero Hicks: University Chancellor, Governor of Guanajuato, and Mexican Federal Senator. In 1988, Juan Carlos and I met at the University of Guanajuato during an exploratory trip to determine if Global Volunteers should develop a Mexico program. He was extremely helpful to us then and became a good friend. On several occasions, I took one or two of you to their summer home in Wisconsin, where we enjoyed their large family and authentic Mexican food. Juan Carlos was tremendously instrumental to our program in Mexico.

Ron Rotell: Salesman. Ron and I attended St. Rose grade school together, along with 113 other classmates. We went to different high schools and colleges but made it a point to connect as often as possible, albeit we often lived in different parts of the country. Ron died too young; he was 63. Nick and I had an enjoyable dinner with Ron two nights before his unexpected death. Ron's son, Chris, asked me to deliver the eulogy at Ron's Memorial Service. It was one of the highest honors of my life. Seven guys, all Ron's grade school classmates, get together every December for the Ron Rotell Memorial Christmas Season Lunch.

Lewie Rydeen: Business Owner and Computer Manufacturing Executive. Lewie was my mentor. He hired me at Sperry Univac when I needed a well-paying job. He promoted me six times during my first two years at Sperry Univac, making me one of the youngest supervisors in the company when I was barely 21. When I left Sperry Univac to join Vista, and that did not work out, Lewie rehired me at a higher paying and more responsible position. Lewie coached me how to think strategically, he taught me how to argue vociferously, and he convinced me that I could do anything I decided to do. Lewie died at 60; I miss him every day.

Martin Sabo: Speaker of the Minnesota House of Representatives and US Congressman. Martin helped me understand the working of the Minnesota legislature. Later, he came to my aid after being fired from my job at the Minnesota Department of Natural Resources. He recommended me for a one-month gig with a US State Department NGO accompanying foreign political and media officials to meetings with prominent US politicians and citizens around the country. This was a critical time for me; I was about to be out of work with nothing on the horizon. Martin's help got me through that difficult time.

Rob Scarlet: International Business Executive and Entrepreneur. I met Rob through mutual friends, and he later served on Global Volunteers Board of Directors for the first six years. When Rob's father died, leaving him responsible for his company, Rob asked me to provide legal counsel. He decided to create an Employee Stock Ownership Plan (ESOP) where the employees would own the company, and I assisted him through that process. Having this company as a client contributed appreciably to my law practice, which allowed our family to help fund Global Volunteers in the early years.

Pat Sheikh: US Government Executive. Pat headed up the office of Capacity Building and Development section at the Foreign Agricultural Services (FAS) and reported to the Administrator who reported to me when I was Deputy Undersecretary at USDA. She helped me understand the essential international roles USDA played, guided me in my work with international agencies, taught me how inter-government agencies collaborated, and explained how USDA interfaced with UN agencies. To the extent I had any successes while at USDA, Pat played a pivotal role.

Ashley Shelby: Autor and Editor. Ashley edited *Conclave Conspiracy*. She suggested innumerable cuts and revisions, most of which I accepted. She helped me delete duplications, improve the story's pace, and clarify sections that were unclear or confusing. Ashley graciously suggested 30 potential book agents, all of whom I contacted, but none of whom offered to help. Ashley is a professional, and I was honored to receive her expert assistance.

Sue Haarman Sindelar: Sue is my older cousin, my mother's sister's only daughter. We were not close growing up, but later, Sue, her husband Tom, and their two sons, Paul and John, lived across Lake Gervais from 2634. Paul babysat for you on many occasions. Sue taught me about the miracle of death. As a hospice nurse and my dad's Goddaughter, Sue attended to my dad during his final weeks. She persuaded me to be present at his death when I was reluctant to continue to respond to the false alarms reporting his impending demise. Because of Sue, I was present to my father's final breath. It was a serene spiritual experience. I hope each of you can be present when I depart this earth.

Greg Skrpeck: Catholic Priest and Prison Chaplin. Greg was a chaplain in the Minnesota Corrections system and the part-time pastor at a small church where I attended until the St. Paul Archdiocese shut it down as a cost-saving measure. He offered excellent Sunday homilies, often drawing on his experiences at the state prison, became a spiritual advisor, and encouraged me to write *Conclave Conspiracy*.

Kenny Slutsky: Attorney and Financial Manager. Kenny served on Global Volunteers Board of Directors from 2003 to 2011. His advice and counsel were always valued, but his most important contribution was his guidance at the beginning of the Great Recession. 2008 was our biggest year ever in terms of volunteers and revenue. Yet in October 2008, Kenny recommended that we substantially cut expenses, which meant laying off staff, reducing the number of service programs, and suspending several of our country programs. He argued that this recession was going to last for years. Kenny was persuasive. Fortunately, the Board of Directors took his advice, and Global Volunteers survived the Great Recession.

Jim Swiderski: Congressional Aid, Teacher, and Author. Jim worked for Global Volunteers in various roles at our corporate offices in Minnesota; in

Xian, China as our Country manager; and in Washington, DC as our government relations manager. Later, he served as a volunteer team leader. Jim's dedicated commitment to the mission and vision of Global Volunteers has always
been appreciated, and our strong mutual friendship endures to this day.

Joe Testa: Business Owner and Entrepreneur. Since 1991, Joe has led more
than 70 Global Volunteers service programs all over the world. He has also
served as our Volunteer Portugal Country Manager for many years. Joe played
a critical role in assisting staff in ensuring purified water at the Ipalamwa RCP
Center, both by getting the water purification equipment donated and instructing staff on the installation, maintenance, and troubleshooting. He and I
conducted an exploratory trip to Cambodia and Vietnam. Joe's a good friend
who has stepped up to the plate whenever asked.

Roger Toogood: Social Worker and Non-Profit CEO. Roger co-managed my
1974 campaign for the Minnesota House of Representatives. His community
contacts, leadership, and hard work significantly contributed to our election
success. There is no question in my mind that I would never have been elected
in my highly Republican district without his leadership. That election opened
many doors—got me admitted to graduate school, resulted in my being appointed DNR Assistant Commissioner, and played a key role in being invited
to join the ICA's consult in Maliwada, India, which focused my study of international development and eventually led to Global Volunteers.

Most importantly, I met your mother because of that election. I owe an enormous debt of gratitude to Roger and all the others who believed in and worked
tirelessly on the 1974 campaign. Later, Roger and Marlys volunteered with
our family in West Liberty, IA, on the Millennium Service Project in 1999 and
served on Global Volunteers Board of Directors for nine years.

Jerry Urban: Grade School Football Coach and Meat Processing Business
Owner. Jerry was the first coach of the St. Rose of Lima grade school football
team. He inspired us to work harder, play tougher, and compete as a team.

Most importantly, he showed us how to win and lose with grace and respect for our opponents. Those were all important lessons for young teens to learn.

David Velde: Minnesota State Government Executive and Attorney. David was Minnesota Deputy Commissioner of Agriculture when I was Assistant Commissioner of DNR. Shortly after that, he and I worked at Rural Ventures, sharing an office at one time. We attended Hamline University School of Law together, both graduating in 27 months. Then we formed Corbid, Philbrook, Velde, and Associates, a legislative lobbying firm focusing on education.

Christie Vilsack: Teacher, First Lady of Iowa, and Government Senior Executive. Tom Bell introduced me to Christie, his younger sister, in 1990, when the two of them helped renovate the office building in Little Canada. Tom gave Christie a Global Volunteers service program in Jamaica as a Christmas present; she later served in Poland. Her husband, Tom, volunteered in San Juan, TX; and their two sons served together in Jamaica. Christie introduced us to local leaders in West Liberty, IA, facilitated our program there during the Millennium Service Project, and she and Tom volunteered with our family in West Liberty in December 1999. Christie continues to support Global Volunteers' efforts in the US by introducing us to key people at colleges and universities across the country.

Tom Vilsack: Attorney, Governor of Iowa, and US Secretary of Agriculture. Tom encouraged and facilitated my political appointment as Deputy Undersecretary at USDA during President Obama's first Administration. Tom is the consummate politician and cabinet-level government executive. He envisions the future and plays the long ball to accomplish critical public goals. While at USDA, I was responsible for much of the department's international activity—primarily food assistance, food security, and ag trade. During this role, I became aware of the UN's *The Essential Package*, which later became the blueprint for Global Volunteers' *Essential Services Prospectus*, which is the basis for our Reaching Children's Potential Program. Because of Tom Vilsack, I was able to learn about and work on the vital issues that ensure every child can reach their potential. Tom and Christie remain dear friends.

Bobbie Walker: Social Worker and Mayor. As mayor of Jonestown, Mississippi, Bobby was Global Volunteers community host when we served there in the 1990s. She and I became good friends. Late at night, after the work was done, Bobby would share with me what it was like growing up in a small Mississippi town as a black girl. I had read about the things she experienced. Still, it took on a terribly different light when she told me about, as a teenager, being treed by big old dogs at the command of their white owners, and when I learned first-hand how even in the 1990s there were white-owned bars and restaurants where she was not welcomed because she was black.

George Warp: University Professor. George chaired the admissions committee at the University of Minnesota School of Public Affairs the year I applied. His intervention allowed me to attend graduate school, even though my undergraduate grades were insufficient to be admitted. It was there that I studied international development, the foundation for Global Volunteers.

Bill Westbrook: Business Owner, Entrepreneur, and Author. Bill showed up at Global Volunteers office one day, offering his remarkable marketing expertise pro bono. Your mother and I accepted. At Bill's encouragement, I wrote the Essential Services Prospectus; Bill designed the Essential Services Triangle. At Bill's suggestion, we established a program in St. Lucia and created the RCP Pilot Project. Through Bill's creativity, we branded our volunteer recruiting efforts as "Leave Your Mark on the World." The RCP Program started in St. Lucia all because of Bill's inspiration. He also served on Global Volunteers Board of Directors for a couple of years. Bill has more positive creative energy than anyone I know.

Dorota Wierzbicka: Global Volunteers 24-year staff person. Dorota volunteered as a Polish translator when she was in high school; then, we hired her. She was promoted from translator to team leader assistant, to team leader, to

Poland Country Manager, to associate director of international operations, then to her current role as director of international operations. Dorota also helped me edit *Conclave Conspiracy*, is a valued member of Global Volunteers staff, and a good friend.

Warren Williams: US Army Colonel (Ret.), Global Volunteers Team Leader, and Professor. Warren and I met in Vietnam when we volunteered in Tan Hiep in the Mekong Delta in October 1995. We established a fast friendship that has flourished over the past 25 years. Warren attended Team Leader Training that December and led over 100 Global Volunteers service programs in the ensuing years, including a stint as St. Lucia Country Manager. He accompanied me on several international excursions, including exploratory trips to Turkey, Greece, and St. Lucia. Warren served on Global Volunteers Board of Directors for 16 years, where his quiet counsel and advice were welcomed, helpful, and appreciated.

Mel Zoff: Mortician. Mel co-managed my 1974 campaign for the Minnesota House of Representatives. Jack Murray had introduced us years before (Mel and Jack were Cretin High School classmates and life-long friends), and Jack suggested that I ask Mel to manage my campaign. Mel agreed on the condition that Roger Toogood would co-manage. I'd never met Roger, so Mel and I went to Roger's home to ask him. After an hour's conversation and Mel's urging, Roger agreed. Winning election in 1974 created the opportunity to meet your mother and opened the initial doors that have allowed us to conduct our life's work.

Anonymous: Philanthropist. One of our multi-time volunteers is the matriarch of a family foundation that has generously contributed the money necessary to construct five of the eight buildings at the RCP Center in Ipalamwa and cover all the health care operation expenses for five years. An ambitious program like RCP could not have gotten off the ground without this family foundation's financial assistance. Then, to put the icing on the cake, the foundation donated $150,000 matching grant so Global Volunteers could expand our impact. In the absence of that matching grant, Global Volunteers could not have survived the COVID-19 crisis.

There are thousands of others—teachers, professors, fellow students, coworkers, colleagues, campaign supporters, law clients, employees, siblings, extended family members, team leaders, community partners, local people, and tens of thousands of volunteers—who have influenced my journey. And, of course, each of you has significantly contributed to the person I've become.

The Lesson: No one does it alone.